Rune Play

RUNE PLAY

A Seasonal Record Book with Twelve New Techniques for Rune Casting

Ralph Blum

Oracle Books
St. Martin's Press
New York

 For information, address Oracle Books/St. Martin's Press, 175 Fifth Avenue, New York, N.Y. 10010.

Edited by Bronwyn Jones
Illustrations by Jancis Salerno

Design by Laura Hough

Library of Congress Cataloging in Publication Data
Blum, Ralph, 1932–
Rune play.
1. Runes—Miscellanea. 2. Oracles. I. Title
BF1779.R86B583 1985 133.3'3 85-11754
ISBN 0-312-69591-8

10 9 8 7 6 5

Dedication

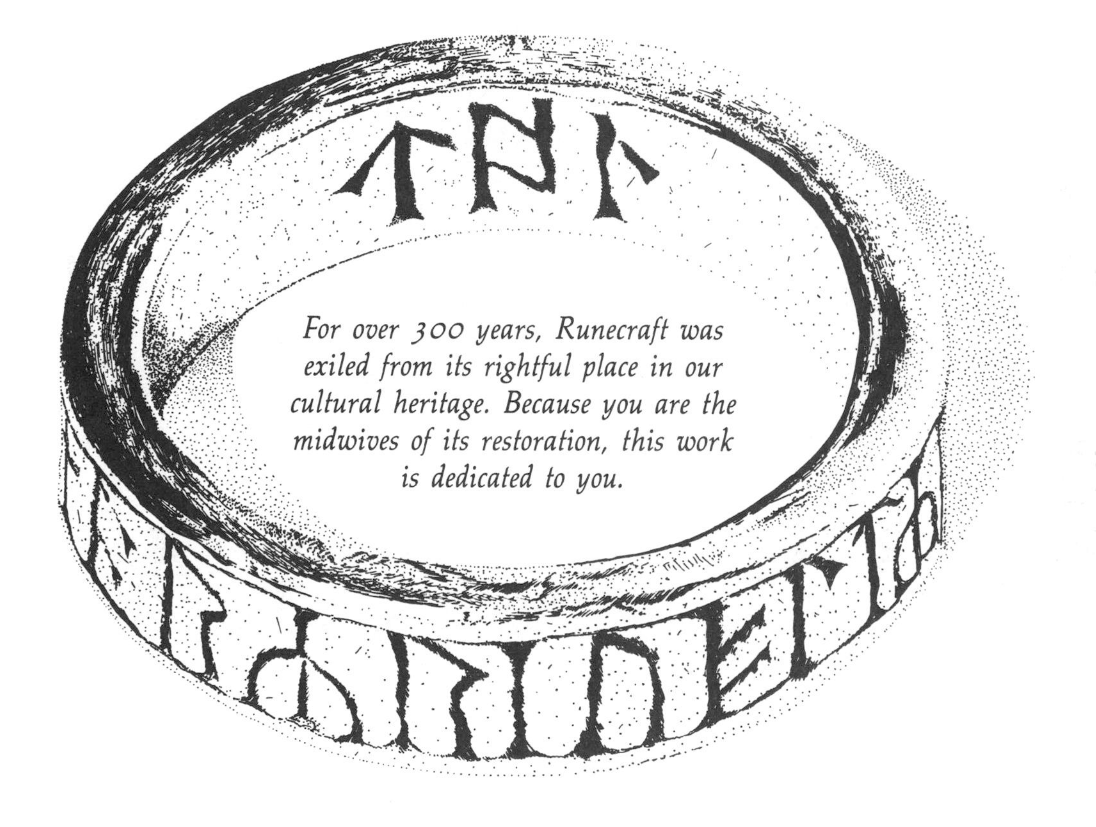

For over 300 years, Runecraft was exiled from its rightful place in our cultural heritage. Because you are the midwives of its restoration, this work is dedicated to you.

Contents

Introduction

To every thing there is a season, and a time to every purpose under the heaven: A time to be born, and a time to die; a time to plant, and a time to pluck up that which is planted. . . .

Ecclesiastes 3: 1,2

Many people have written to ask when we were planning to offer a workbook or, as one reader of *The Book of Runes* put it, "a kind of logbook where I can set down my daily Rune castings and begin to identify patterns." Others have suggested a learning tool, "a place to record my daily Rune readings, to familiarize myself with the Runes and get to know them." One user of *The Book of Runes* asked for a workbook that would assist her "to research myself . . . to serve as the basis for psychological profiling of the mechanisms and turning points in the process of self-change." Still others among the growing number of subscribers to our newsletter, *The New Oracle News & Rune Digest,* have asked for "new techniques and spreads that must have occurred to you since you first published *The Book of Runes.*"

As is my wont at the start of a new project, I consulted the Runes concerning the timeliness of the undertaking. I drew three Runes and received ᛜ, *Inguz,* ᛈ, *Perth, Reversed,* and ᚨ, *Ansuz.*

ᛜ, *Inguz,* the Rune of Fertility and New Beginnings, represents the *Overview* of the project. The essence of ᛜ is "the completion of beginnings" and its message is that one now has "the strength to achieve completion, resolution, from which comes a new beginning."

In the second place came ᛈ, *Perth, Reversed,* the Rune of Initiation, Something Hidden, in the sense that "becoming whole, the means of it, is a profound secret" quite beyond our frail manipulative powers. ᛈ represents the *Challenge* to be met by this new project. Reversed, this Rune treats any obstructions as "an obstacle course, a challenge specific to the initiation you are presently undergoing." One passage from ᛈ seems particularly appropriate to quote here:

> The old way has come to an end; you simply cannot repeat the old and not suffer . . . call in your scattered energies and concentrate on your own life at the moment, your own requirements for growth. More important, *Perth* counsels you not to focus on outcomes, or to bind yourself with the memory of past achievements; in so doing, you rob yourself of a *true present,* which is the only time in which self-change can be realized.

This is the core, the heart briar, the essential message of *Rune Play.* The preparation of this book, then, seems timely for all of us concerned with the process of self-change.

The third Rune, representing the *Action Called For,* was ᚨ, *Ansuz,* the Rune of Signals, the Messenger Rune. With ᚨ we are in the realm of communication, especially that between the ego self and the Higher Self; it symbolizes "the urge to integrate unconscious motive with conscious recognition." Following the theme enunciated by *Perth, Reversed,* ᚨ is a reminder that "you must draw first from the well to nourish and give to yourself. Then there will be more than enough to nourish others."

The challenge was this: to prepare a book that was appropriate to people working with the Runes in a systematic or even casual way. This is not, in any ordinary design sense, a journal, organizer, or appointment book. Nor is it a workbook, since regularity and consistency are lesser virtues in Runecraft than is the personal sense of what is appropriate. You will notice the absence of dated pages, for although this book is divided into weekly segments, the intention is that you can pick it up when you will, record readings and comments when you will, without feeling obligated to make regular entries. Yet the framework is there for those who have established a practice of starting each day by drawing a *Daily Rune* or, put somewhat differently, a Rune that stands for a personal weather forecast for this day in your life.

Over time, many people have found that to draw a single *Daily Rune* or Rune of Right Action, was sufficient to indicate the "key" in which their day was written. As one longtime Runecaster put it, "If I'm in for heavy weather, I can put on my long underwear when I get up." From the mail we have been receiving, it is clear that *Daily Rune* is a singular success. And not only for its rewarding way of providing short-term guides for conduct. Picking a Rune each day is the perfect way for someone new to the Runes to learn their meanings effortlessly. You are, so to speak, studying a Rune a day, familiarizing yourself with the interpretations, coming to terms with Reversed readings, *not* as "bad" but as phases of your own cycle—the sun working through clouds, the shadow side of your development. *There is no good or bad but thinking makes it so* is a powerful theorem from the "Owner's Manual of Your Own Life."

The Book of Runes suggests that "when it has been a particularly trying or exhilarating day, you may wish to consult the Oracle again in the evening for an evaluation of how you've conducted yourself." We call this the *Results Rune* for it answers the question "What has today brought?," providing an overview of the day's challenges and how you have responded to them. Again, almost invariably, those who use the Runes in this way will experience subtle shifts in emphasis, and rewarding new ways of interpreting ordinary events.

Everyone has days that are memorable for their overload of demanding decisions. The outworking of a critical situation in the course of a day may impel you to turn to your Runes for "a good second opinion" more than once. We call these *Outworking Runes* (*OR* for short). With practice, you will quickly discover ways of integrating these sequentially derived insights into the fabric of your life. This practice will help you not only to mark your present course position but will also assist you to identify patterns and to better understand your life process. Position. Pattern. Process. The three "P's" of self-change.

Many of us have discovered the advantage of being able to access and refer back to previous Rune readings. Perhaps you have recently undergone a series of upheavals in your life, events that have led to major modifications in attitude, career, dwelling, or ways of doing things. By reviewing the clustered Rune readings from such intense periods, recurring life patterns can be identified. Once you recognize the pattern, you can begin to change it.

The idea of marking a year of life by the seasons comes from my friend Dean Loomos, who, perhaps thanks to his Greek heritage, has a considerable gift for consorting with Oracles in general, and with the Viking Runes in particular. It was his suggestion that the World Tree, *Yggdrasil,* should appear on *Rune Play* pages with appropriate foliage, reflecting the changing seasons.

For this is where it all began—when Odin hung himself on the tree in order to win wisdom.

The Viking Runes run on any time *but* clock time. Dream time. Mood time. The time it takes for intuition to mark territory through action. Closest to home, the Runes work on *beauty of the earth time.* Look back through the images and metaphors found in *The Book of Runes.* You can hear the falling leaves and watch the turning tides. From understandings gleaned out of *The Book of Runes* this new book is organized and offered. Part of the harvest was a yearning for a new relationship to time. An impeccable attitude toward time.

What if you buy or receive this book in March? Remember as a kid, coming in at the middle of a movie and staying until your friend tugged your sleeve with "This is where we came in?" That's how to use this book. Open to the season of spring: March is counted as the first month of the season. Write in the date of the current week and you are ready to begin. When you come around to the place where you began, you may recognize that place in a new way, according to a new sense of time.

There is an underpinning to the Viking Runes that is both subtle and heartening. It partakes, consciously, of the flow of beings into their forms; of the attunement to natural rhythms and the endless going and return that is our life. The seed in the earth, the budding and flowering, the fruit ripening in the sun, the husks crumbled into loam, the fallow time that follows the harvest, the new seeds in the earth once again.

As the seasons move, different clothes protect us, different foods nourish us, different activities sustain us, different attitudes inform us. We are talking about differences—changes—rather than stress-and-strain notions like "more" and "faster" and "time running out." It is our intention with this book to be in harmony with the natural rhythms of moons waxing and waning, the running of tides, the procession of solstices and equinoxes that hold and enfold us all.

So we offer you a book of days, with the days gathered and bound by the seasonal focus, keeping us mindful of nature's time as our time. Since this is a book of thanksgiving, it is well that it begins with the season of autumn. The Rune of Harvest, remember, is ᛃ, *Jera,* a Rune of thanksgiving for your own process "which, in its season, leads to the harvest of the self."

Gud blessi thig!

Invocation

I honor your gods
I drink at your well
I bring an undefended heart
    to our meeting place.
I have no cherished outcomes
I will not negotiate by withholding
I am not subject to disappointment.

How to Use This Book

Rune Play is divided into four seasons, with monthly intervals of approximately five weeks each. Each week is laid out on two facing pages that provide space for each day's Rune readings. Additional space is provided at week's end for summary, review or comments.

Since *The Book of Runes* was published, a number of new techniques and spreads have suggested themselves. Each new method of Rune casting brings with it a wider experience of the diversity and usefulness of the Viking Runes. Runes found in nature, Runes and personal health, Runes and group relationships—these are among the new techniques presented here for the first time.

These twelve new techniques appear at monthly intervals and as separators between seasons. Following each technique a page is provided where you may try out the technique and record your observations.

You will notice that each daily space contains three Rune blanks in which to draw your *Daily Rune*, *Outworking Rune, and Results Rune.* If picking more Runes or employing a spread is appropriate, simply draw your own blanks on the page for the additional Runes required.

Do not feel obliged to stay within the space provided for each day. If, for example, on a certain Tuesday events occur that call for extended self-exploration and evaluation, feel at liberty to expand into the space provided for the coming days. Hopefully, there are enough extra days included to see you through. With that flexibility in mind, *Rune Play* offers something new: the five-week month.

SAMPLE DAILY READINGS

Here are some of the techniques used by people of different temperaments and outlooks. The first is taken from the journal of a young New York businessman at a time when his company was merging with another company. Though regarded as an up-and-coming manager, he was concerned over his uncertain future at a time when the policies of new management were not yet clear. His Daily Rune was ᛁ *Isa,* Standstill, which he used as the Overview Rune for a three-Rune spread. He wrote in his journal:

7:30 A.M. *Daily Rune,* ᛁ, Whose Standstill? Corporate or mine?
11:55 A.M. *Issue*: Does my future lie with
[new company name]? ᚹ, Joy, Light. Good.
I just got my appetite back.
4:30 P.M. *Issue*: My boss is slated for a position
on the new team. How can I support him?
ᛒ Growth, *Reversed.* So I wait.
Nothing to be done— the Standstill
is mine.
10:45 P.M. *Issue*: An overview of how I conducted myself.
ᛖ, Movement. Gradual development
and steady progress in a time of transit
and transition. Face the future assured.

The young man has been keeping a Rune Journal for over a year. He commented: "I've learned to have greater trust in myself through Rune play. Keeping this record helps when I want to review the anatomy of any personal crisis and see how I handled it."

Here is a journal entry from a Minneapolis woman, a single working mother. She uses the Runes to hold conversations with herself and employs a question-and-answer format. This passage was recorded at a time when she was feeling exhausted and badly in need of a break.

Q: What happens if I leave the kids with Mom and take 3 days off, get away, think only of me? The *Issue* is taking time off.

A: ᚲ, *Kano,* Opening. Good, I'll come back with "renewed clarity," just as I thought.

Q: Ted [new boyfriend] wants to go with me and "share" my three days. I am torn, but it doesn't feel right. What happens if I let him come with me? The *Issue* is my relationship.

A: ᛉ, *Algiz,* Protection, *Reversed.* "Be thoughtful about your health, look carefully at all the associations you form at this time." *All* means you too, Ted. Important to see whether he takes my refusal personally or understands and accepts my need to spend some time alone.

Her comments: "The Runes I draw seem to reflect what I already subconsciously know, but sometimes find hard to admit or accept without reassurance or confirmation. They make me feel more tranquil and help settle inner conflicts even though their message is not always what I want to hear. Since starting this journal, I often catch myself 'making nice,' putting everybody's wants and needs ahead of my own. Next time a similar situation confronts me, I'll go back, find today's page number, enter it on the current page. By comparing the Runes I drew on both occasions, my behavior patterns really jump out at me. I am taking responsibility for my own needs at last."

Jason is a fifteen-year-old California high school sophomore who has been recording his Rune readings ever since his grandmother gave him *The Book of Runes* "by mistake" last Christmas ("She bought it thinking it was some kind of game. Was she ever right!"). His hobby is cycling; his secondary concern is dating and being able to stay out late on weekends. As a regular practice, he picks a Rune in the morning and another before he goes to bed, "to get the Runes to give me a grade on how I did today." When there is a special issue, Jason records the essentials as they affect him and his family, as though he were telling a friend. He has his own four-part technique:

> *Situation:* What's really big for me right now is a new bicycle I want to buy for $350. No one else in the family wants me to buy it and it's really causing problems.
>
> *Issue:* The new Peugeot ten-speed bike.
>
> *Rune:* H, *Hagalaz,* Disruptive Natural Forces.
>
> *Comment:* "Change, freedom, invention and liberation" is what I want, all right. And "disruption" is what the bike will cause with Mom and Dad. It'll bother them for a while, but it's something I really want and eventually things will smooth over.

He bought the bike and, as Jason predicted, things did smooth over.

Another issue arose concerning a girlfriend who is sixteen and is allowed to use her family's car sometimes while she saves to buy her own.

Situation: Saturday is Marcie's birthday. She wants us to drive to San Diego, go to the zoo and go to a party at S.D.S.U. [San Diego State University]. No way we'll get back before 1:00 A.M. My limit is 11:30 P.M. I don't know about permission to make the trip.

Issue: What do I tell my Mom when she asks where we're going?

Rune: ᛇ, *Eihwaz,* Defense.

Comment: So this is a test and not telling Mom would be a lie. I guess I'm being told to think of the consequences before I act. And that through "inconvenience and discomfort" I'll get promoted growthwise. Just what I wanted to hear.

Jason played it straight. The outcome: His mom talked to Marcie's mother. It was agreed that the kids could go to San Diego and stay over at the college dorms, returning on Sunday.

The next example comes from the files of a Houston marriage counselor who uses the Runes as part of the therapeutic process. First the issue is discussed with her client; next she has the client lay out a Three Rune Spread in order to provide a different perspective. Then the issue is once again discussed in the light of any new insights.

Here is how the therapist used the Runes with a couple in crisis, hardworking professionals who come home at the end of a long day needing to be nurtured. Neither has the energy to give the other the attention they need, and both are feeling hurt and resentful. The issue is their relationship. The three Runes chosen by the wife were: (1) *Issue:* ᛞ, *Dagaz,* Breakthrough; (2) *Challenge:* ᚹ, *Wunjo, Reversed,* Joy; (3) *Action Called For:* ᚠ, *Fehu, Reversed,* Possessions.

Drawing *Dagaz* calls for a major transformation in attitude and counsels her to not collapse herself into worries about the future. *Wunjo, Reversed,* the Challenge Rune, indicates that she is going through a difficult period, but that she should see this time as a test, stay focused in the present, and trust her process. *Fehu, Reversed,* the third or Action Called For Rune, signifies, once again, considerable frustration that she needs to examine from the point of view of lessons to be learned. She is dealing with the shadow side of her nature here and is asked to consider where her "true nourishment lies."

After a fruitful discussion of areas of dissatisfaction and how they might be improved, the couple saw clearly that a change in attitude was called for. They both realized that their expectations upon arriving home were unrealistic. By giving each other time alone to go through the mail, change clothes, read or just lie down and close their eyes for a while, they found that they had something to give when they finally came together to welcome each other home.

Although the examples of Rune recording given above are quite detailed, most of the people asked to test out sample pages from *Rune Play* kept their entries brief. The overall pattern was to set down key phrases from *The Book of Runes* that were meaningful to them, then add a few words by way of comment. Some people referred to other readings that shed light on the present issue, or to the way they had handled similar challenges in the past. Many entries included readings done for friends. A few people included Rune readings concerning the state of the nation and the world.

Extra Rune blanks are to be added by you as needed. Draw in the blanks by hand whenever and wherever you wish to undertake or expand a spread. The pages of this book have been made from the sturdiest and most pleasing paper stock available. Your ordinary pen (or pencil) should suffice. If you find the ink bleeds through—rare but not impossible—perhaps you can select another pen with which to record your process in *Rune Play.*

This is your book. As you use it, *Yggdrasil,* the Tree of the World, will speak to you. And as you discover new and creative ways to use its benefits, you will speak back.

The following entries were made by a woman at a time of intense life pressure: a pending divorce, a fire in her home, and her birthday, all in one week's span. Despite the demands being made upon her time and energy, she saw reason to use her Daily Rune castings as a means of clarifying while she persevered. Even in the midst of chaos and crises, she also persevered in her sense of humor and play.

An example of how flexible and adaptable these pages are is found in her Friday, 3/15 entry. She simply ignored the Friday Daily Rune routine and did a Three Rune Spread, writing beneath the three blanks provided the words *Overview, Challenge,* and *Outcome.*

For the week of *March 11*

Mon 3/11

Mannaz, Reversed. Blocked again. How like me! Admit release. Don't turn to others. I'm getting good at that. And what blocks the self? The momentum of past habits

DAILY RUNE

OUTWORKING RUNE

Fehu, Reversed. Frustration! Everything I did today didn't quite work. the lesson must be self-nourishment. That's all I got

Not Bad.

RESULTS RUNE

Tues 3/12

Fehu, Reversed. Not again! Well my life right now is full of "doubtful situations." I want to ask about one of them. The letter I must write to S.

DR

Signals, Reversed. I'll say the well is clogged. Clean it out. Suggest to S. that "adversity" equals opportunity.

OR

Breakthrough. I feel good about today Leapt into the void a couple of times. Being a Spiritual Warrior does take work. [ᛞ] goes under my pillow tonight. You never know.

RR

Wed. 3/13

Hagalaz. Freedom through disruption. Events beyond my control. I like it. Growth is coming very fast. Growing pains for adults. In two days I'll be 45.

DR

The Blank Rune. Meeting with S.'s father. So the issue here is relinquishing control. His turn. It's about time. Give him [ᚺ]. Both Barrels.

OR

Defense. The meeting was great. I said things that had to be said. Surprised everybody.

Yeah team!

RR

Thurs. 3/14

Separation. Well it's certainly a time of separating paths. This marriage is gone. Now I have to give up my attachment to it. Time to find out who I am without the marriage. Meeting with lawyer this afternoon.

DR

OR

Self, Reversed. Twice in one week. Facing Up can be exhausting. Maybe I will, Maybe I won't. Face Up. I mean. Old habit patterns are the worst addiction.

RR

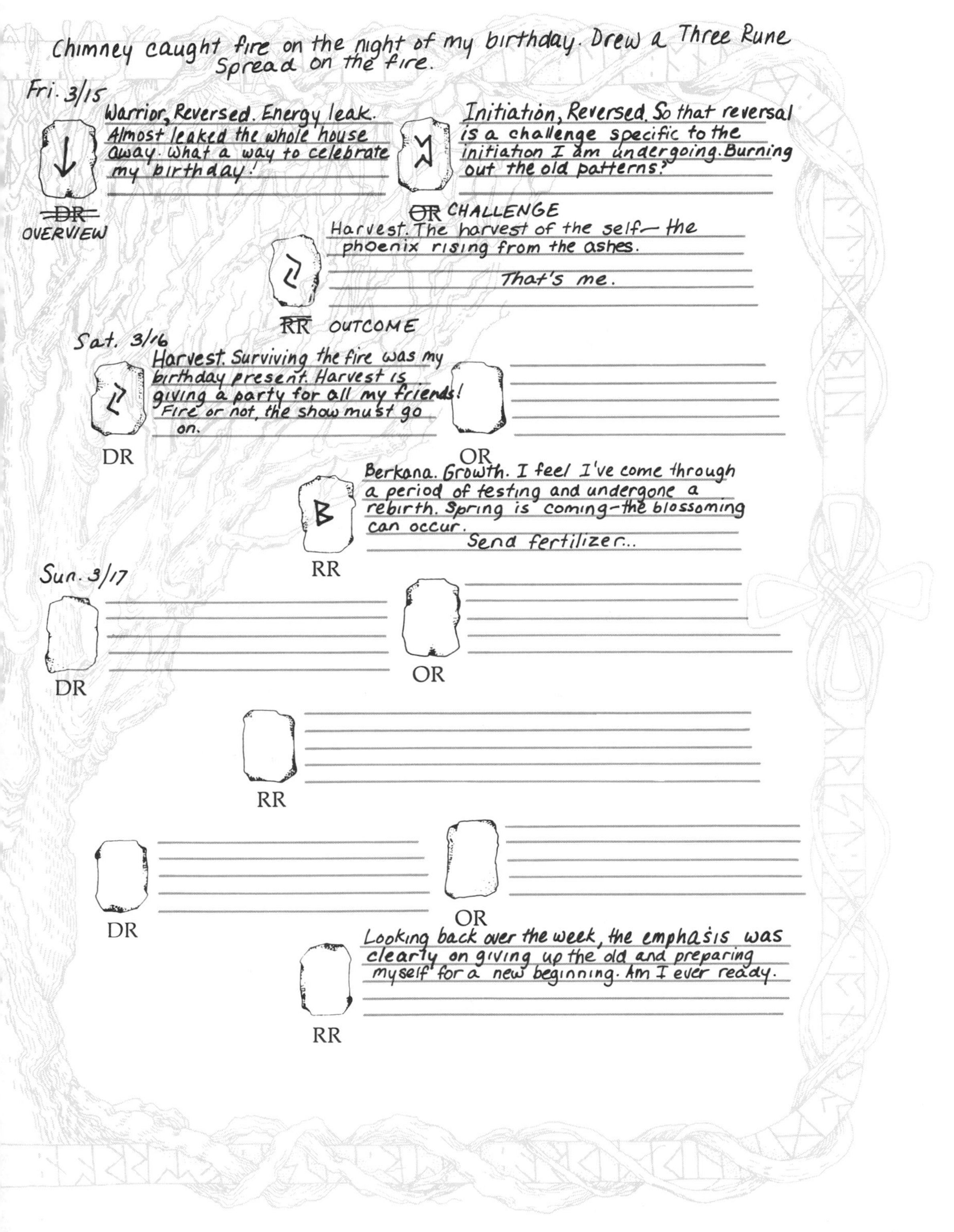
Chimney caught fire on the night of my birthday. Drew a Three Rune Spread on the fire.
Fri. 3/15
Warrior, Reversed. Energy leak. Almost leaked the whole house away. What a way to celebrate my birthday!
DR
OVERVIEW
Initiation, Reversed. So that reversal is a challenge specific to the initiation I am undergoing. Burning out the old patterns?
OR CHALLENGE
Harvest. The harvest of the self— the phoenix rising from the ashes.
That's me.
RR OUTCOME
Sat. 3/16
Harvest. Surviving the fire was my birthday present. Harvest is giving a party for all my friends! Fire or not, the show must go on.
DR
OR
Berkana. Growth. I feel I've come through a period of testing and undergone a rebirth. Spring is coming—the blossoming can occur.
Send fertilizer...
RR
Sun. 3/17
DR
OR
RR
DR
OR
Looking back over the week, the emphasis was clearly on giving up the old and preparing myself for a new beginning. Am I ever ready.
RR

AUTUMN

Runes of Well-Being

At certain times in our lives it is comforting to have immediate access to information about our overall well-being, our physical, mental (emotional), and spiritual health. A fitness report, so to speak, from an expert—the expert being *you.*

Such reassurance might be called for after a disturbing visit to your doctor, therapist, or a troubled friend. The "damage report" can be rendered less awesome when buffered by a second opinion from "that part of you which knows everything you need to know for your life now."

As is the way with the Viking Runes, the operative word in the last sentence is *now.* The spread presented here is a *true present printout from your own biocomputer.* While interpreting the *Runes of Well-Being,* pay particular attention to the ratio of balance/imbalance, deprivation/nourishment, awareness/unconsciousness.

THE SPREAD

Nine Runes are selected, one at a time; each Rune is replaced in the bag after it has been recorded so that each issue is addressed with all 25 Runes in the bag. Three Runes will be chosen for placement under these three headings: (1) *Body;* (2) *Mind;* (3) *Spirit.* In descending order, these Runes stand for (1) *Overview;* (2) *Challenge;* (3) *Action.* Here is the pattern for casting the Runes of Well-Being:

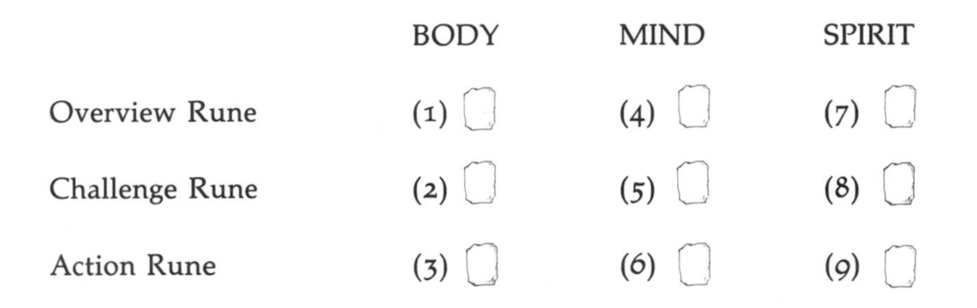

	BODY	MIND	SPIRIT
Overview Rune	(1)	(4)	(7)
Challenge Rune	(2)	(5)	(8)
Action Rune	(3)	(6)	(9)

A SAMPLE READING

THE QUERENT

A woman is currently subject to maximal stress coming from enough directions to confound Wonder Woman, including: the recent death of her father who was actually "a mother" to her as well; the throes of a shattered marriage; the trauma of various surgical procedures recently performed on her body; blocked feelings that have been putting her into emotional overwhelm.

THE SPREAD

	BODY	MIND	SPIRIT
Overview Rune	(1) ᚲ	(4) ᚷ	(7) ᛟ
Challenge Rune	(2) ᚨ	(5) ᛇ	(8) ᛦ
Action Rune	(3) ᚺ	(6) ᚠ	(9) ᚾ

THE READING

(1) BODY: *Overview Rune*

ᚲ, *Kano,* is the Rune of Fire, of Opening, and bespeaks a new and greater clarity in which to begin the work of restoring her body to optimum health; it affords light in which to see what is trivial and outmoded in her conditioning. Since she is a person who invariably tends to the needs of others while pushing her own needs firmly aside, ᚲ reminds her: "Simply put, if you have been operating in the dark, there is now enough light to see that the patient on the operating table is yourself." So get on with it, this Rune is saying.

(2) BODY: *Challenge Rune*

ᚨ, *Ansuz,* the Messenger Rune. Not surprisingly, given the strength and durability of her outmoded conditioning, the Challenge Rune is ᚨ, the Messenger Rune, the Rune of Signals. "Even a warning when timely may be seen as a gift." The Challenge is one of a new life unfolding, the new pathways, connections, and linkages that open and form at such a richly creative time. At stake is the possibility of a special new integration between unconscious "motive" and conscious "recognition." Again, a point is made that is paramount to a healthy policy of self-care and maintenance at all levels:

> You are reminded that you must draw first from the well to nourish and give to yourself. Then there will be more than enough to nourish others.

The dominant theme for the entire Well-Being Spread is being estabished in this first level.

(3) BODY: *Action Rune*

ᚺ, *Hagalaz,* Elemental Power and Disruptive Forces. This woman has reached an age (early forties) where she must look squarely at issues of "change, freedom, invention, and liberation." The *Action* is already under way; she can resist it or support it, but from the body level up

> the onset of power may be such as to rip away the fabric of what you previously knew as your reality, your security, your understanding of yourself, your work, your relationships or beliefs.

She is put on notice that sustaining loss or damage isn't what matters here. Change is what matters: "The universe and your own soul are demanding that you do, indeed, grow."

(4) MIND: *Overview Rune*

ᚷ, *Gebo,* the Rune of Partnership. She is being asked to befriend her own mind, to enter into a new union, a creative partnership—of the very sort she yearns to have with a man—with her own mind. True partnering, the Runes remind us, can only be accomplished between equals. "Take me, I'm yours" doesn't work anymore. The truth is this: *You must start by being a good partner to your self.* Otherwise how can you hope to understand the mechanism of partnership with others, or with the Divine? The gift of partnership is the gift of freedom.

(5) MIND: *Challenge Rune*

ᛇ, *Eihwaz,* Defense, Avertive Powers. The querent is encouraged to understand that she is being tested, in the sense of tempering the warrior's sword of clear understanding. Old debris must be hauled away. By being tested she will come to recognize the areas in her life where blockage and defeat occur; she will become sensitized and empowered to manage the very thinking and conduct that bring her to grief. The testing time is also a waiting time: A new "aware" quality of patience is called for. And with it, tolerance of the "inconvenience and discomfort" through which new growth, a new mental health is being promoted.

(6) MIND: *Action Rune*

ᚠ, *Fehu,* the Rune of Possessions, Nourishment. This Rune is concerned with fulfillment at every level. Nourishment, as used here, includes everything "from the most worldly to the sacred and Divine." While she practices patient understanding of all that is challenging her, she is required to undertake "a deep probing of the meaning of profit and gain" in her life. She is urged to review her priorities and remember that true nourishment, true well-being, begins with self-rule and the growth of a will.

(7) SPIRIT: *Overview Rune*

ᛟ, *Othila,* the Rune of Inheritance, Separation, and Retreat. In medieval times, there was a "test of condition" known as *Einmannkampf,* or "one-man combat," a situation where a knight, armed but alone, went up against a vastly superior force. The single warrior could not win, was not expected to win. *The warrior was judged according to how he handled himself in defeat.* Similar tests of condition confront the Spirit today, in every life. What the querent has inherited and clung to as her salvation must now be shed before she sinks in its leaden embrace. The orders ring with hard words: submission . . . retreat . . . separation. And yet this is a healing separation which will free her to become more truly who she is.

(8) SPIRIT: *Challenge Rune*

ᛦ, *Algiz,* the Rune of Protection. *Reversed.* The entire issue of what Protection means in her life must be reviewed. There is major unfinished business in this area, and it is keeping her toxic. This is a time of transition, rich not only in healthy opportunities and challenges, but also in "trespasses and unwanted influences." Unhealthy associations can no longer be entered into under the guise of seeking protection. Once she has taken full responsibility for herself, the benefits will begin. And herein occurs the only other echo of *Einmannkampf* in the Runes: "You may not win, but you will never lose, for you will always learn from what takes place."

(9) SPIRIT: *Action Rune*

ᚾ, *Nauthiz,* the Rune of Necessity, Constraint, and Pain. This Rune is the most challenging and, at the same time, has the greatest potential for healing of the 25 Runes. With it comes the energy to make straight the crooked places in ourselves. Adversity is the ally. Looking on this Rune with a smile will be evidence that she recognizes "the troubles, denials and setbacks of life as your guides, teachers and developers." She must now work with what she has denied and disowned in her own nature. And the call to action is both clear and gentle: "Let the constraints of the time serve you in righting your relationship to your Self." And to your *self.* As above, so below; as within, so without.

In the life of the Spirit, so say the Runes, we are always at the beginning. Even a situation resembling a battlefield at the moment of gravest peril and uncertainty *is* a new beginning. The battlefield could be a courtroom where you are on trial, a hospital emergency room, a marital bedroom. The best outcome is the *greatest good;* the strategy is *healing.*

All this being examined and considered, the querent chose a Rune for summation, the "in a nutshell" or "gist" of the situation Rune. The Rune she chose was ᚱ, *Raido,* the Rune of Communication, Union and Reunion, Journey. It is the Rune of the Spiritual Warrior on her quest. Body serving Mind, Mind honoring Spirit, the Journey is the soul's journey. To have undertaken this spread is ample evidence that the querent is well and truly on her way. She is advised to ask for what she needs. "Ask through prayer," is ᚱ's counsel:

> through addressing your own knowing, your body knowing, the Witness Self, the Teacher Within. Once you are clear, then you can *neutralize your refusal to let right action flow through you.* Not intent on movement, be content to wait; while you wait, keep on removing resistances. As the obstructions give way, all remorse arising from "trying to make it happen" disappears.

Body, Mind, Spirit—the vital signs, free of illusions. As always, the journey is toward self-healing, self-change and union.

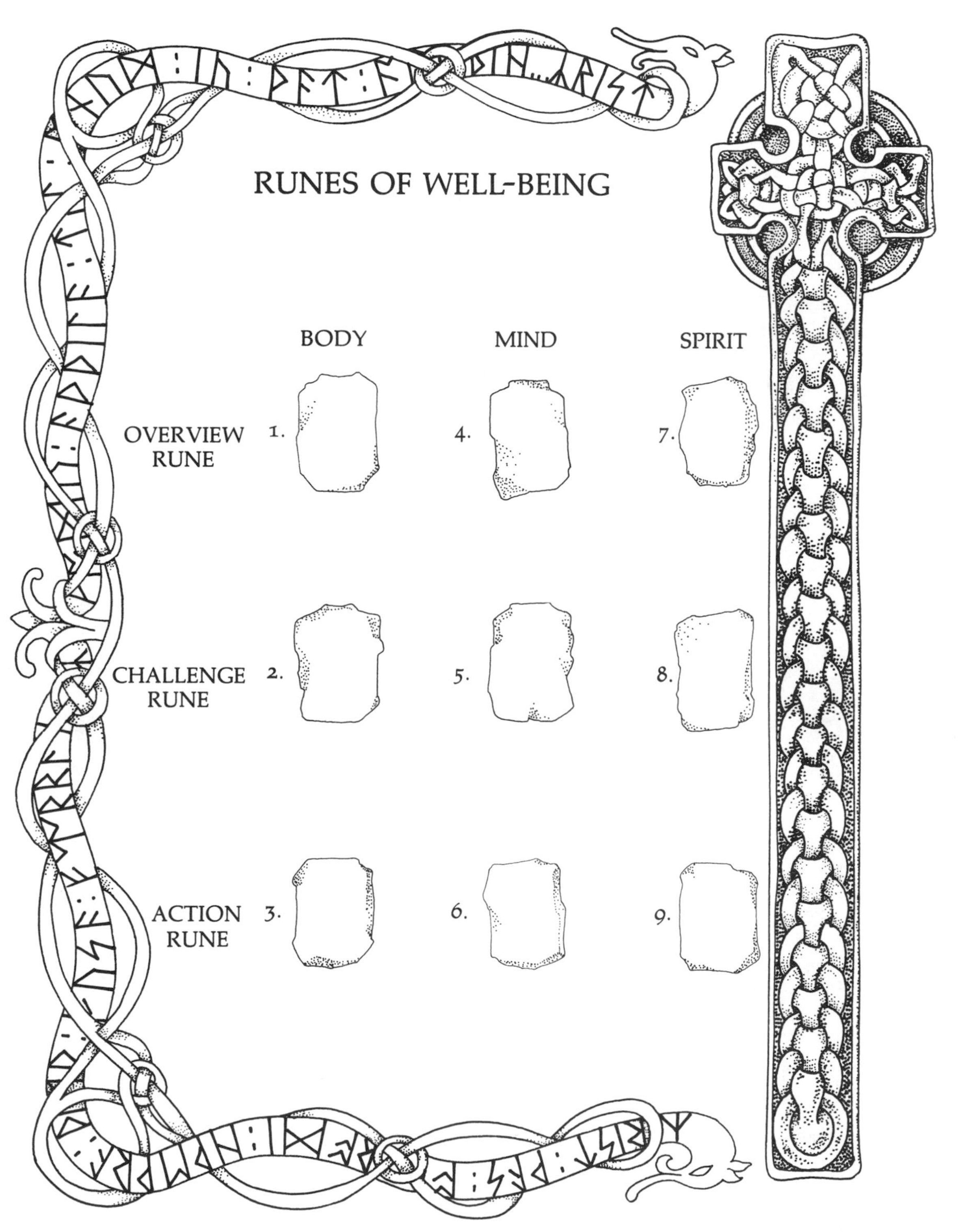
RUNES OF WELL-BEING
BODY
MIND
SPIRIT
OVERVIEW RUNE
1.
4.
7.
CHALLENGE RUNE
2.
5.
8.
ACTION RUNE
3.
6.
9.

For the week of ____________

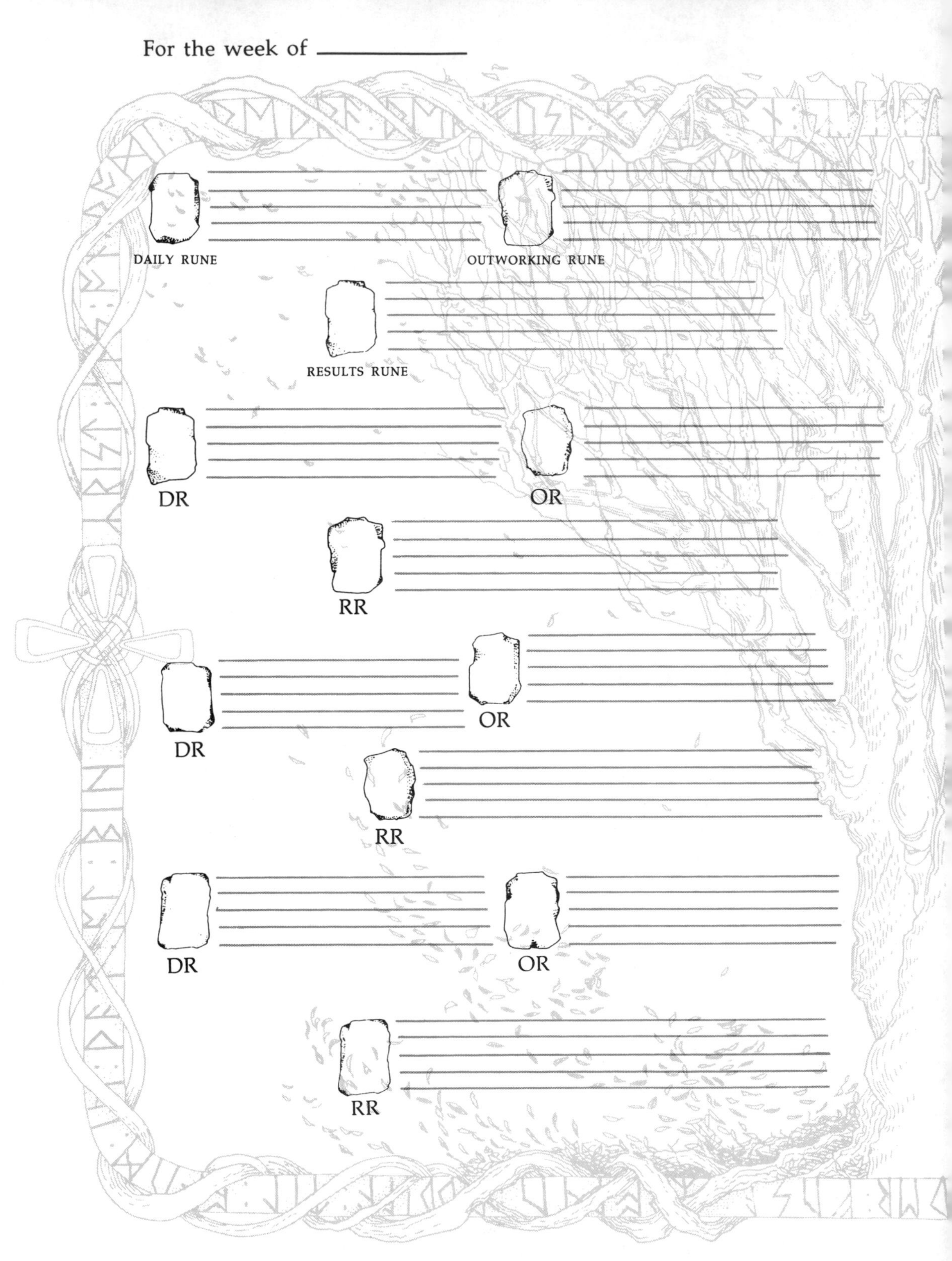

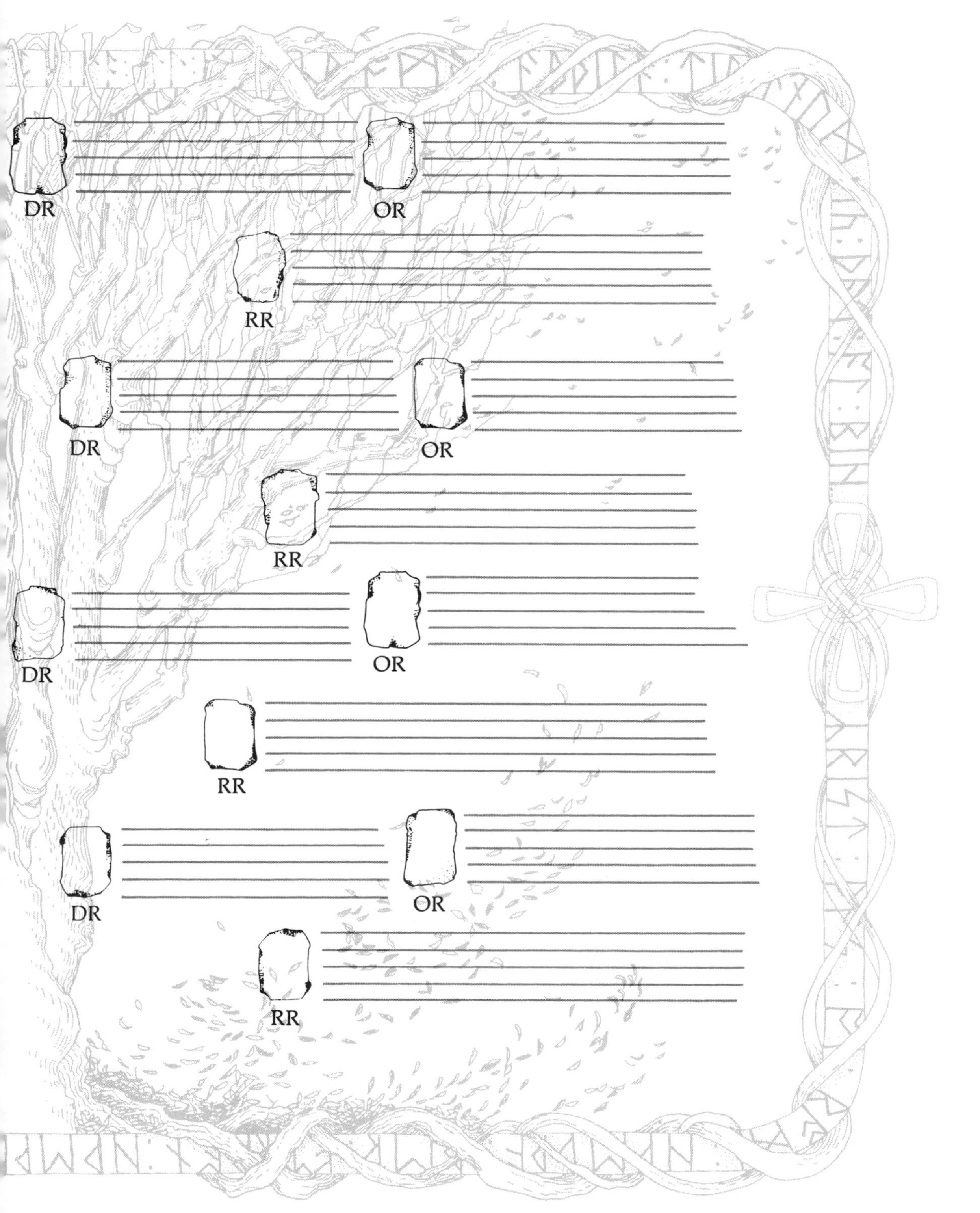
DR
OR
RR
DR
OR
RR
DR
OR
RR
DR
OR
RR

For the week of ______________

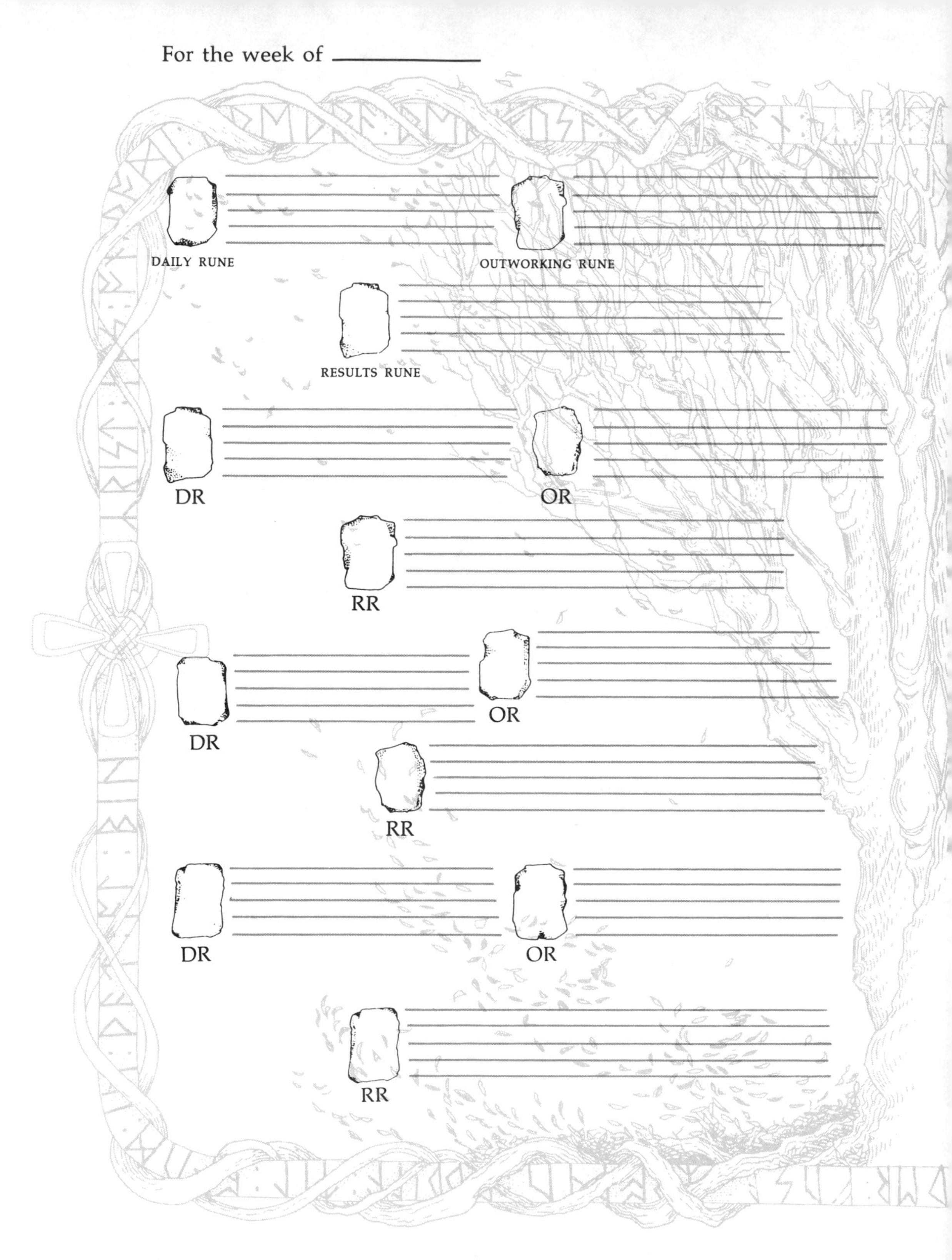

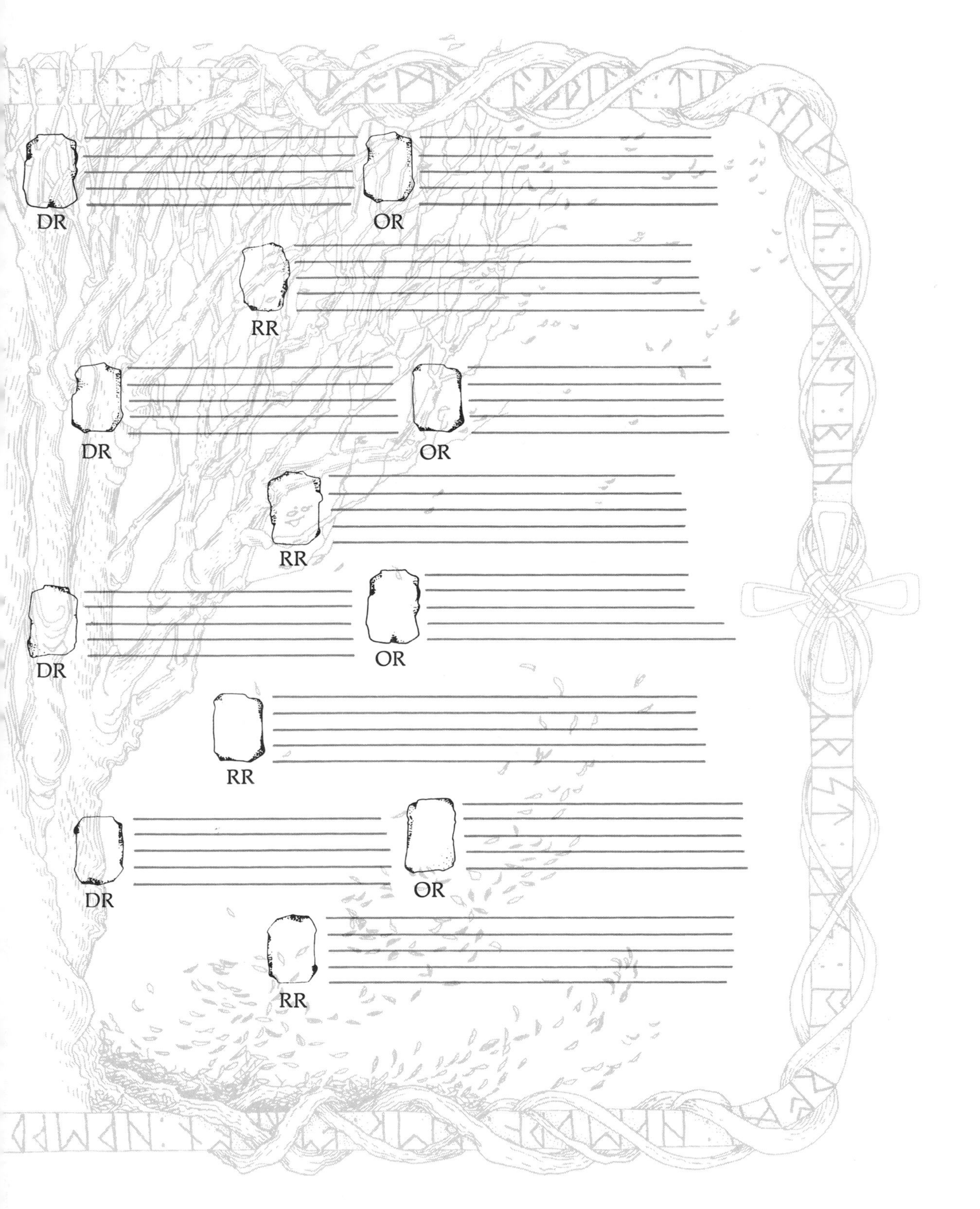
DR
OR
RR
DR
OR
RR
DR
OR
RR
DR
OR
RR

For the week of ________________

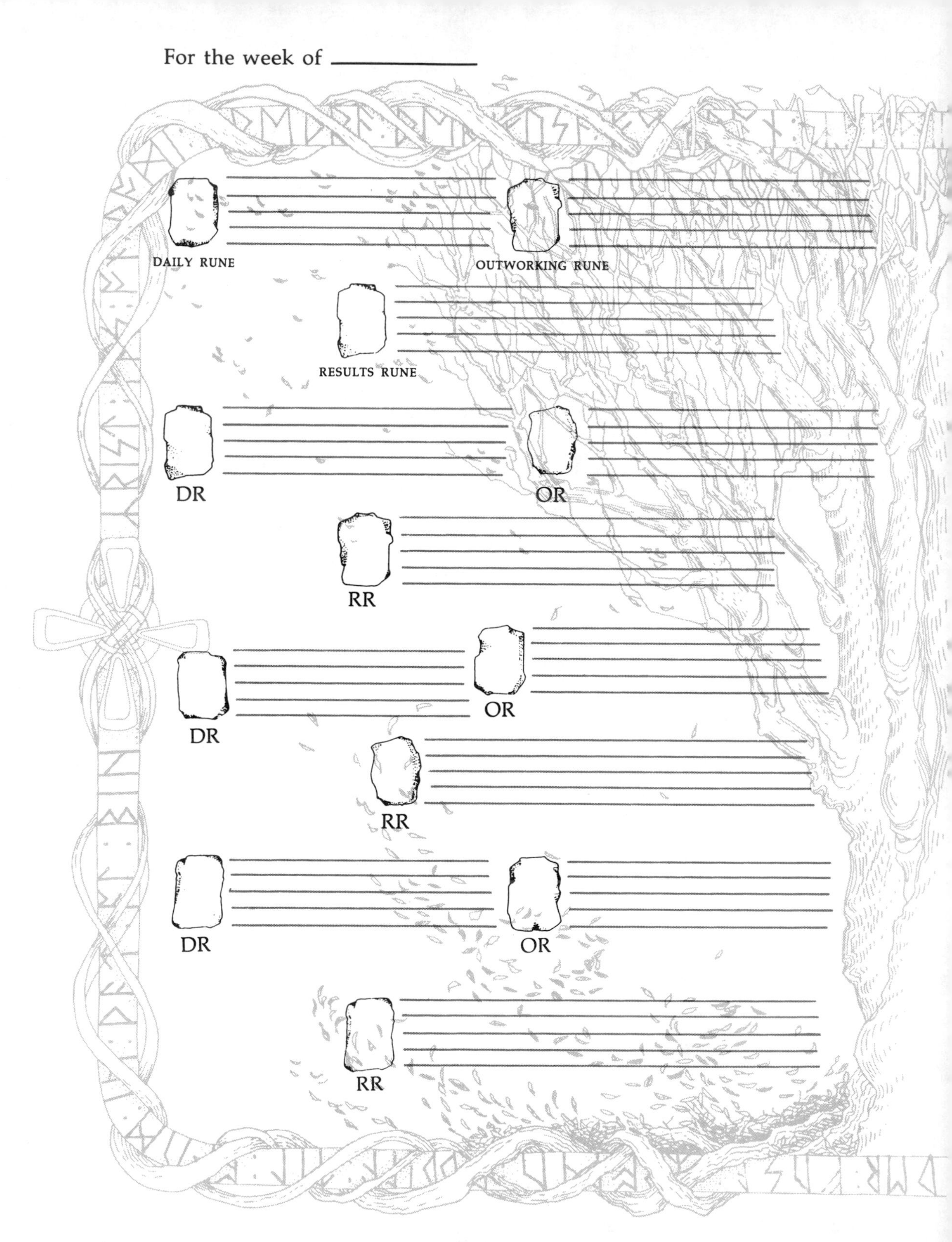

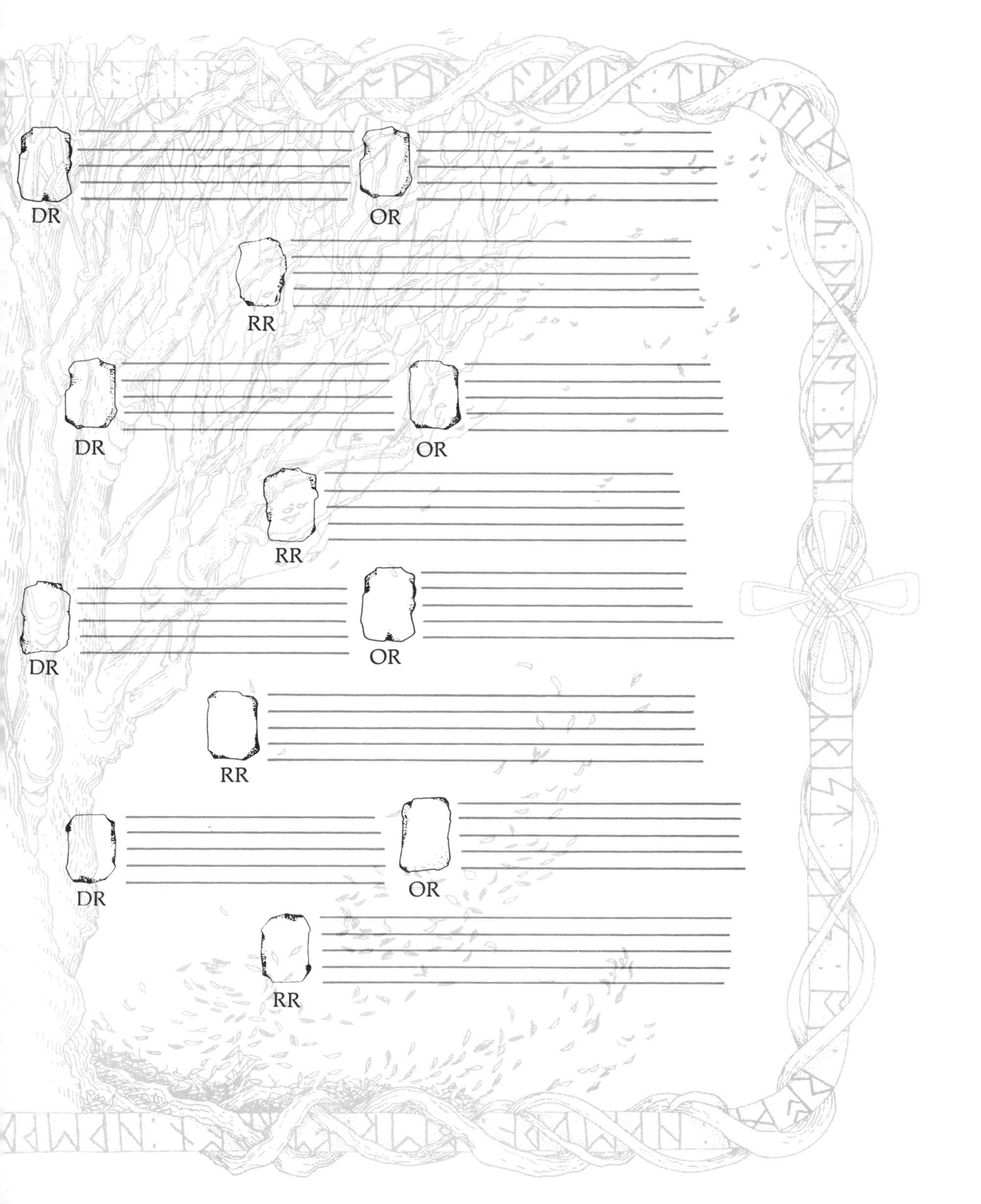
DR
OR
RR
DR
OR
RR
DR
OR
RR
DR
OR
RR

For the week of ____________

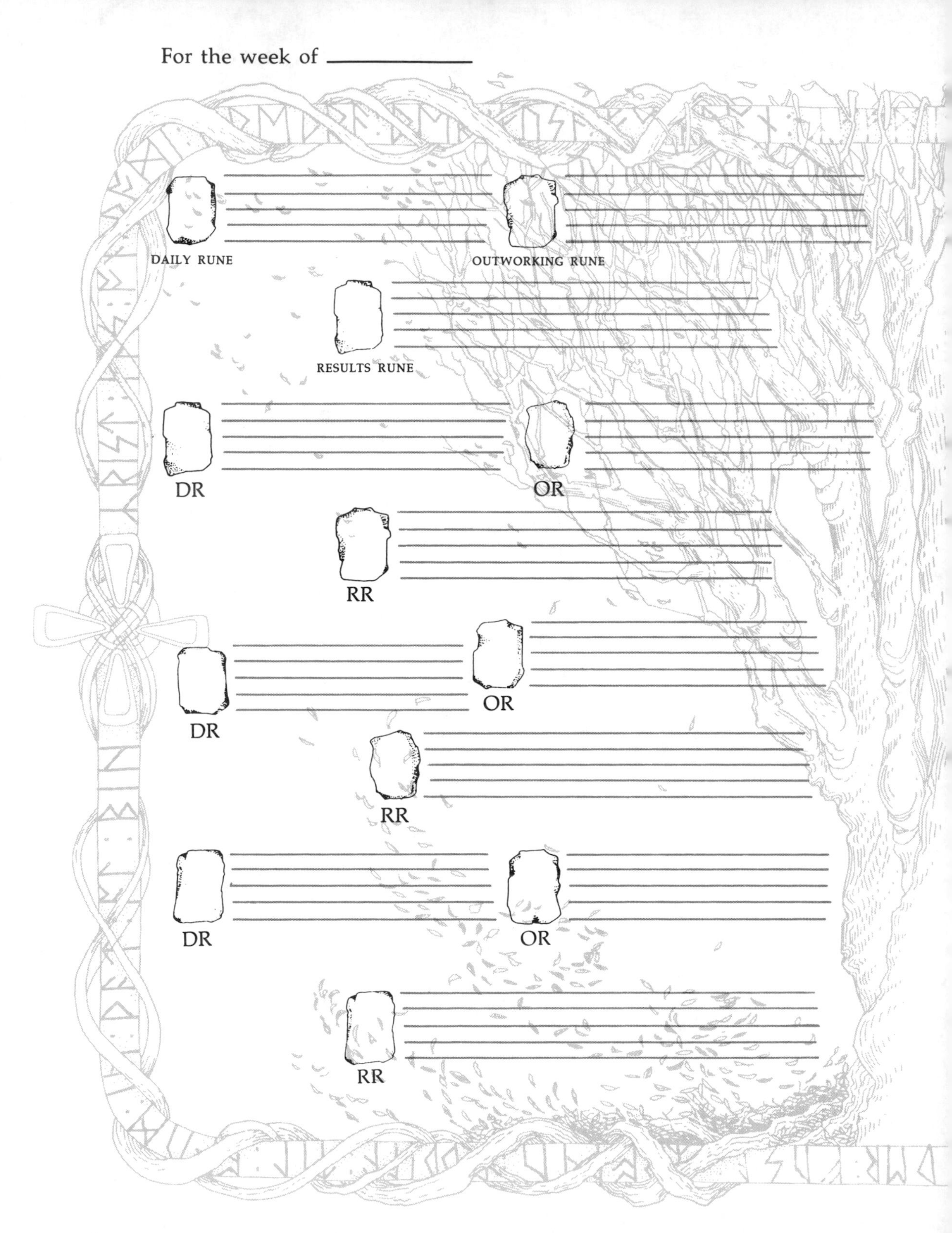

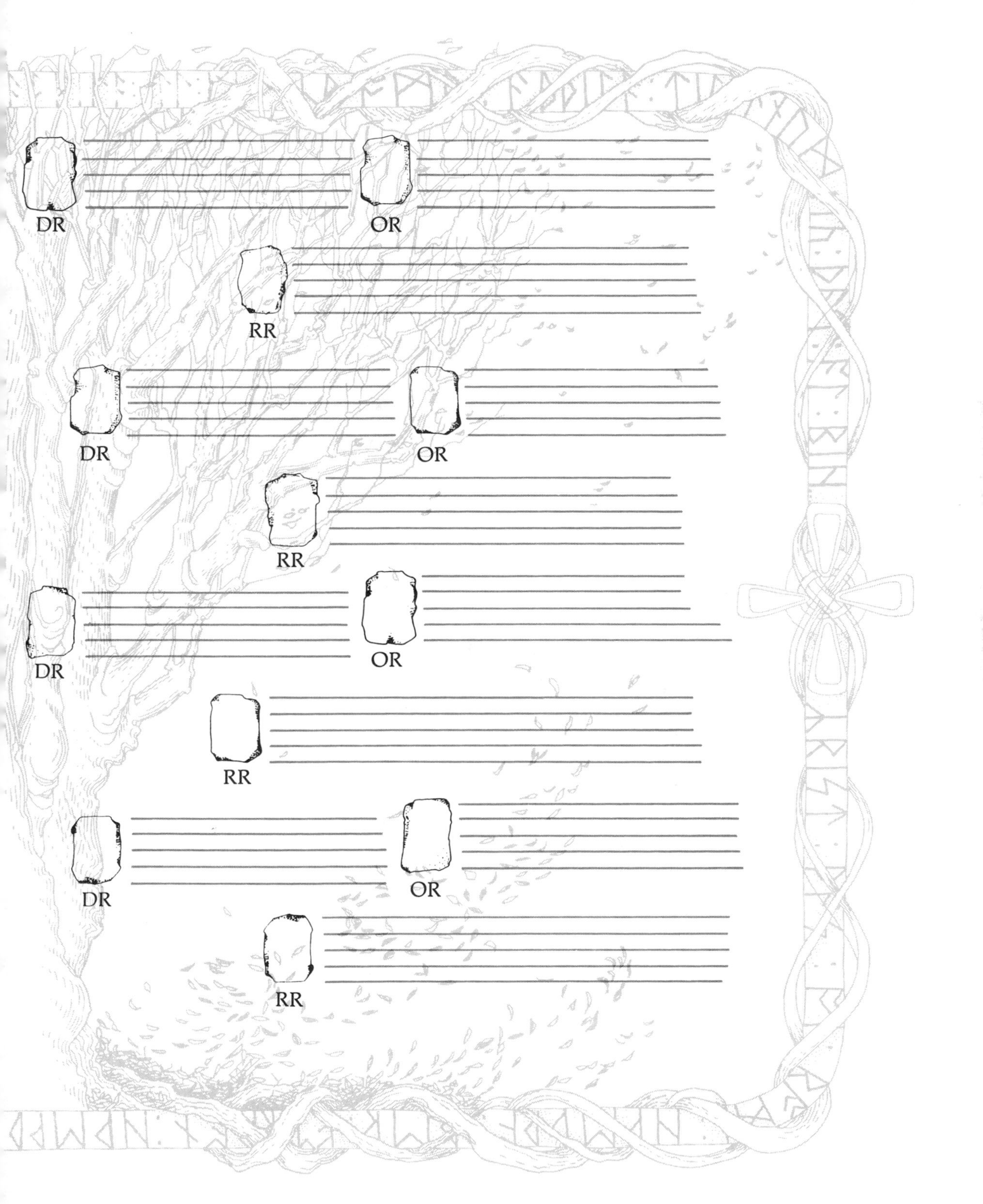
DR
OR
RR
DR
OR
RR
DR
OR
RR
DR
OR
RR

For the week of ____________

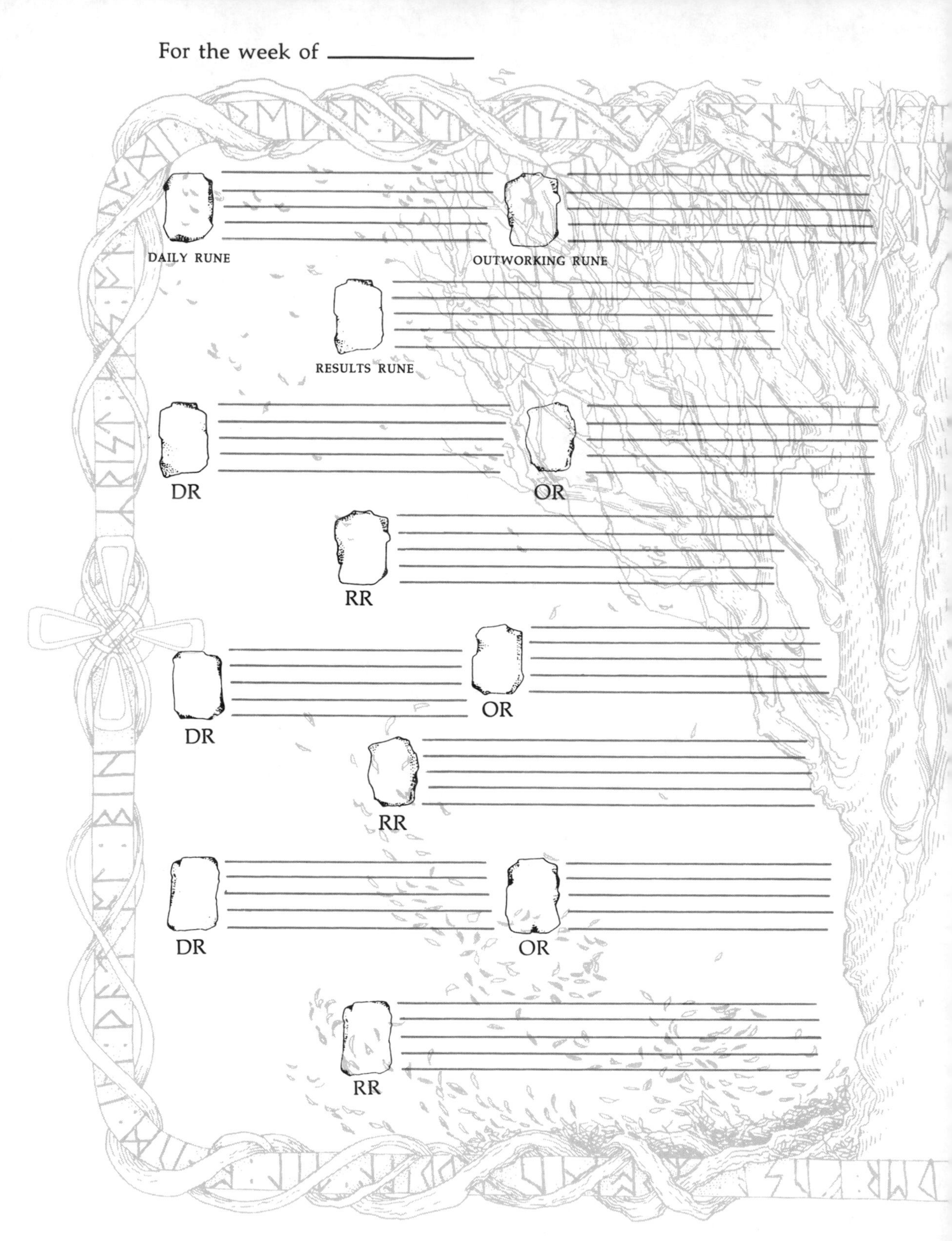

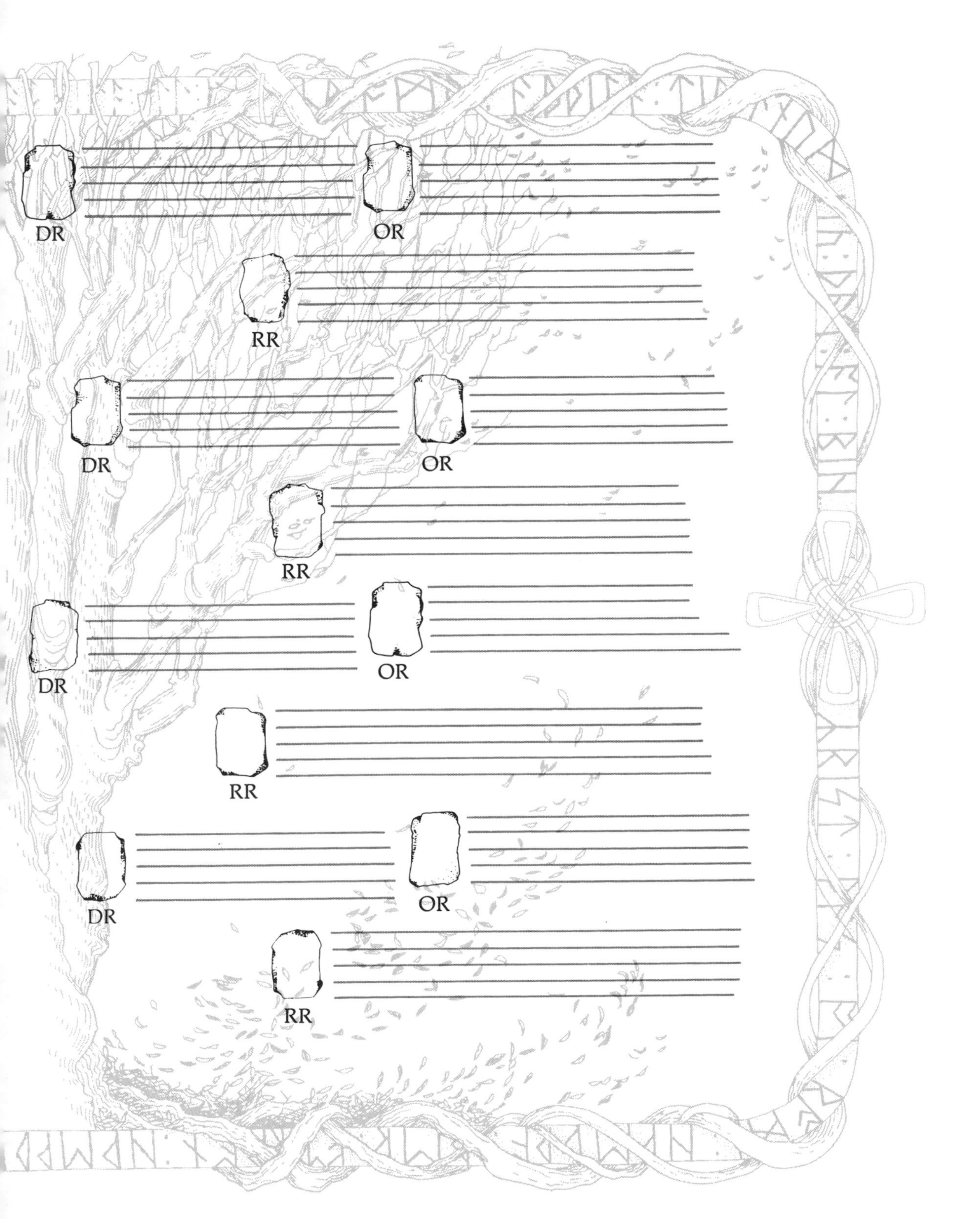
DR
OR
RR
DR
OR
RR
DR
OR
RR
DR
OR
RR

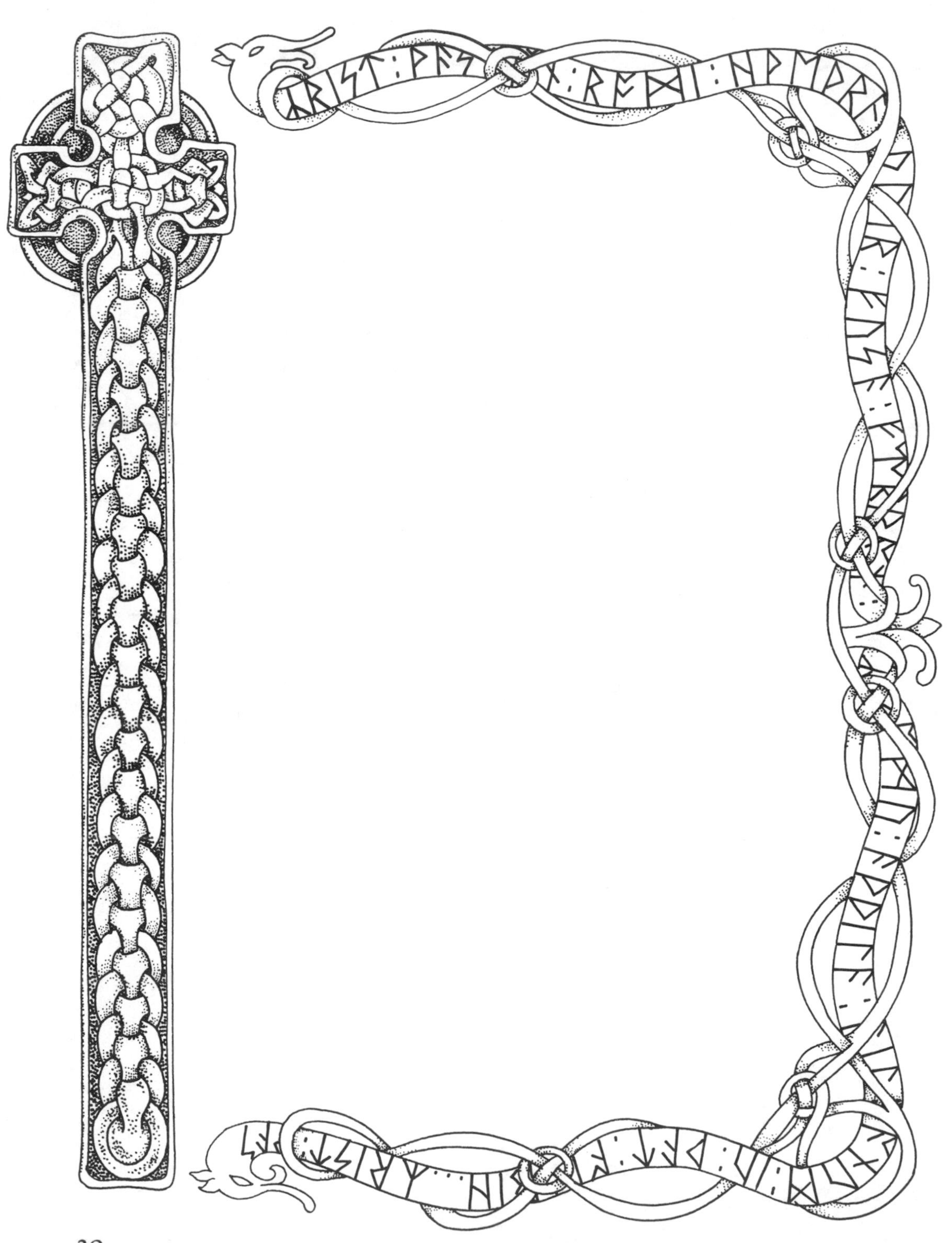

Rune Play

Do you remember, as a child, sitting in the dentist's office, finding comic book drawings of a dense, leafy jungle, and being asked in the caption: "How many monkeys can you find hidden in the jungle?" And when you really looked there they were: monkeys outlined in tree bark, monkeys stitched from vines, monkeys made from the outlines formed between leaves; trunk monkeys, branch monkeys, root monkeys! Well, the Viking Runes have their own monkeyshines. They offer themselves in profusion, in our daily lives, for those who have eyes to see.

Sometimes Runes appear in nature's forms. Just when you are thinking that maybe you had better call the doctor, a cloud combed by the wind stretches itself into the soft lightning-bolt form of ᛋ, *Sowelu,* the Rune of Wholeness and Life Forces. Environmental Runes are all over the place. License plates and bridges scaffoldings, splashes of paint on a wall, cracks in the pavement—all can serve to keep you mindful of your Daily Rune.

Say you selected a Daily Rune and it is ᚠ, *Fehu,* the Rune of Nourishment and Possessions. Be on the lookout for *Fehu* throughout the day. Find ᚠ in the twisting branches of a favorite tree; recognize it the moment your arms reach up as you hold a picture against the wall or stretch a piece of laundry to pin it on the line.

The following are suggestions of ways you can "play" your Daily Rune, the idea being to imprint the unconscious with the essence of *Fehu.*

(1) During a meditation or while resting, visualize ᚠ and keep the image on your mental screen.
(2) Stand in front of a mirror and make ᚠ by stretching.
(3) Do it while floating in a pool, hot tub or ample bathtub; a river, a lake, the ocean.
(4) Draw ᚠ, doodle.
(5) Spot ᚠ in textures, on surfaces, everywhere.
(6) Write in this book a new thought about Possessions at some level in your life.
(7) Let the last image you hold in your mind before you drift off to sleep be ᚠ.

This is the short list. No doubt you can come up with other forms of *Rune Play.*

Rune Play can be enjoyed by people of all ages. In fact, it appears that the unconscious or difficult-to-articulate concerns of young children can often be identified when you and your child play at finding hidden Runes.

The most delightful forms of Rune Play are those you invent for yourself, to play by yourself or with others. Have a good time!

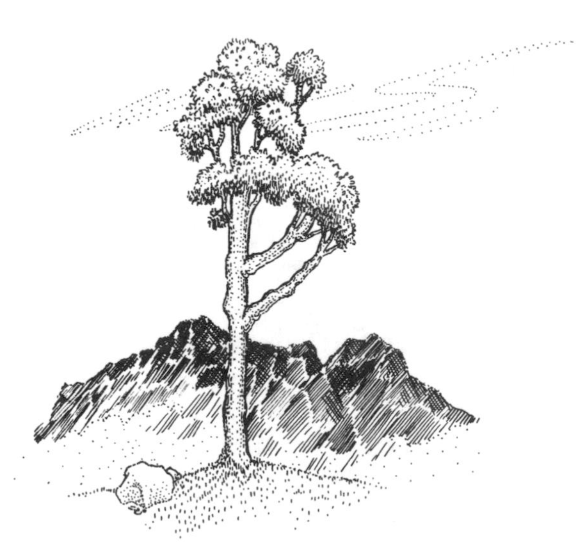

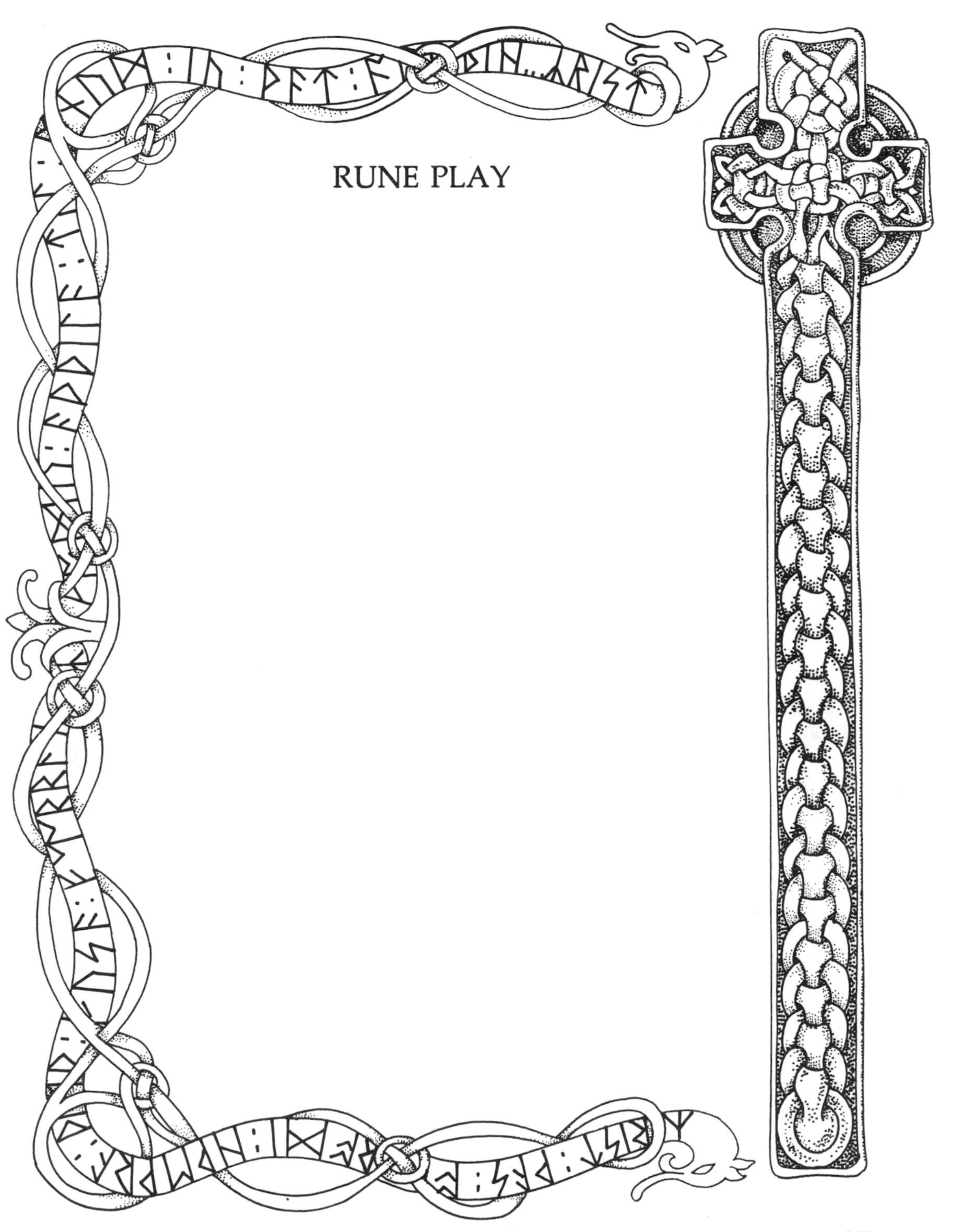

RUNE PLAY

For the week of ____________

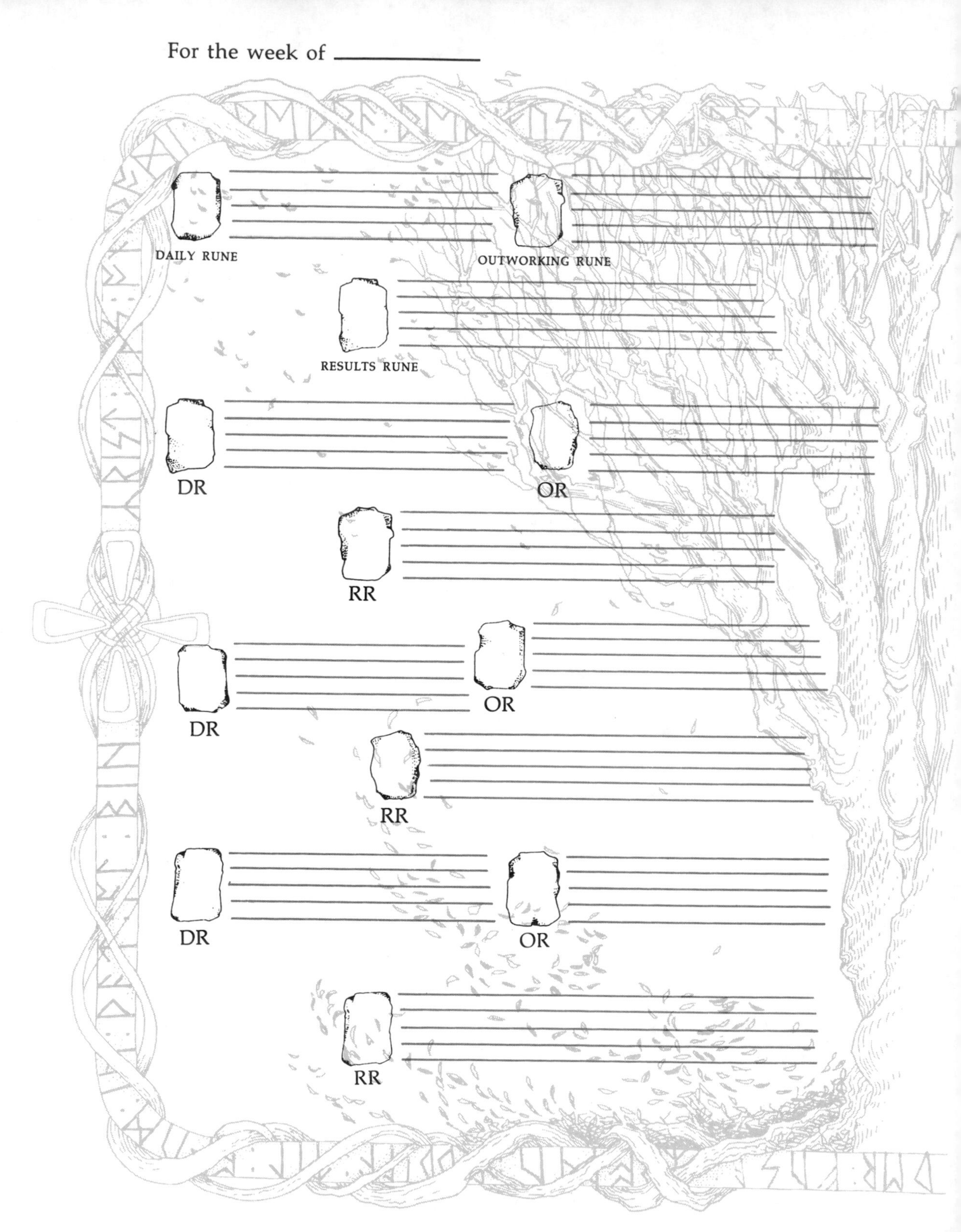

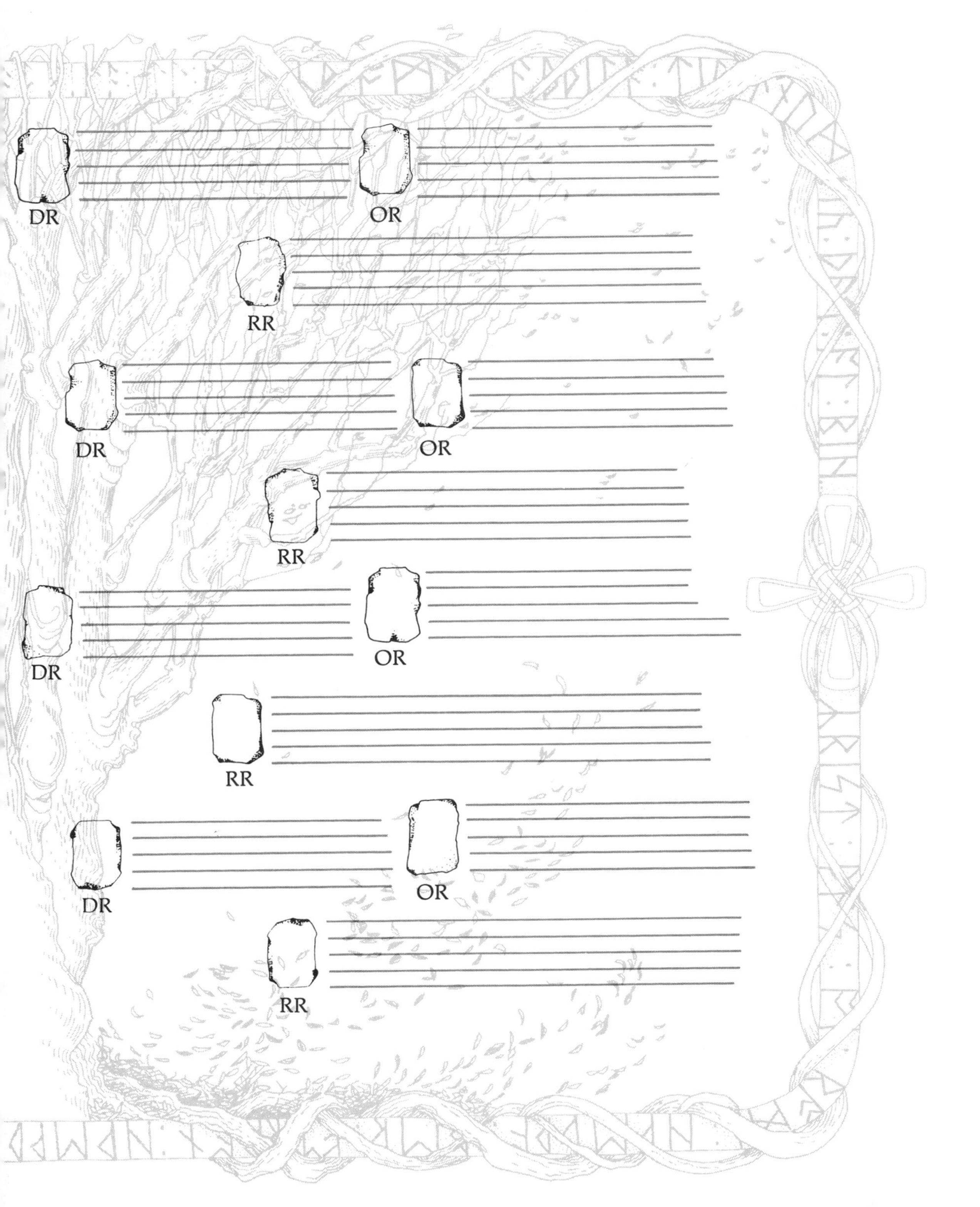
DR
OR
RR
DR
OR
RR
DR
OR
RR
DR
OR
RR

For the week of ___________

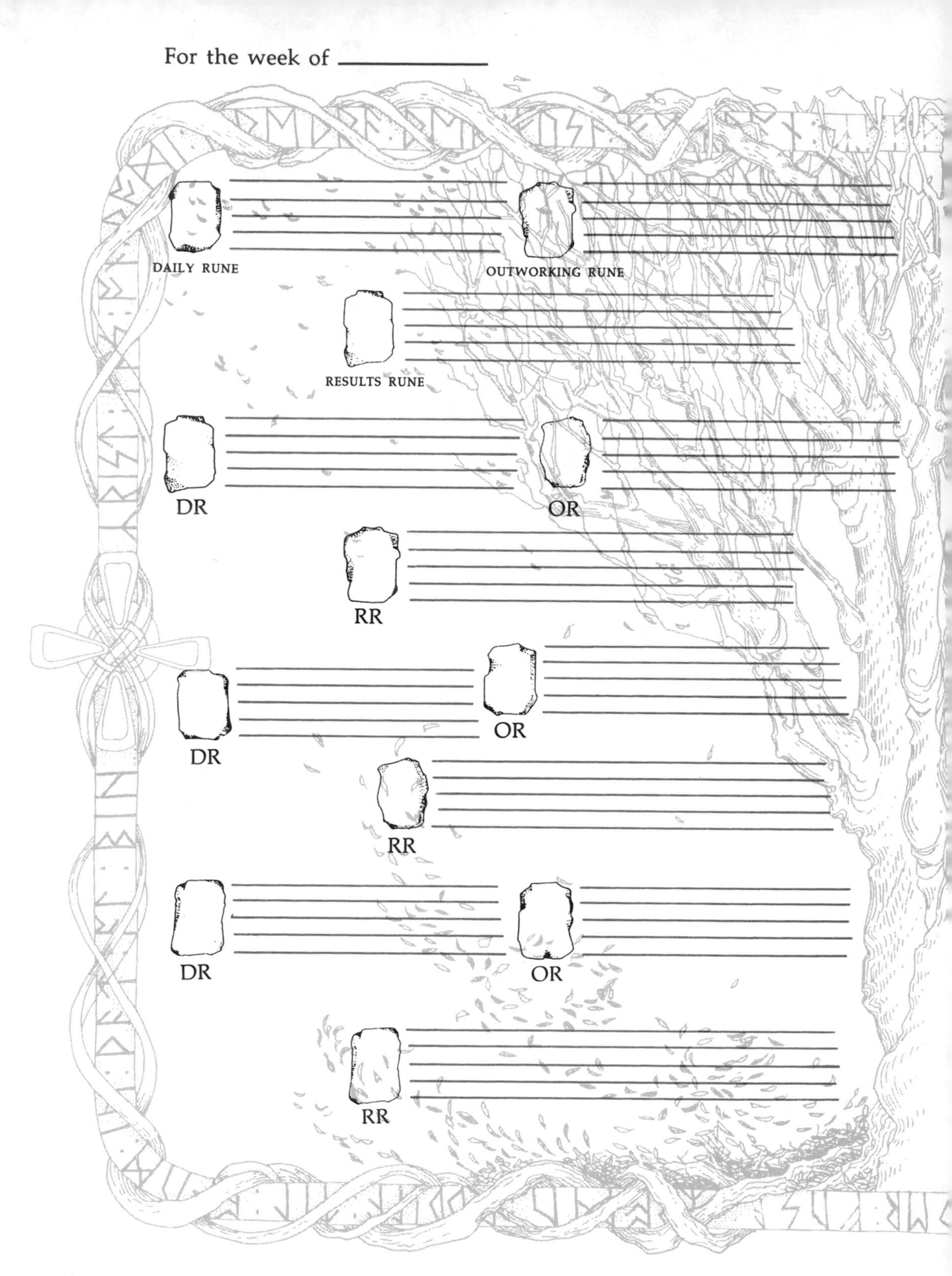

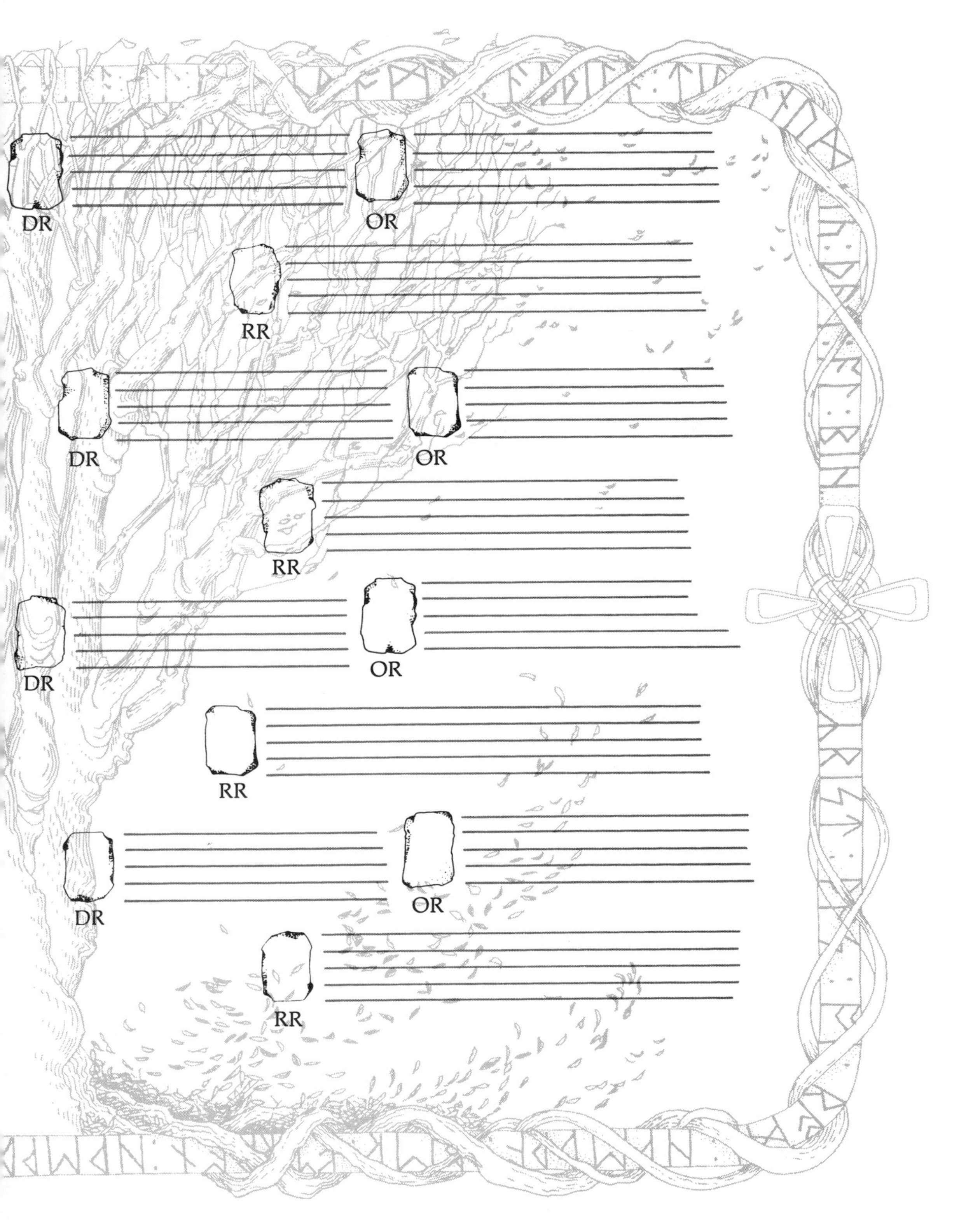
DR
OR
RR
DR
OR
RR
DR
OR
RR
DR
OR
RR

For the week of ____________

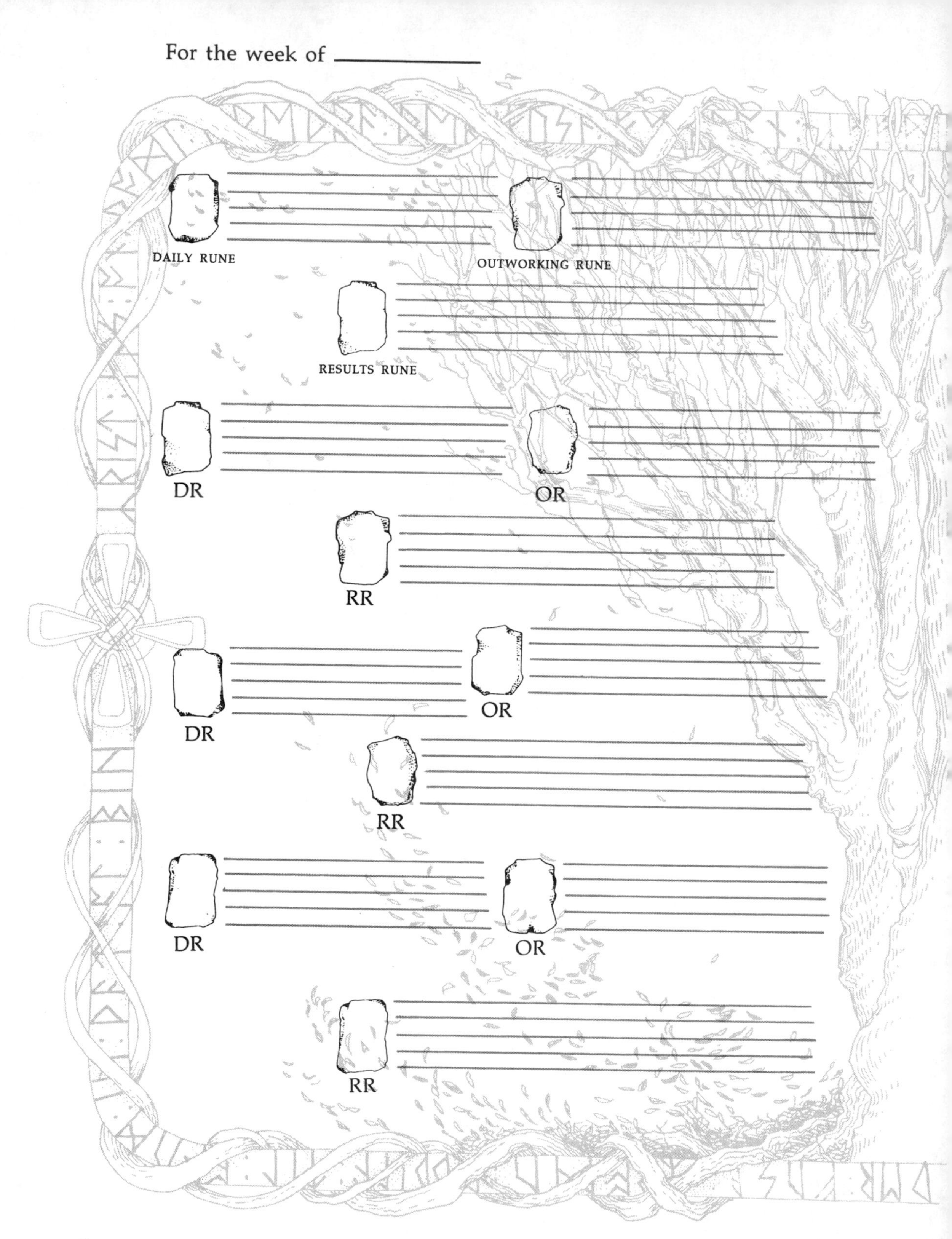

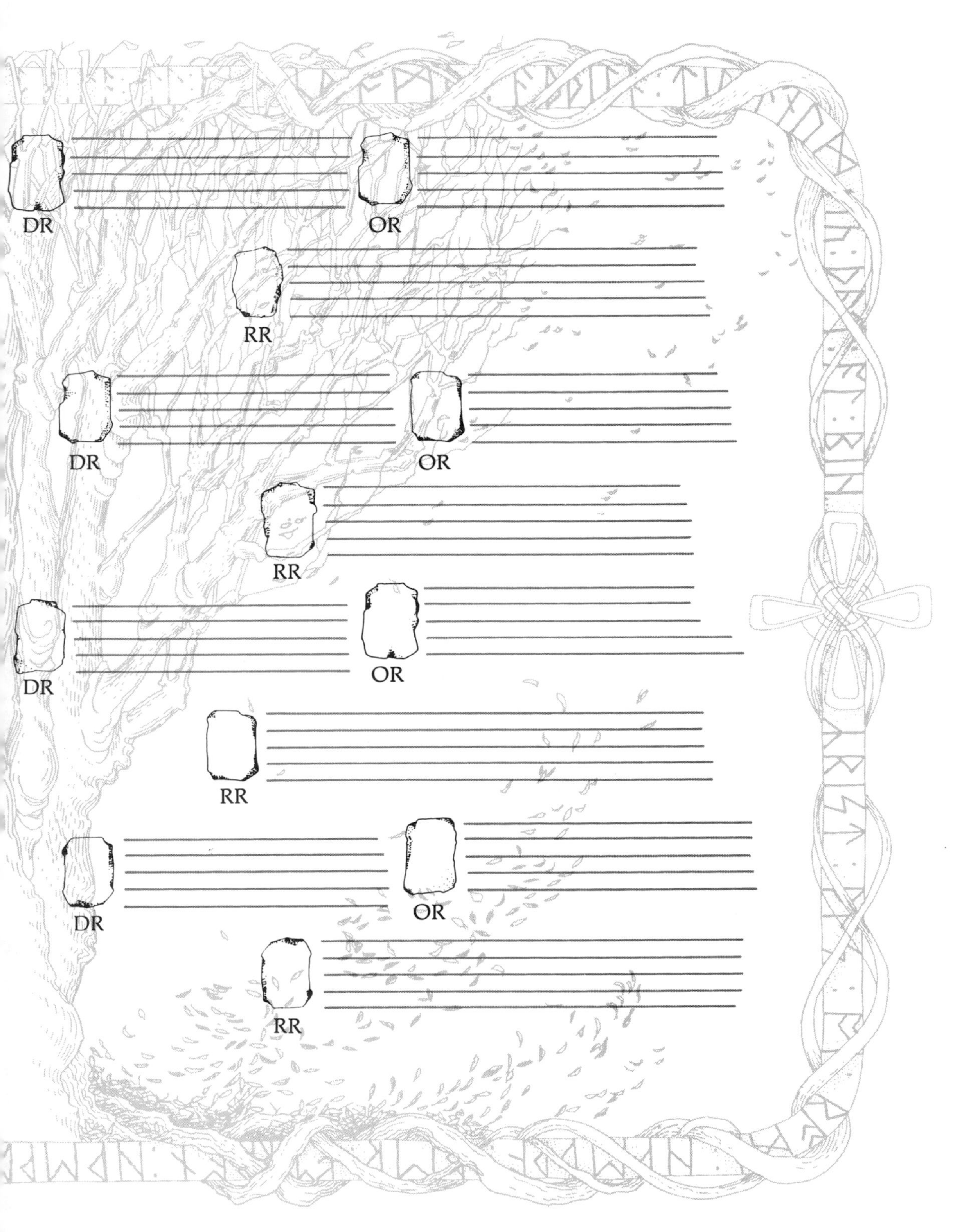
DR
OR
RR
DR
OR
RR
DR
OR
RR
DR
OR
RR

For the week of ____________

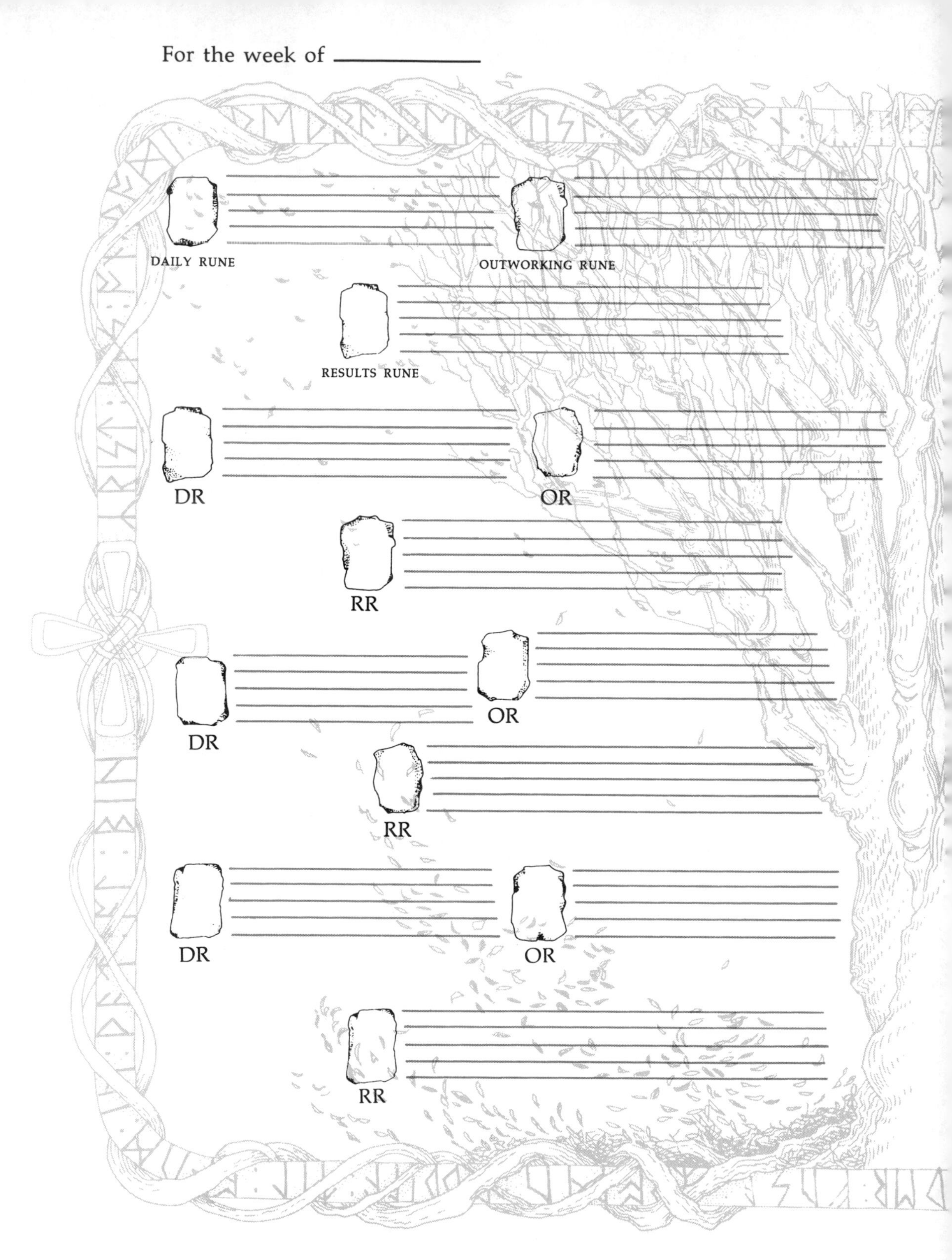

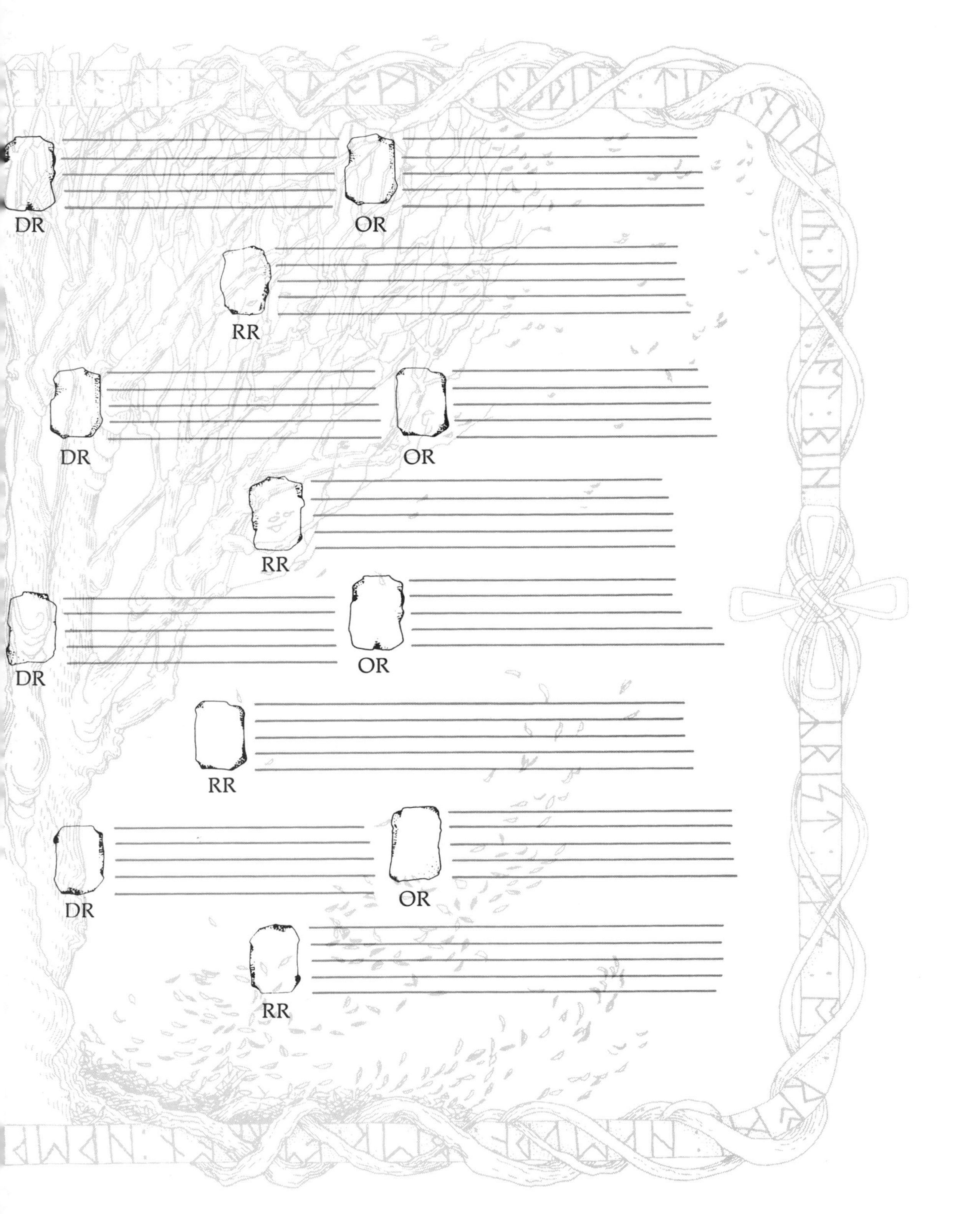
DR
OR
RR
DR
OR
RR
DR
OR
RR
DR
OR
RR

For the week of ____________

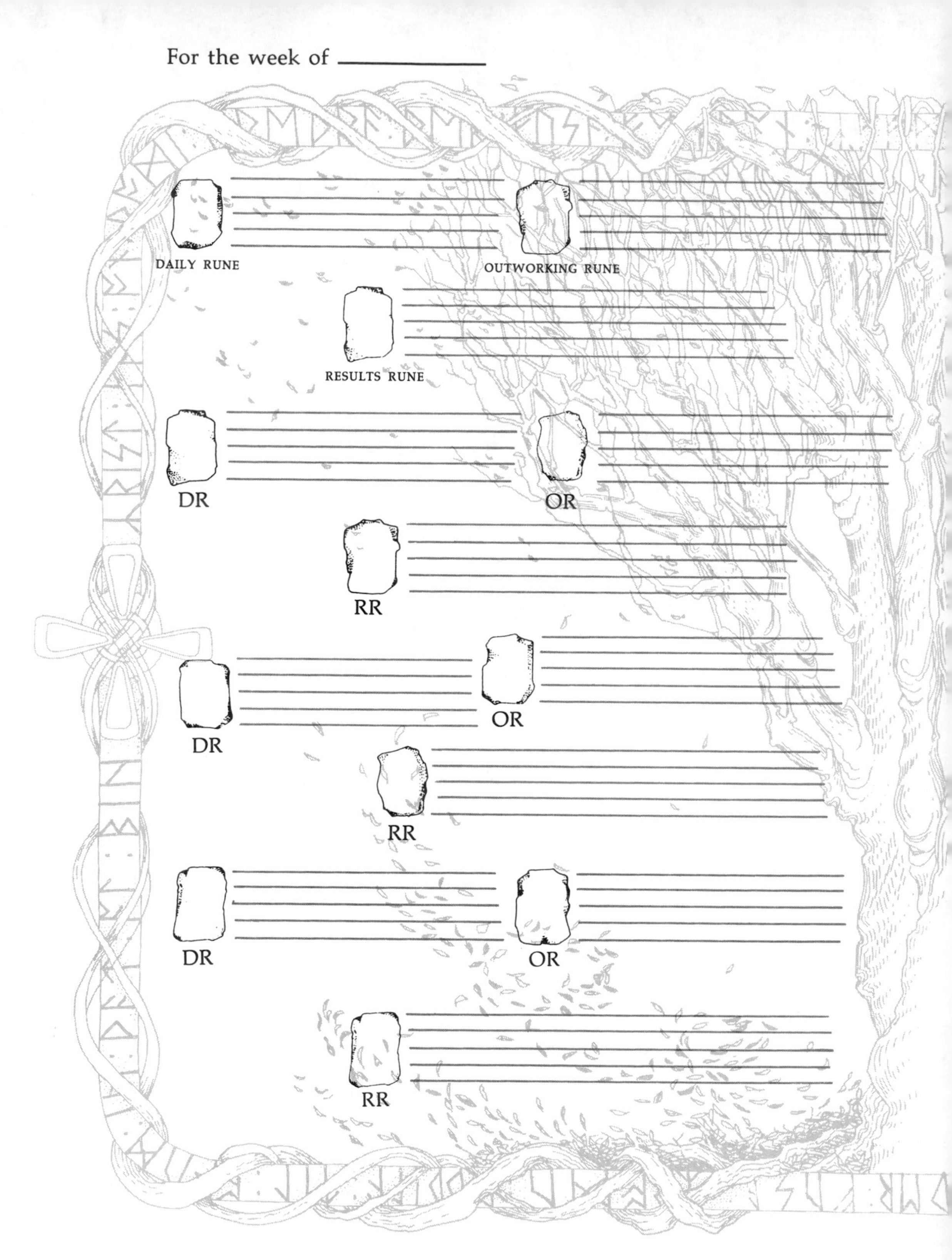

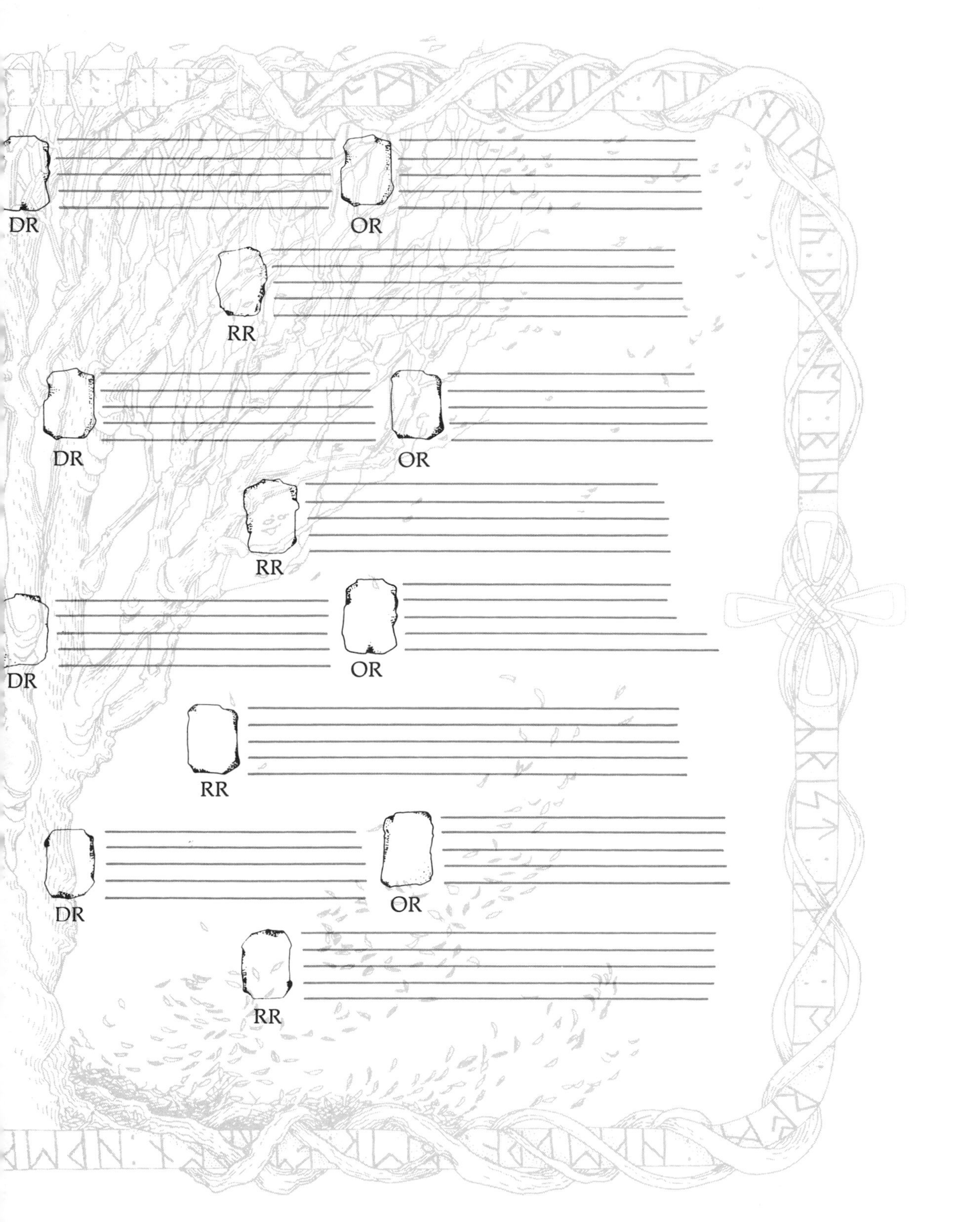
DR
OR
RR
DR
OR
RR
DR
OR
RR
DR
OR
RR

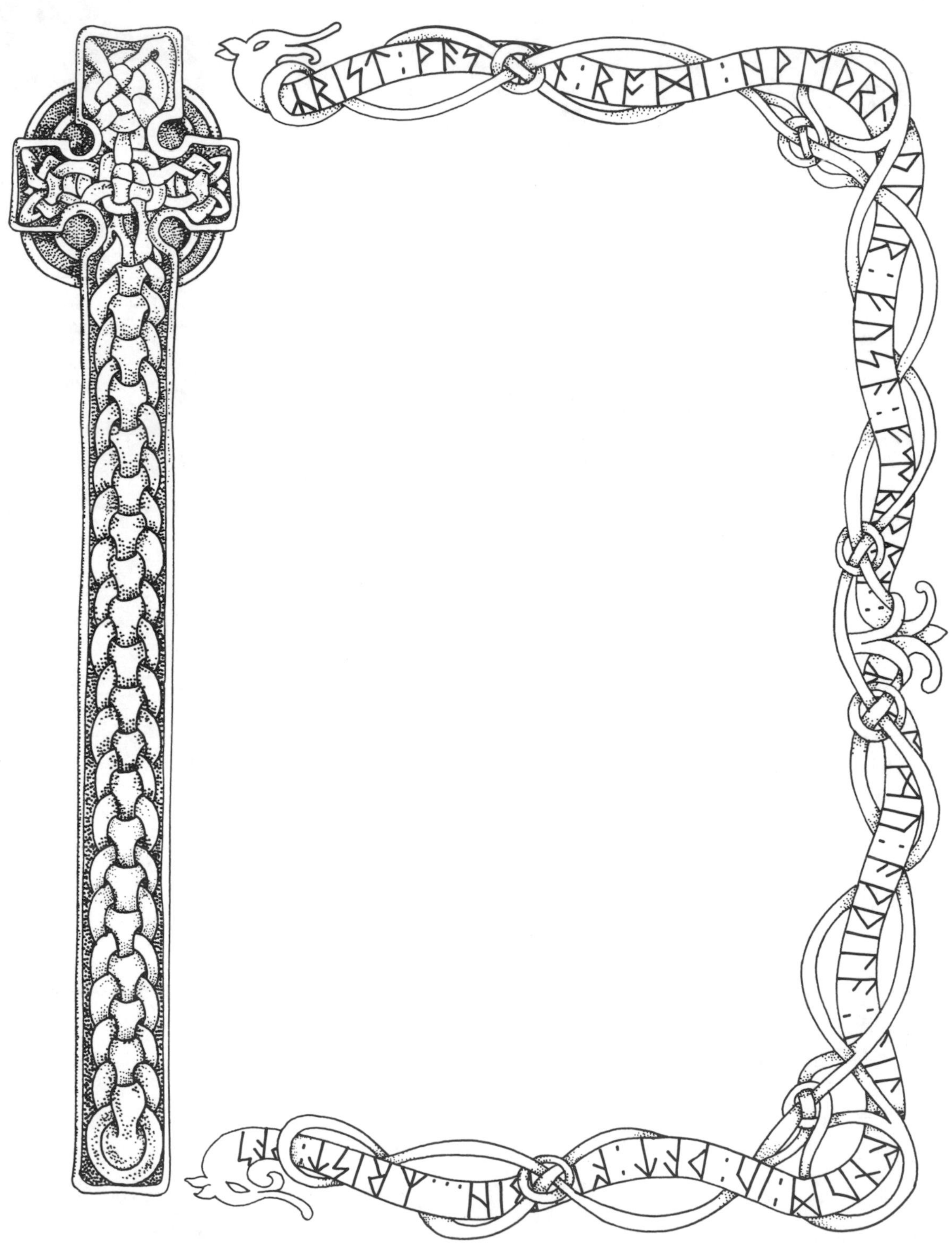

Outworking Runes

he *Daily Rune* has energy aspects which can be identified and made use of by drawing additional Runes at key moments during the course of your day. Let events cue you as to when another Rune—an *Outworking Rune*—can serve to illuminate your condition as it develops and evolves.

If your Daily Rune is X, *Gebo,* Partnership, you are put on notice that partnering of all kinds is central to your day's focus. Since partnership begins at home, pay particular attention to your relationship with yourself, because establishing an open, flowing channel between the self and the Self is the ultimate form of human partnership.

Mark down the Rune glyph or symbol. Draw it on a mirror; leave it on the kitchen table or on your desk. The point being: Let this cue to Right Action sink in. Use the Rune as an *aide-mémoire,* a string tied around the finger of the unconscious.

Sometimes things happen during the day that capture your attention by their severity or irregularity. The school principal calls you at work to inform you that your child has chicken pox. A check bounces that was supposed to cover your rent. You come out of the dentist's office to find you have a flat tire. . . . Instead of going into terminal shock, consider this: *The higher the degree of strangeness of an event, the more information it brings you.* So don't take it personally; look at the event strategically. Perhaps you can avoid calling up a friend to chatter about "what just happened to me." *Keep the energy at home.* Take a deep breath and pick an Outworking Rune.

The time is: 10:55 A.M. The Outworking Rune you pick is ᚹ, *Wunjo,* Joy and Light, *Reversed.* "Things are slow in coming to fruition." There may be snafus, mixups, confusion, which you are counseled *not* to react to. You are not one of Pavlov's dogs—ring a bell and I salivate . . . things go wrong and I blame others. "Seen in its true light, *everything is a test."* Don't take it personally, but do give it your attention. Find the laughs in what is happening. Find a way to break the circuit, to interrupt the automatic abuse of yourself /others that comes when you are feeling angry or afraid.

Again, as the day progresses, you may sense new energies in play. The Outworking Rune is fascinating to observe when you are able to cast part of yourself in the role of *witness.* This movie *is* your life, after all.

Pick another Outworking Rune. Note the time: 3:25 P.M. The Outworking Rune you draw is ᚾ, *Nauthiz, Reversed.* Terrific! You were expecting relief and you get "Pain, Necessity, and Constraint." Consider whether something within you is being ignored or disowned and, like the neglected child, is making its bid for your attention. Run a quick survey: Begin with what is most difficult and proceed to what is easy. Or if that is too overwhelming, begin with what is easiest and proceed to what is most difficult. It is through constraint and limitation that we come to understand our strengths as well as our weaknesses. So, "No suffering over your suffering" this Rune is saying, and remember, "Modesty and good temper are essential at such a time."

You may or may not see fit to draw further Outworking Runes during this hair-raising day (the furnace goes out; *all* the kids have chicken pox . . .). By the end of the day you may want to choose a final Rune simply to see how well you have progressed. Have you met "deferred joy" and "constraint and pain" with the heart of a Spiritual Warrior? Have you kept your perspective, your good humor? If so, you might draw ᛞ, *Dagaz,* the Rune of Transformation and Breakthrough. Congratulations. Take heart from these words:

> A major period of achievement and prosperity is sometimes introduced by this Rune. The darkness is behind you; daylight has come.

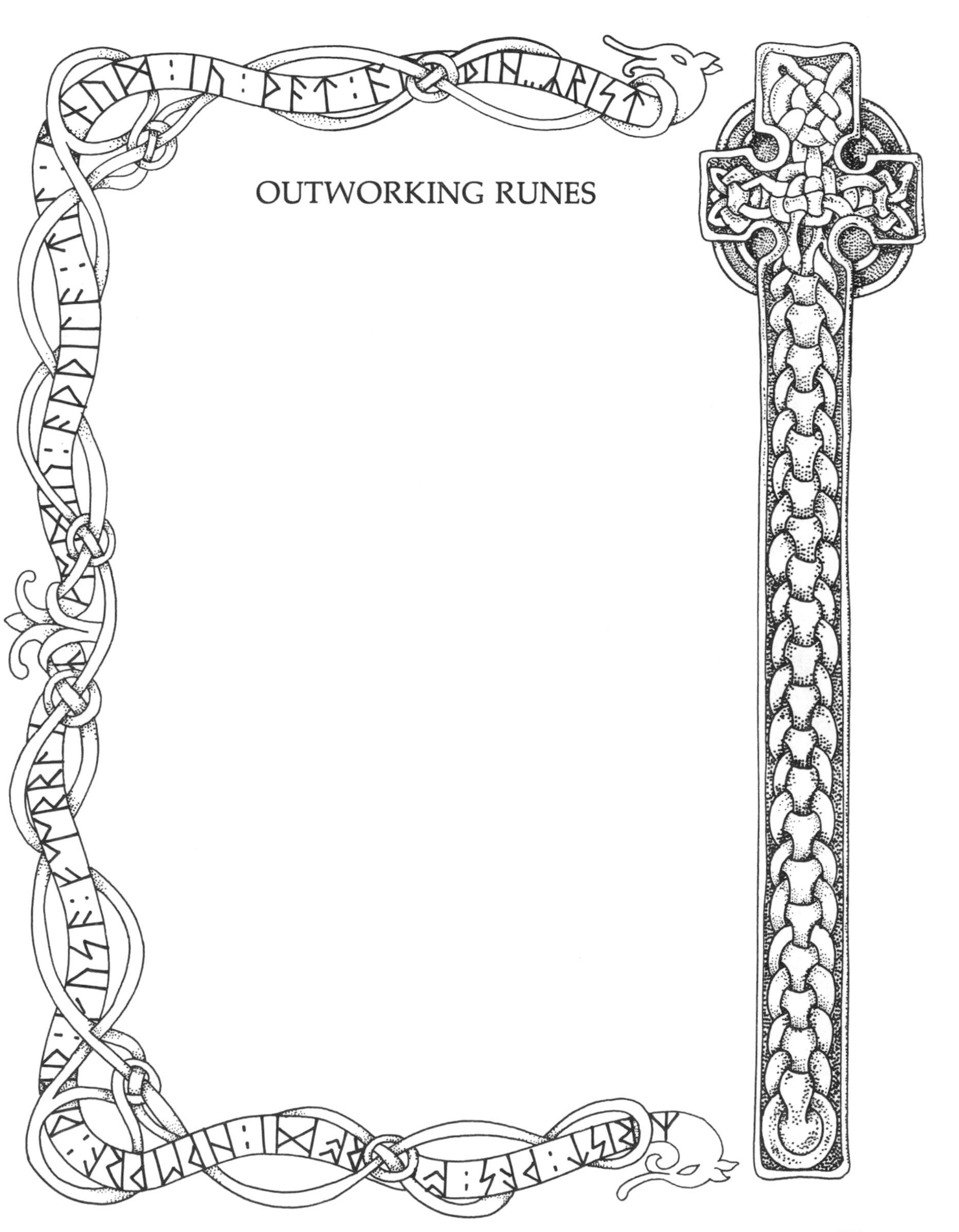

OUTWORKING RUNES

For the week of ______________

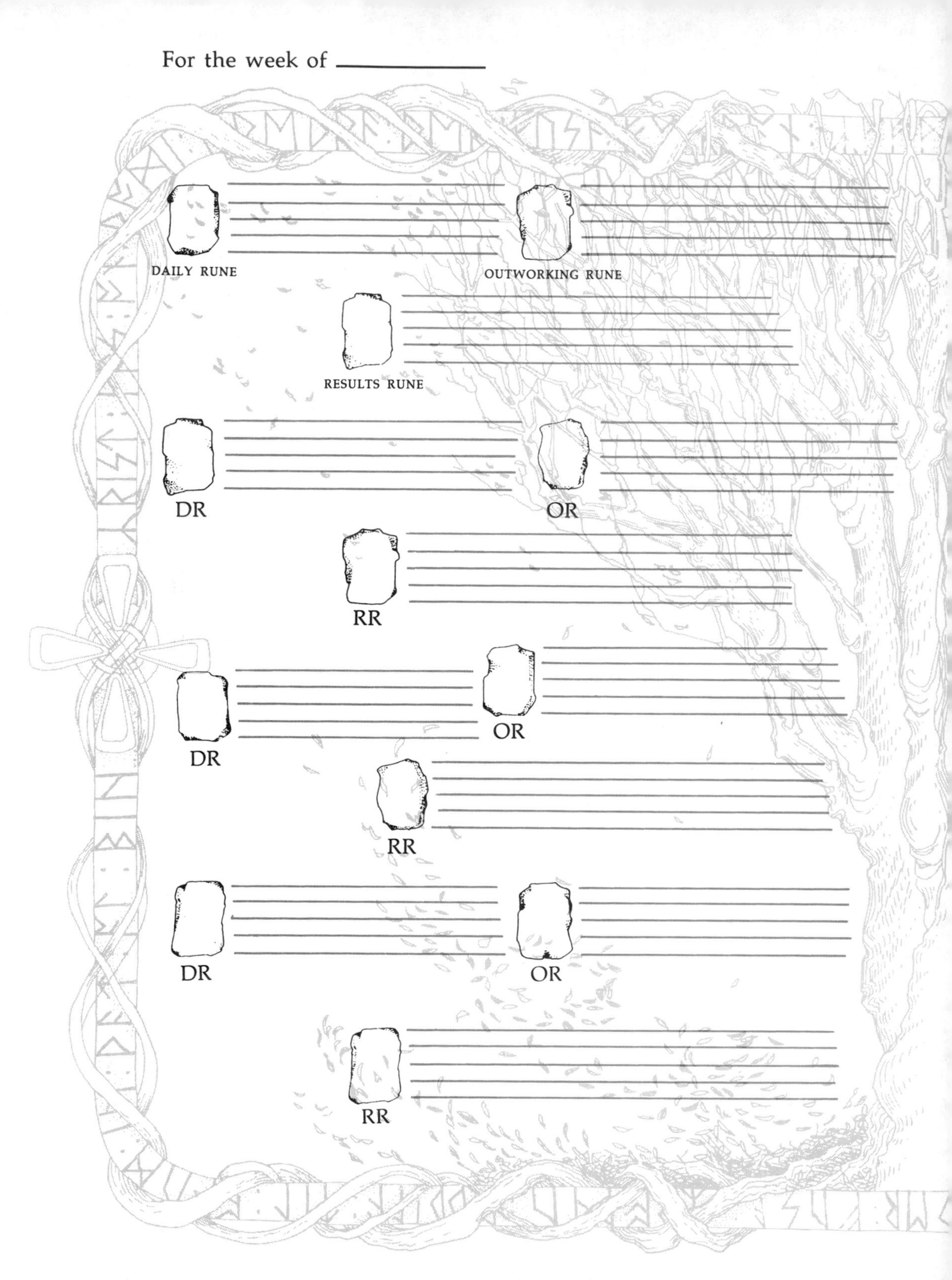

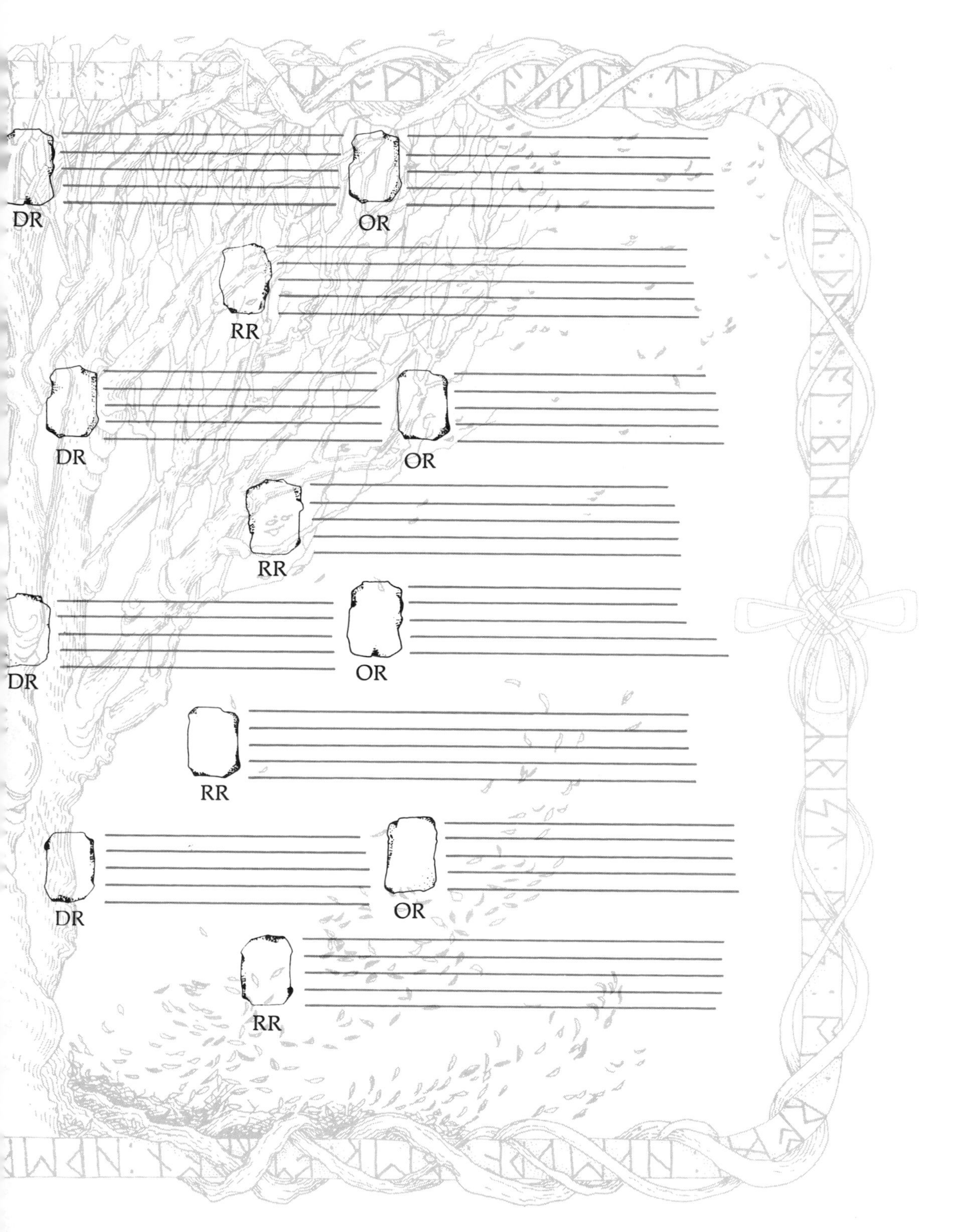
DR
OR
RR
DR
OR
RR
DR
OR
RR
DR
OR
RR

For the week of ____________

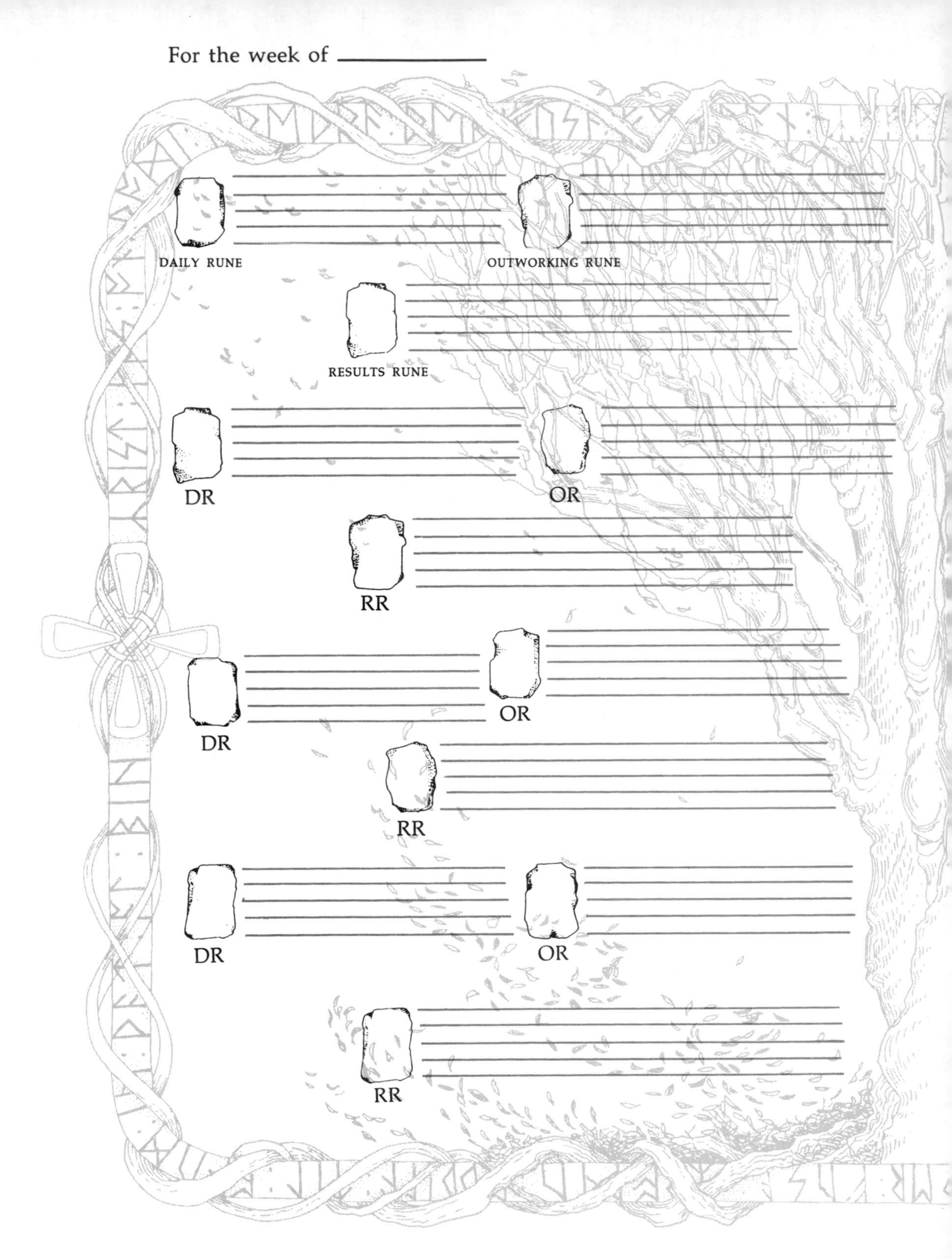

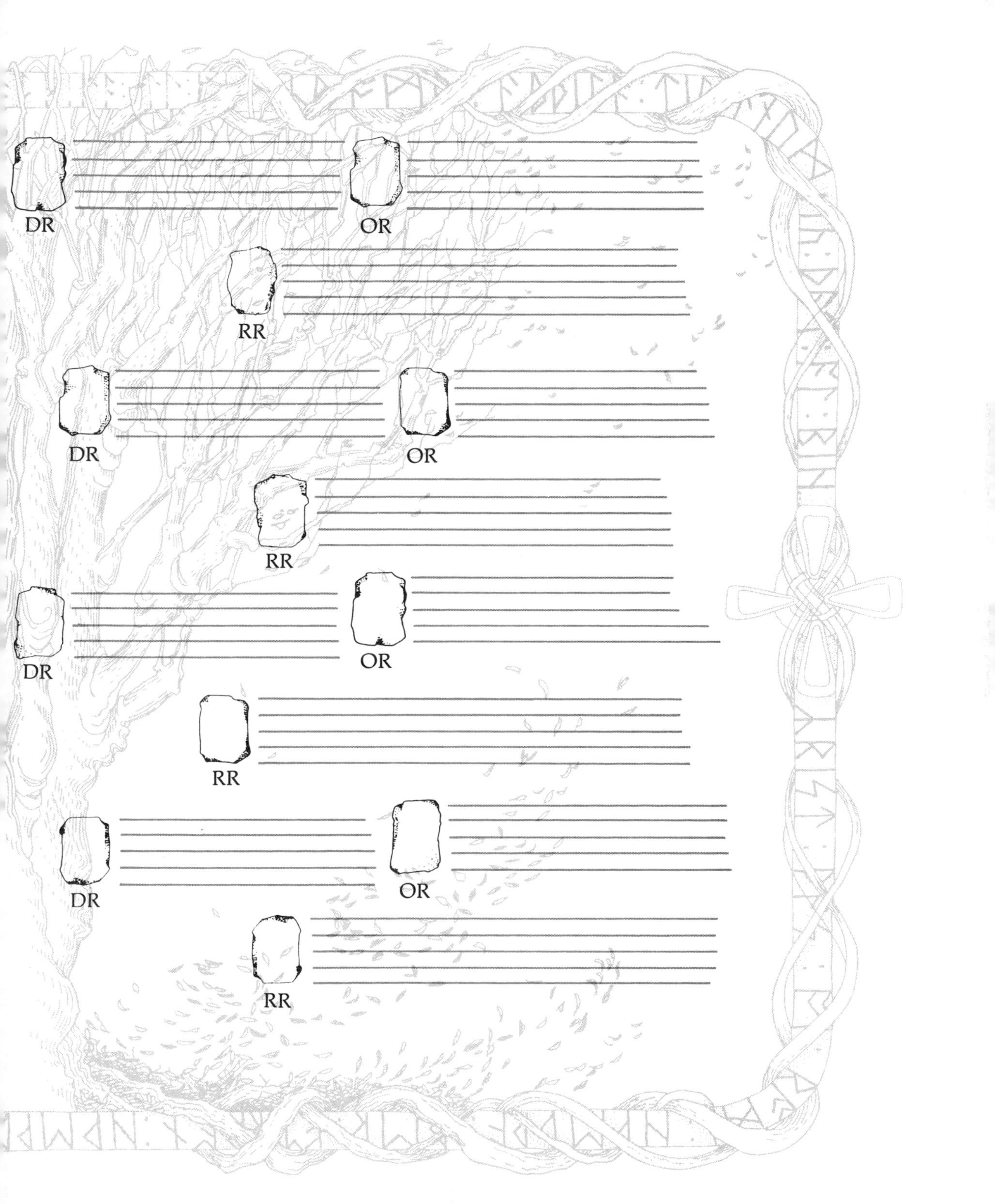
DR
OR
RR
DR
OR
RR
DR
OR
RR
DR
OR
RR

For the week of ___________

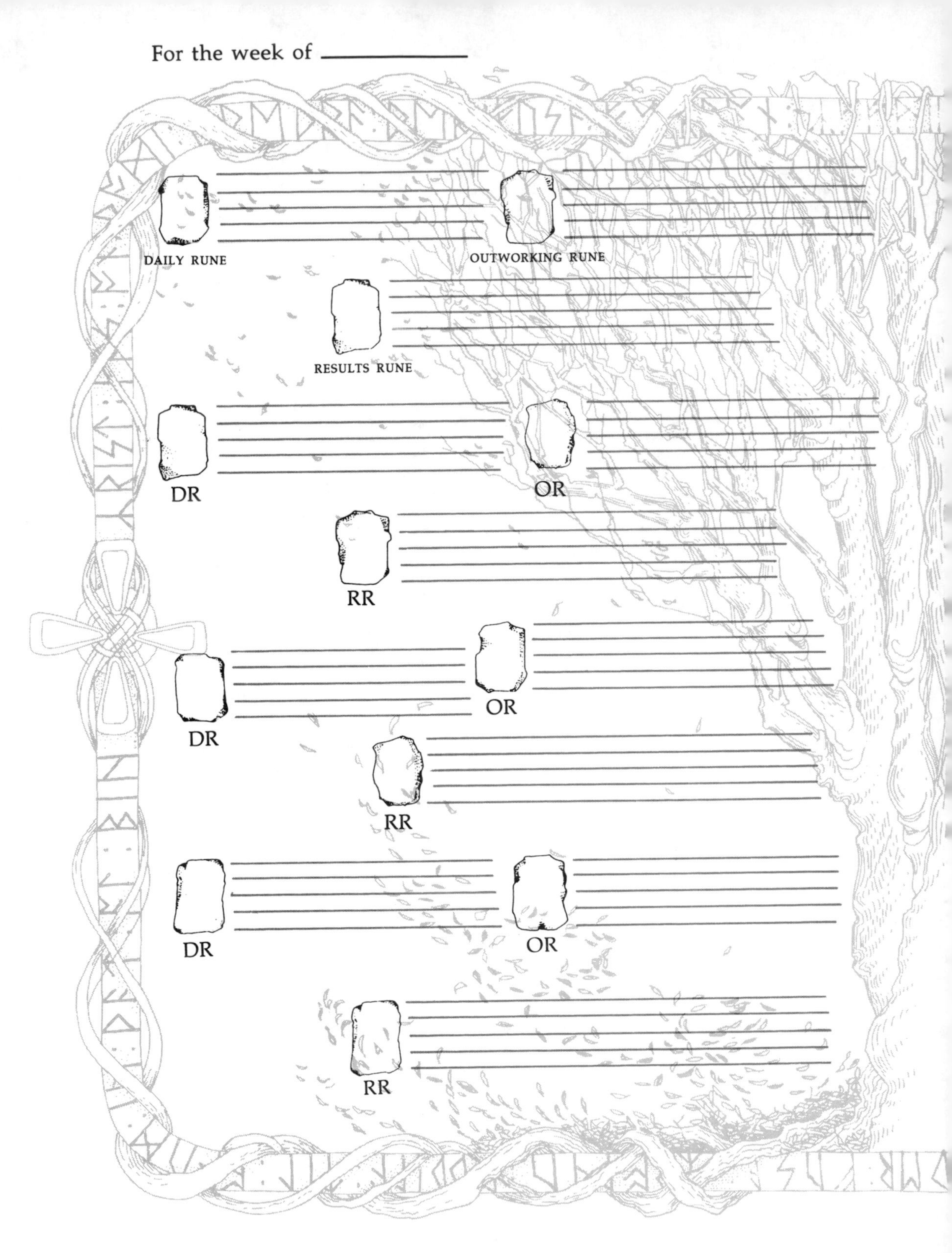

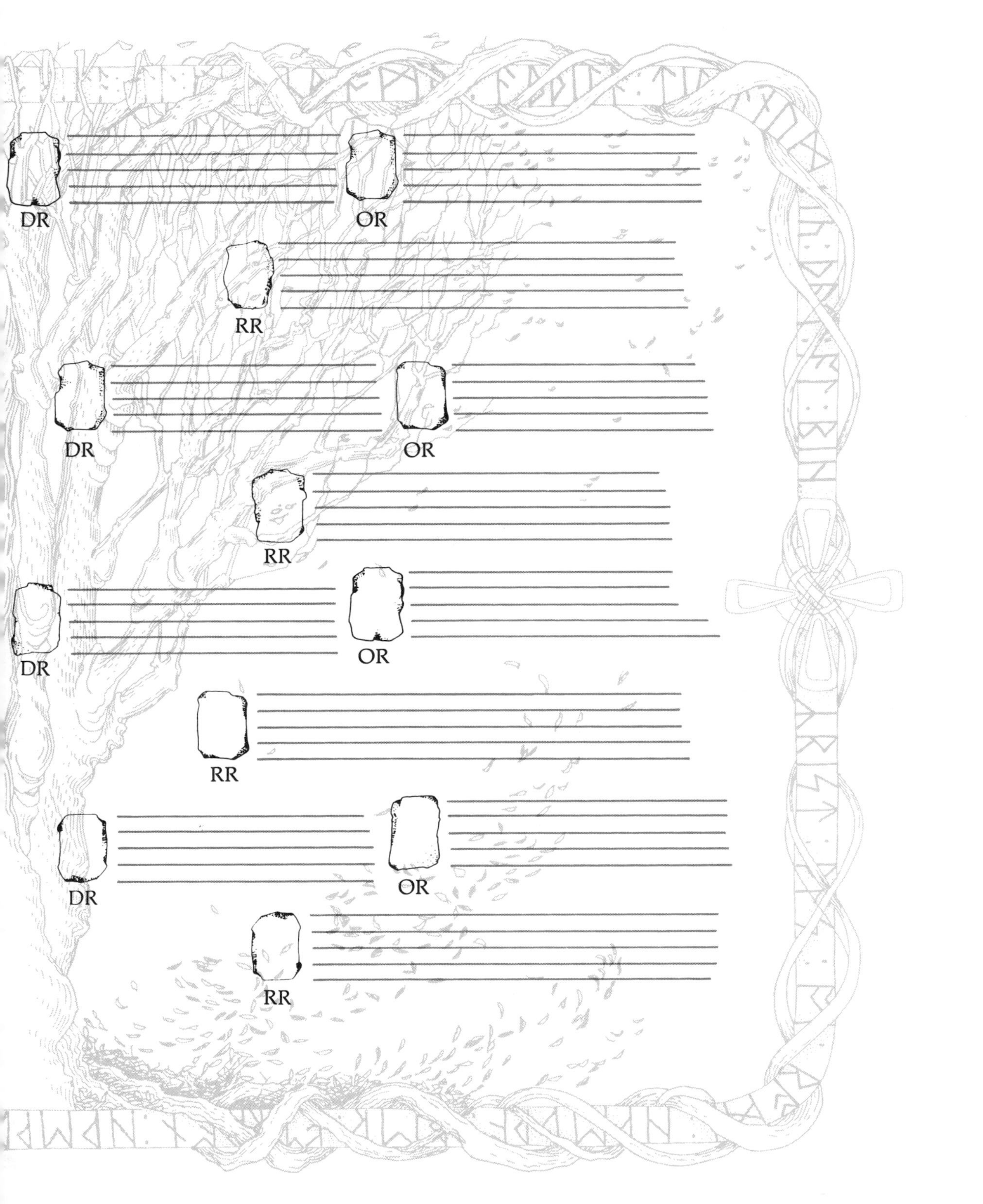
DR
OR
RR
DR
OR
RR
DR
OR
RR
DR
OR
RR

For the week of ___________

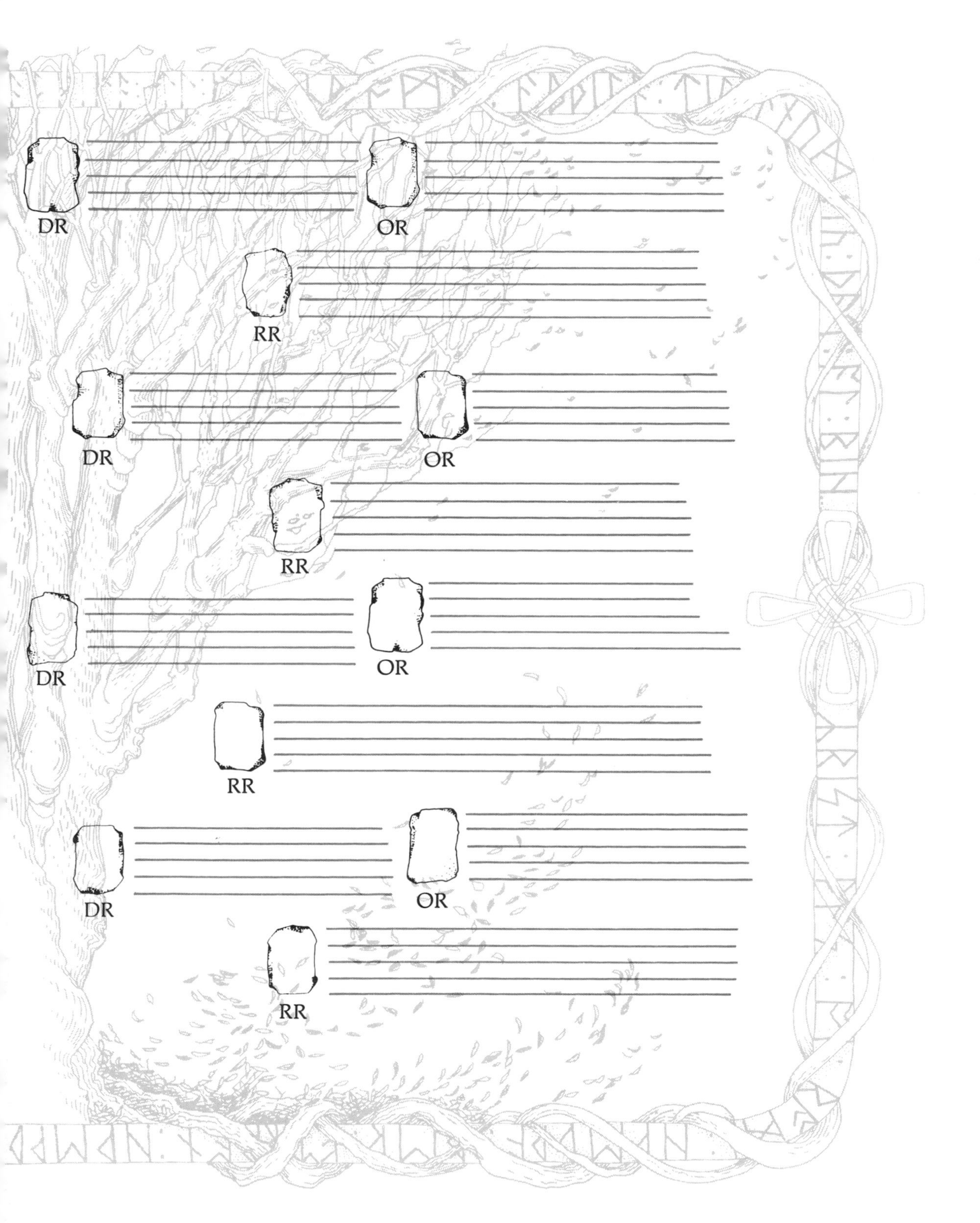
DR
OR
RR
DR
OR
RR
DR
OR
RR
DR
OR
RR

For the week of ____________

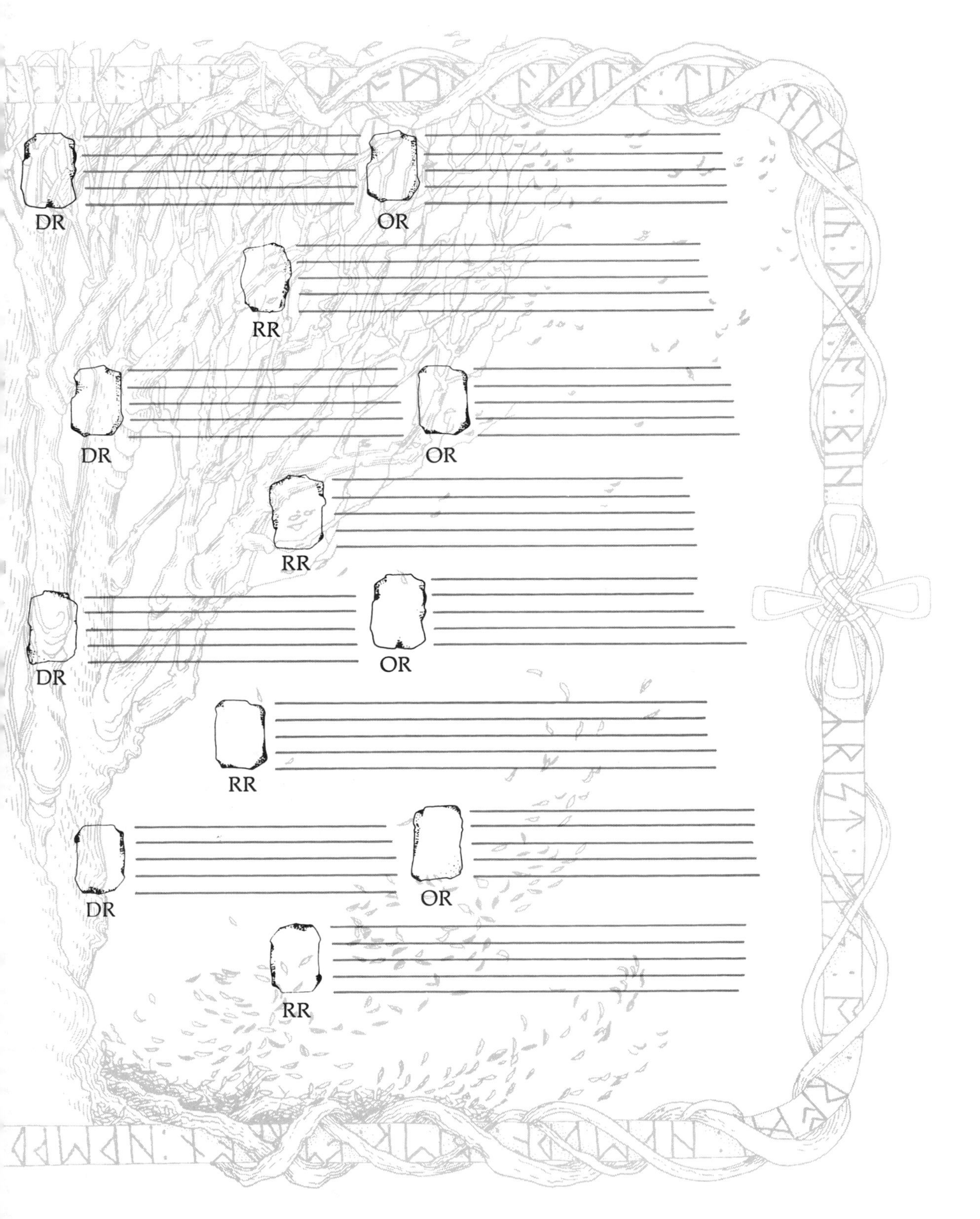
DR
OR
RR
DR
OR
RR
DR
OR
RR
DR
OR
RR

WINTER

℞: Runes of Healing

The Runes as described here are healing, merciful Runes; they will do you no harm.

Martin D. Raynor, Ph.D.
Preface to *The Book of Runes*

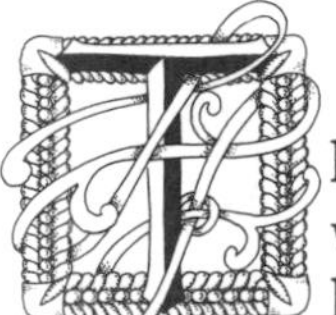

here is sufficient evidence from the length and breadth of the Viking world that Runes were used for healing. The Vikings are known to have painted Runic glyphs on staves and on their skin for the healing of battle wounds. The Runes served them well in the ceremonial act of healing.

When asked the question "How can little marked stones facilitate healing?" the Runes replied with ᚱ, *Raido, Reversed,* which deals with "ruptures . . . disruptions," and calls our attention to that quality of perfection which includes even our pain. The healing begins with unblocking a point of view, with the providing of a new optic on just how things actually work. Once this opening has been accomplished

> what you regard as detours, inconveniences, disruptions, blockages, and even failures and deaths will actually be [seen as] rerouting opportunities, with union and reunion as the only abiding destinations.

A number of people have written to describe healing experiences in which the Viking Runes appear to have played some part, including one letter from an Episcopal priest who works with laying on of hands. The priest did not cease the laying on of hands; he merely added *Runes of Healing* to the ceremony.

Theorem: When Runes are marked over a wound or an area of pain (on the skin, a cast, or bandage), an energy field is created that facilitates healing.

Say you have just broken your leg. The cast is in place. What can be done by competent practitioners of allopathic medicine has been done. Pick a Rune for the crack in your tibia. You pick the *Blank Rune;* ink that on the cast over one side of the break. Replace the Rune and select another. You pick ᚨ, *Ansuz, Reversed.* Now ink that on the other side of your cast, directly opposite the *Blank Rune.* Then wait and see. Test it out yourself and record your experience: Is the normal healing time accelerated enough to surprise your doctor?

The next time you, or someone you know, comes down with the flu and is feeling depressed, pick a Rune. Pick two. Pick three. If it's a bad cold and it's still in your head, mark the Runes over your sinuses to work on the problem, and put blocking Runes on the throat, chest, etc., to inhibit the cold's progress. The R_x is yours to concoct and administer.

"What?" you say. "And go to the office looking like this? Or see my doctor, my psychiatrist, or—heaven forbid—my mechanic, with ᚾ on my jaw!" This is personal business, not show-and-tell business. If you are dealing with any part of the body other than your face or hands, you can felt-tip yourself in perfect privacy and then get on with your normal life. Wear the glyphs until they wash off or until you get a feeling that it is time to replace them with different Runes.

The following is a report from a thirty-seven-year-old woman who had been suffering periodically from migraine headaches. The headaches came, "lasted for two hours, then gradually subsided, leaving me utterly exhausted and depressed."

It occurred to her to consult the Runes. First, she drew a Rune asking about the timeliness of healing herself through the Runes. She drew ᛇ, *Eihwaz,* the Rune of Defense. Noting particularly the counsel about avoiding stressful situations that brought about the blockage she identified with the headaches, she wrote: "To me this Rune said that there are three elements. The headache. The cause of the headache. And the Rune. I had to look at my relationships, things that angered me, areas where I was suppressing, stifling, even strangling myself. I made a clear decision to let go of whatever was causing my migraines."

Next, she asked for a Rune to end the headaches. She drew ᛚ, *Laguz, Reversed,* the Rune of Water, Flow and "that which conducts." First blockage then flow. She read the appropriate passage and then, as soon as she came home from her office, she inked the two Runes on her temples. In the morning, she left the faintest trace of the Runes on her face. "During the day," she reported, "on bits of paper I'd write the Rune for Flow over and over again, sometimes drawing ᛚ on a simple picture of my face. I kept that Rune in my hand while I was driving. Finally, I made myself a *Laguz* amulet and hung it around my neck. I also did a lot of thinking about my relationship with my husband and children. And about everything I could see in my life that appeared to be blocking. Soon the headaches came less frequently. Now I rarely get a migraine, and when I do, I can short-circuit it fast."

A migraine headache is not likely to be made worse if you pick a Rune and use it to do some thinking and clarifying. You may find, as this woman did, that the Rune helped her to identify the underlying cause. If the Rune selected is not, practically speaking, an antidote, perhaps it serves in ways we do not yet understand to help restore balance at the energy level. And always remember: *The Runes are not a substitute for your doctor.*

Available information on the art of Runic healing is, for the most part, anecdotal. Perhaps it is well that it remain so, for this is not the province of organized medicine, but rather a folk art at the disposal of all whose Faith is not confined within the boundaries of traditional medicine. When in doubt, before undertaking such a procedure, place yourself and your health and all outcomes in the Light or in the keeping of Holy Spirit.

The *why* and the *how* of Rune healing are of less significance at this time than that something is accomplished. Pick a Rune, trust it, use it, record the process, learn from it.

RUNES OF HEALING

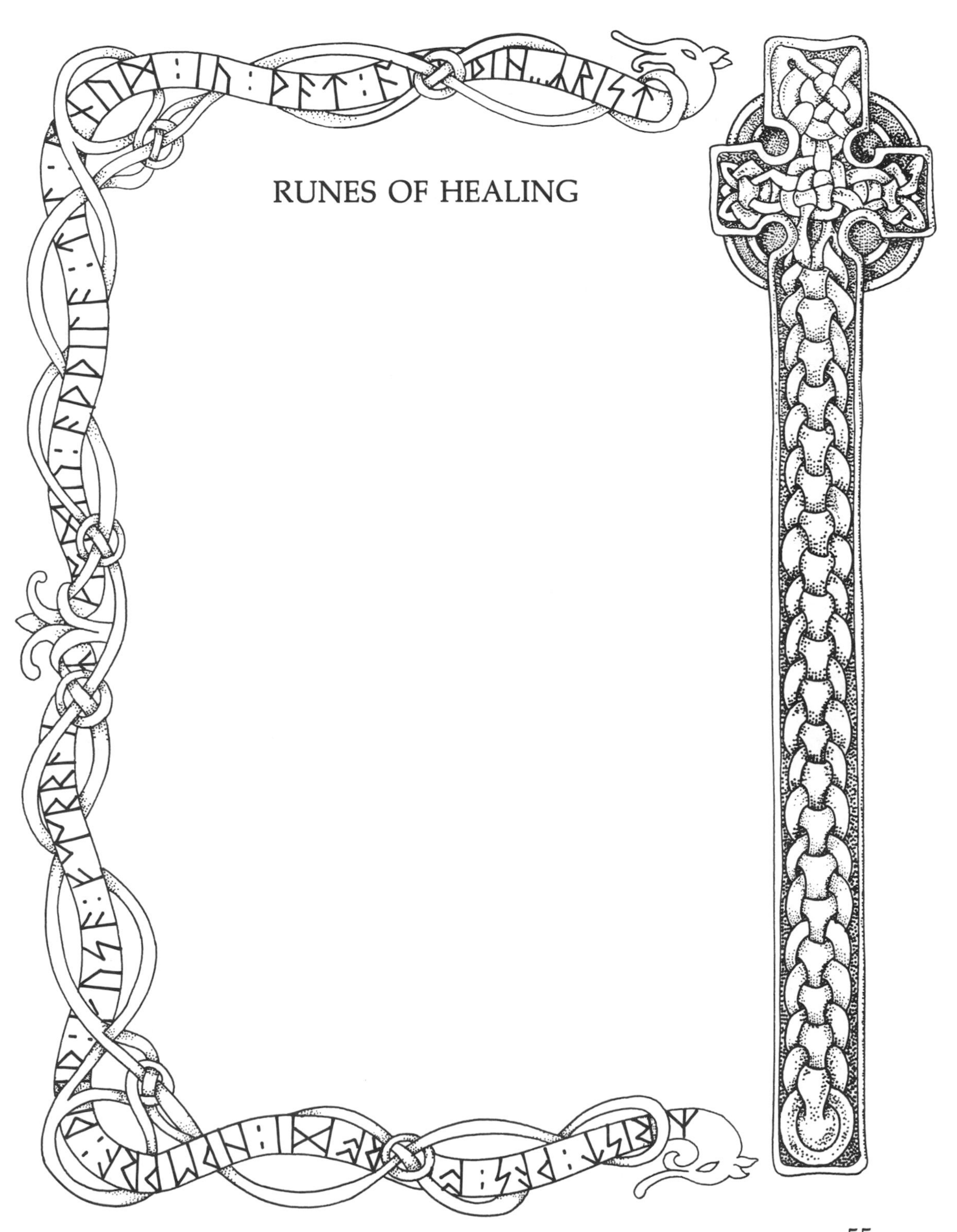

For the week of ____________

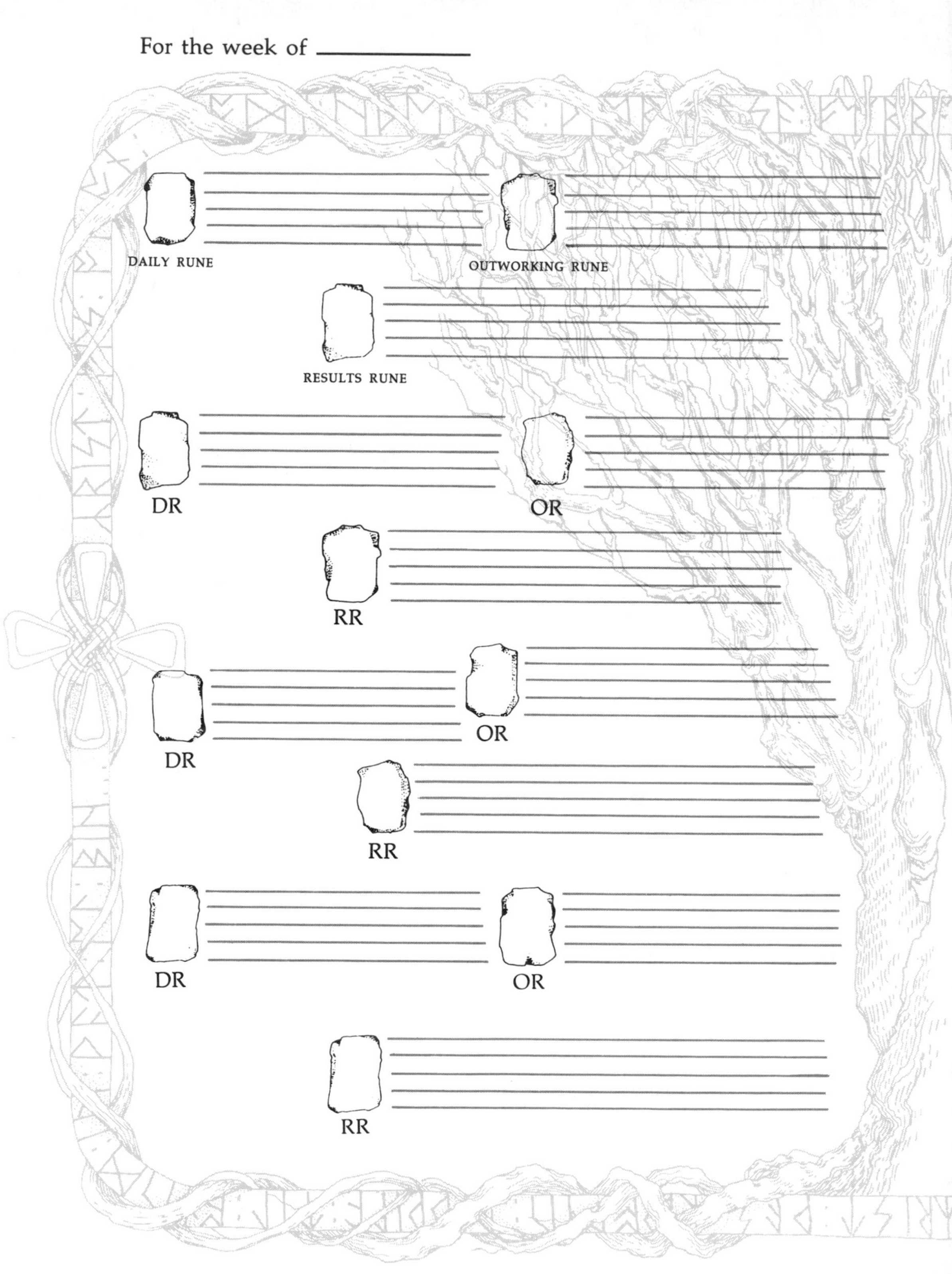

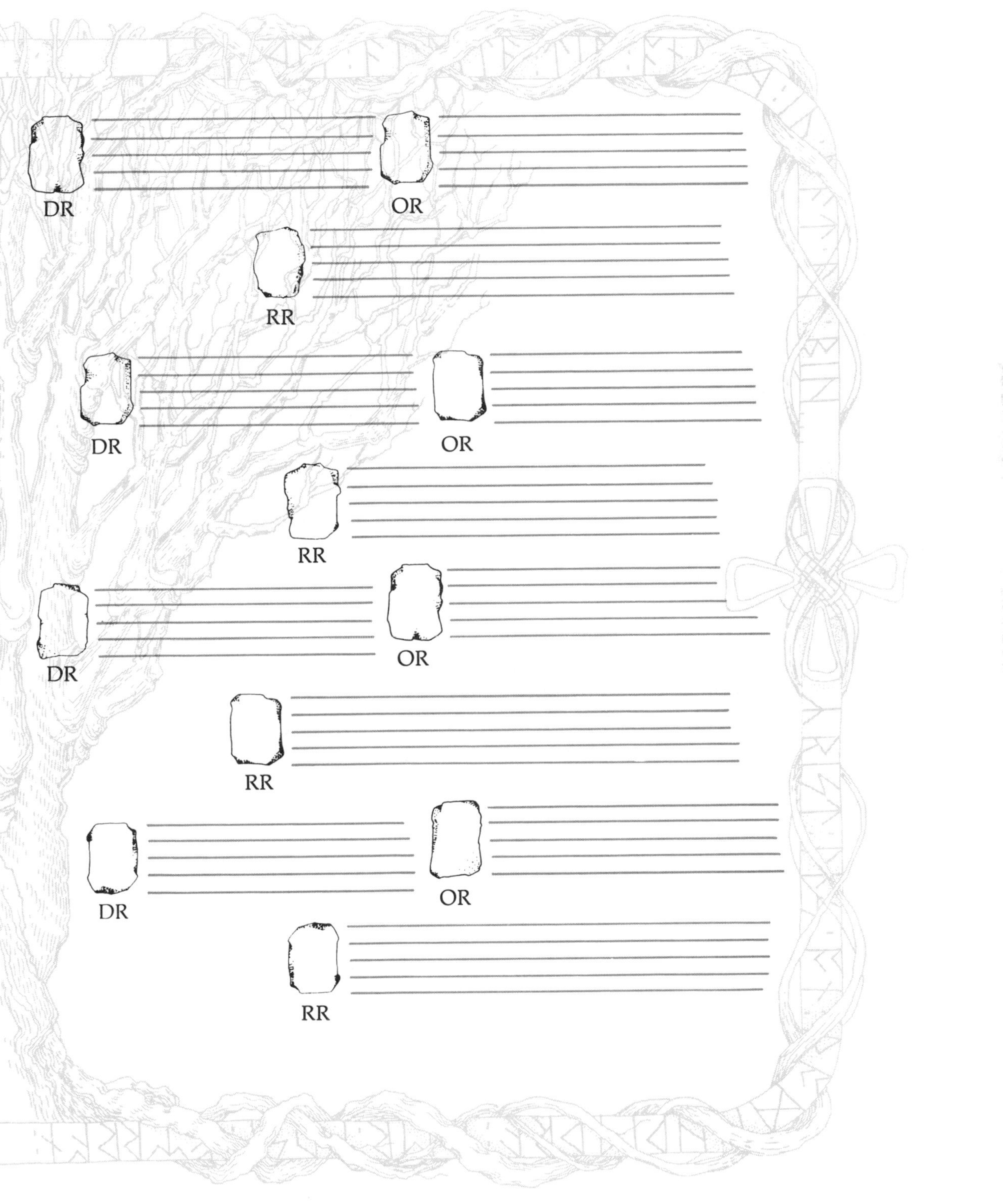
DR
OR
RR
DR
OR
RR
DR
OR
RR
DR
OR
RR

For the week of ____________

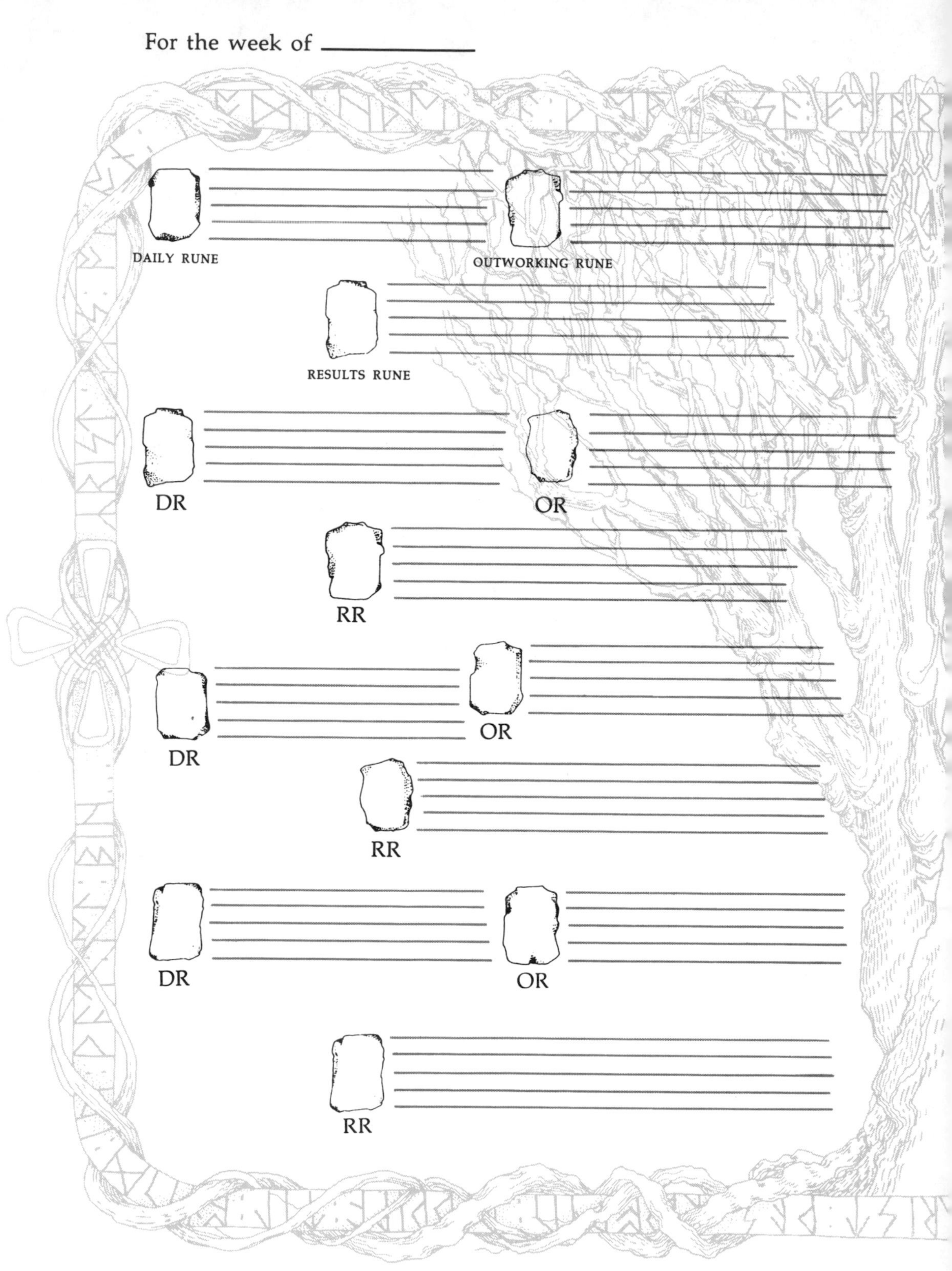

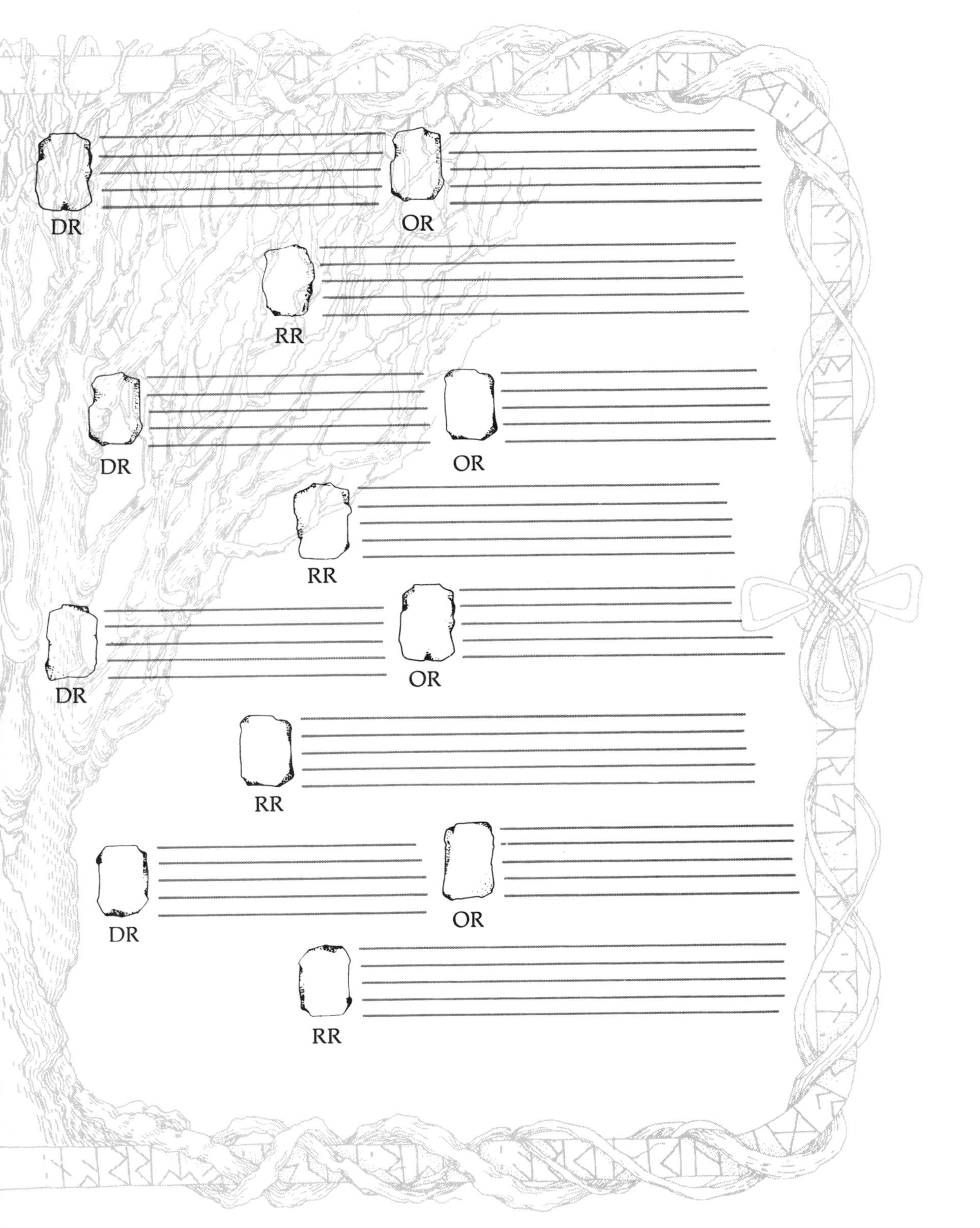
DR
OR
RR
DR
OR
RR
DR
OR
RR
DR
OR
RR

For the week of ______________

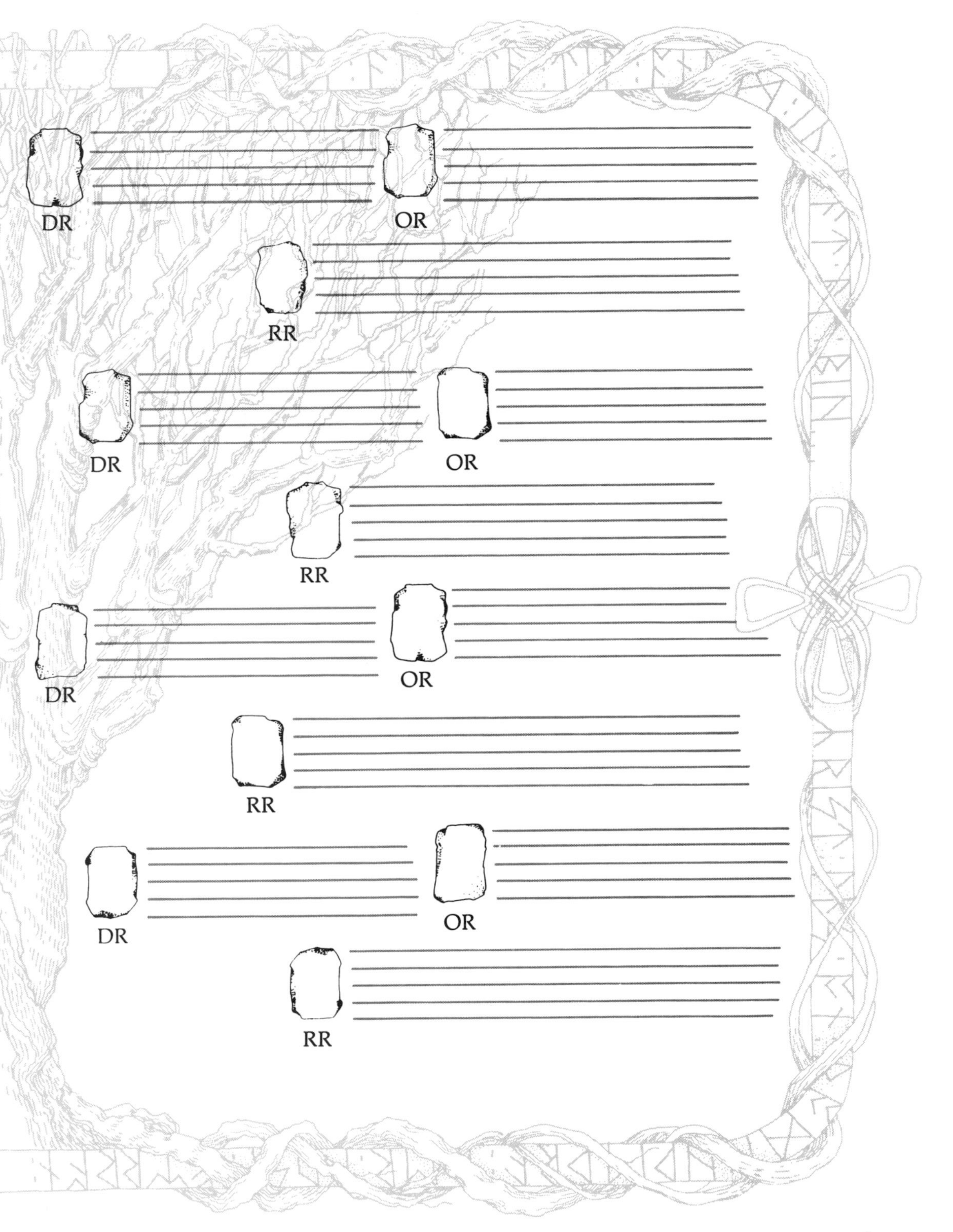
DR
OR
RR
DR
OR
RR
DR
OR
RR
DR
OR
RR

For the week of ____________

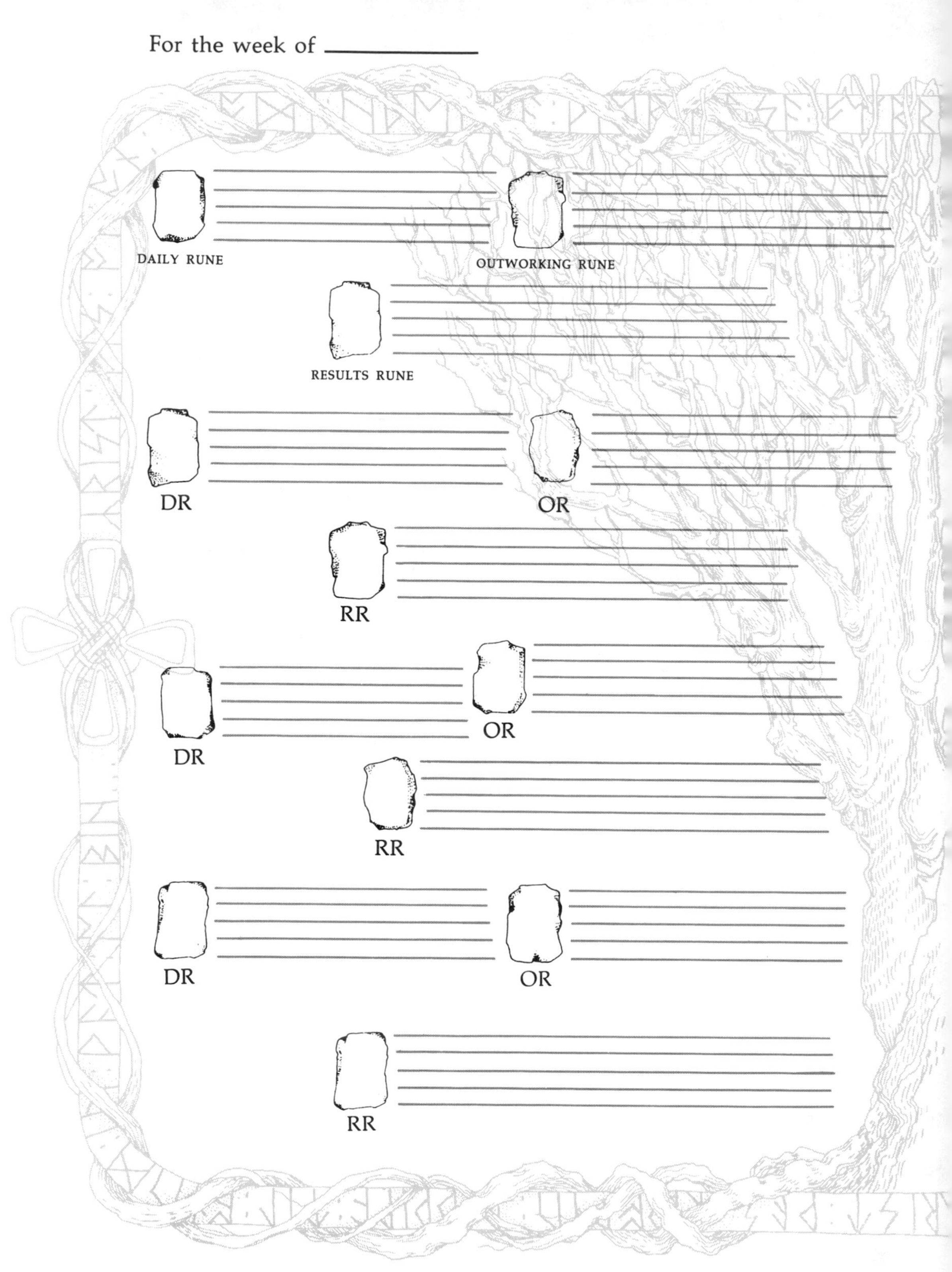

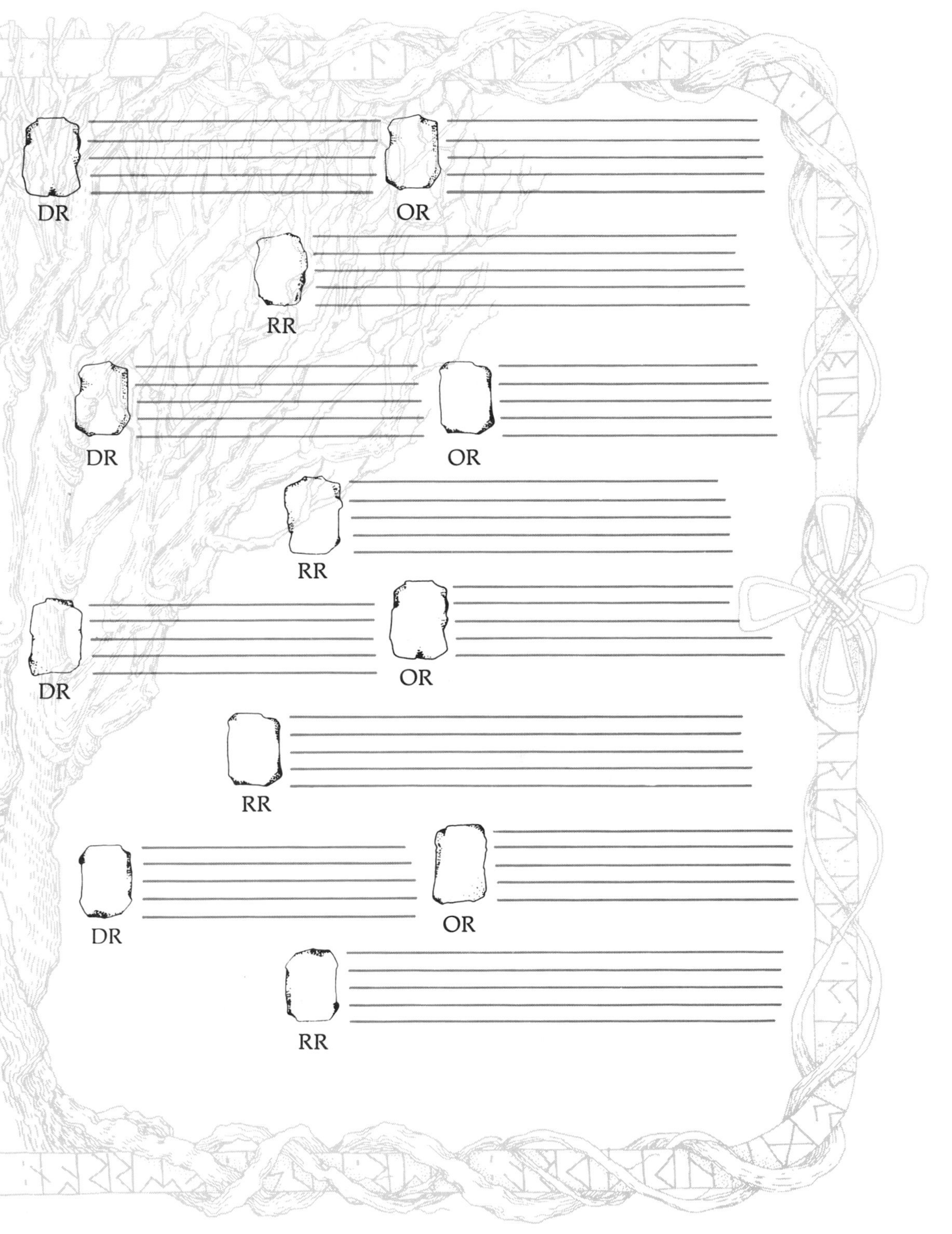

DR
OR
RR
DR
OR
RR
DR
OR
RR
DR
OR
RR

For the week of ___________

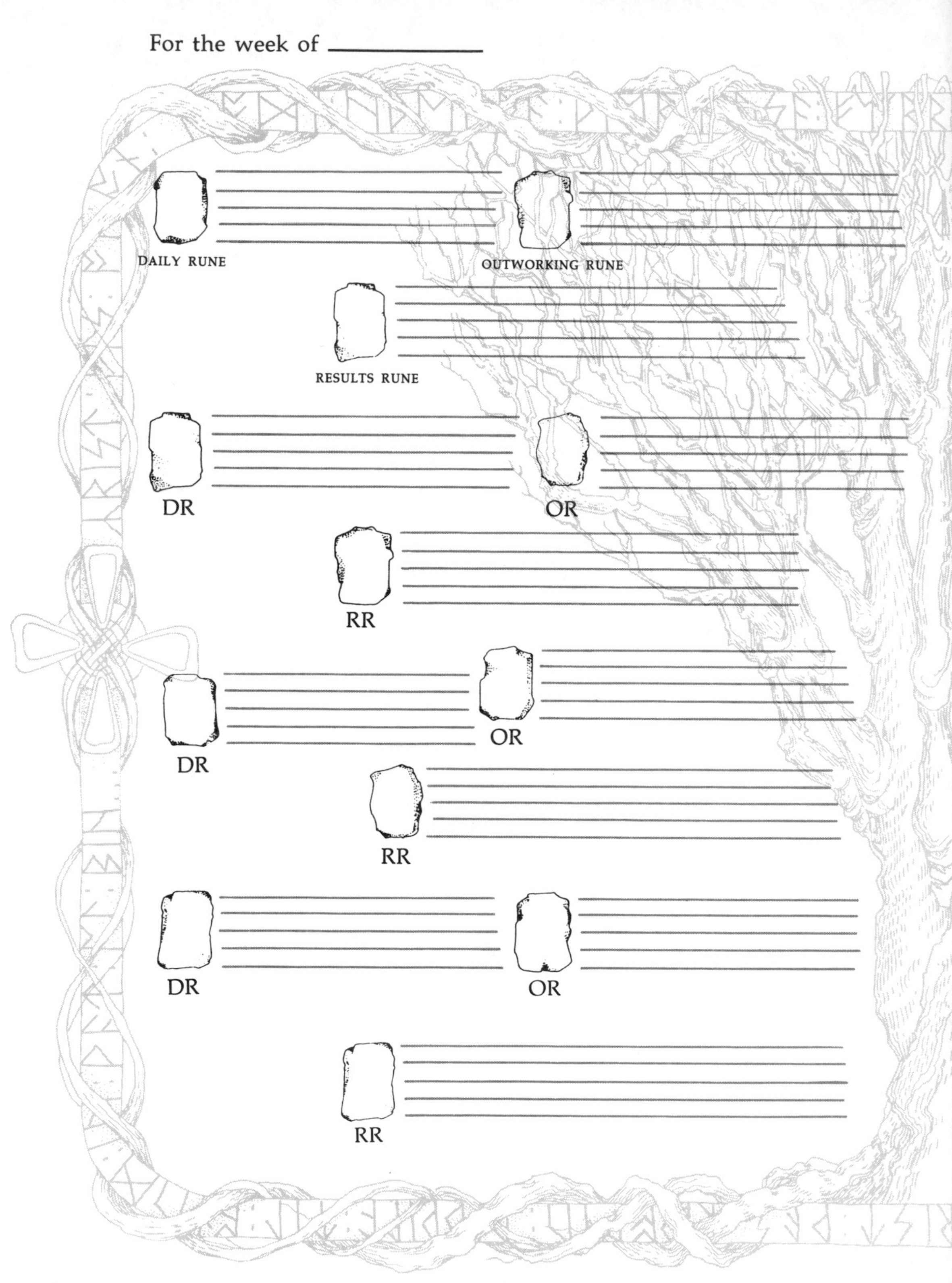

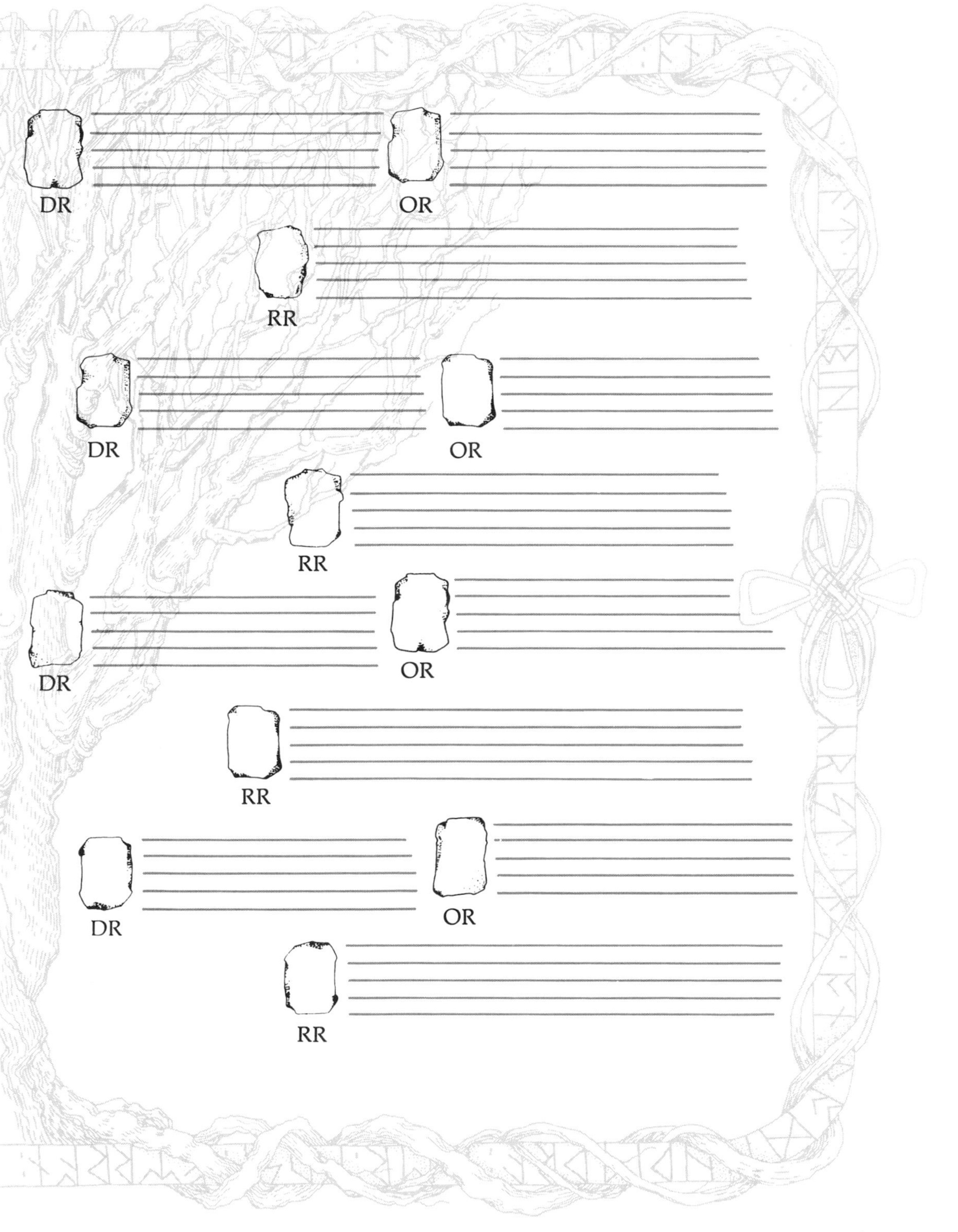
DR
OR
RR
DR
OR
RR
DR
OR
RR
DR
OR
RR

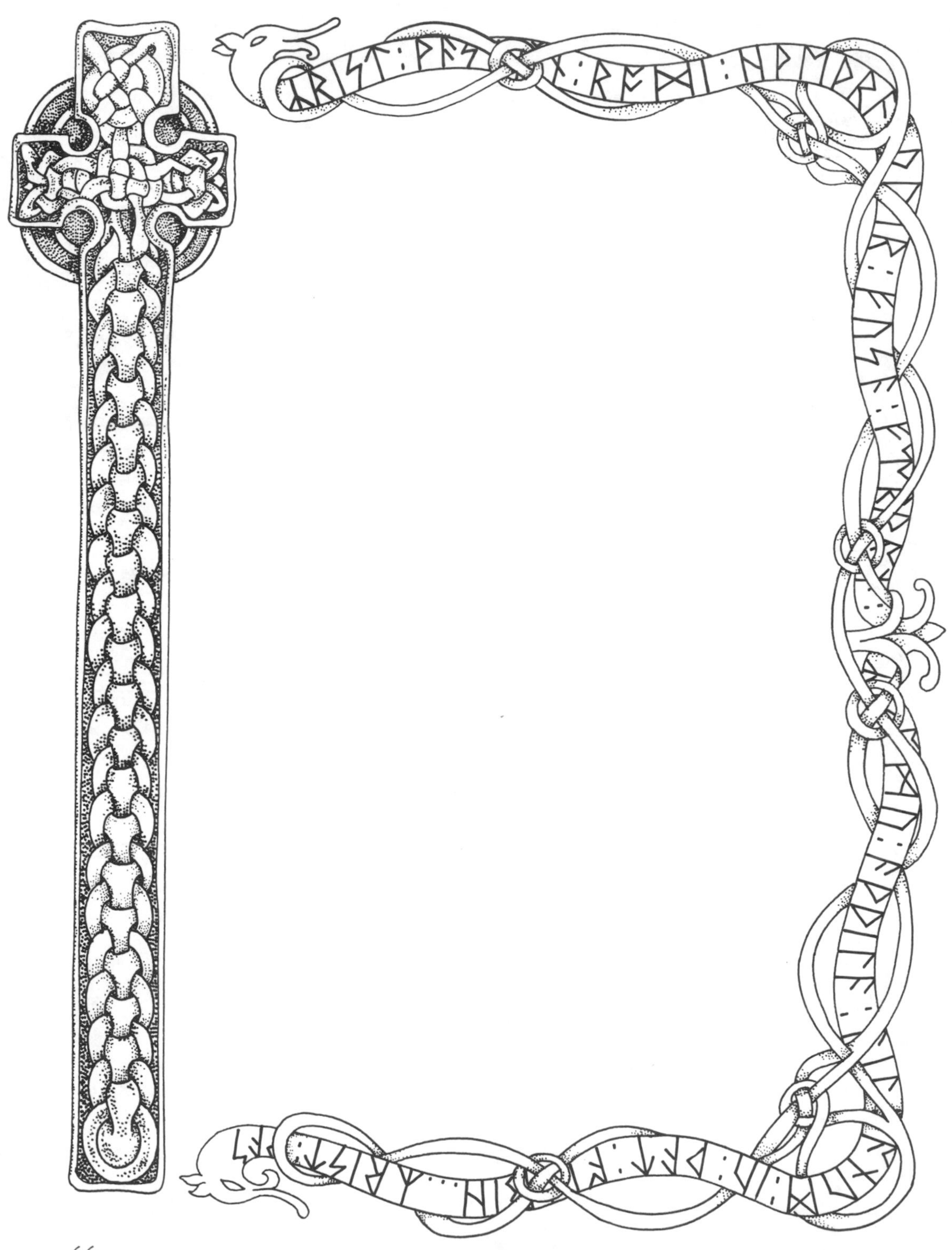

Two Bags Reading

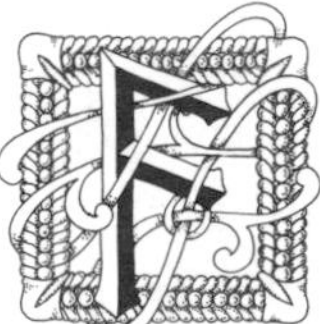

or this casting you will need one set of Runes and two bags. It is precisely at times of great stress—when there doesn't seem to be enough time and the needle on your pressure gauge is tilting into the red—that the Two Bags Reading recommends itself.

Find a quiet place. This is not always easy in the midst of job or family demands. Yet even in our complex culture there are safety zones, places where the world thinks twice before trying to get at you. Best bet: the bathroom. Next best: your own car. On the way to somewhere, nothing says that you can't stop on a country lane or park in a shopping mall. Remove yourself from the action; simply use your wits and the available possibilities.

Decide on the issue of primary concern. Take the full bag and begin, one by one, to remove the Runes from their bag and drop them into the empty bag. As you do this, slow your breathing while concentrating on the issue that is your immediate concern. Use each outbreath to release your hold on any "cherished outcomes," replacing them with a fresh curiosity and appetite for the insight the last Rune in the bag will hold for you.

It is this last remaining Rune that will provide the new clarity and perspective you require.

The Two Bags Reading can be used profitably by two overwrought people. You will need two sets of Runes and four bags to do this simultaneously or, if only one set is available, one person will do it at a time in order to have a full set of Runes to draw from. When each of you has reached the final Rune and considered its message, you may then want to exchange Runes and consider how the two Runes interconnect. This is a very powerful and healing form of Rune Play when entered into by two who share interests, conflict, and growth.

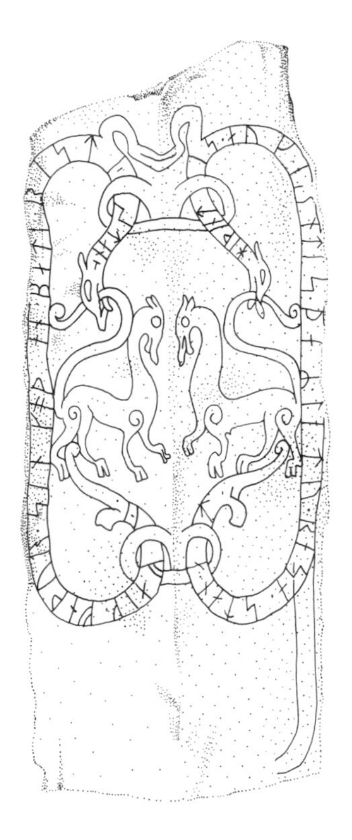

TWO BAGS READING

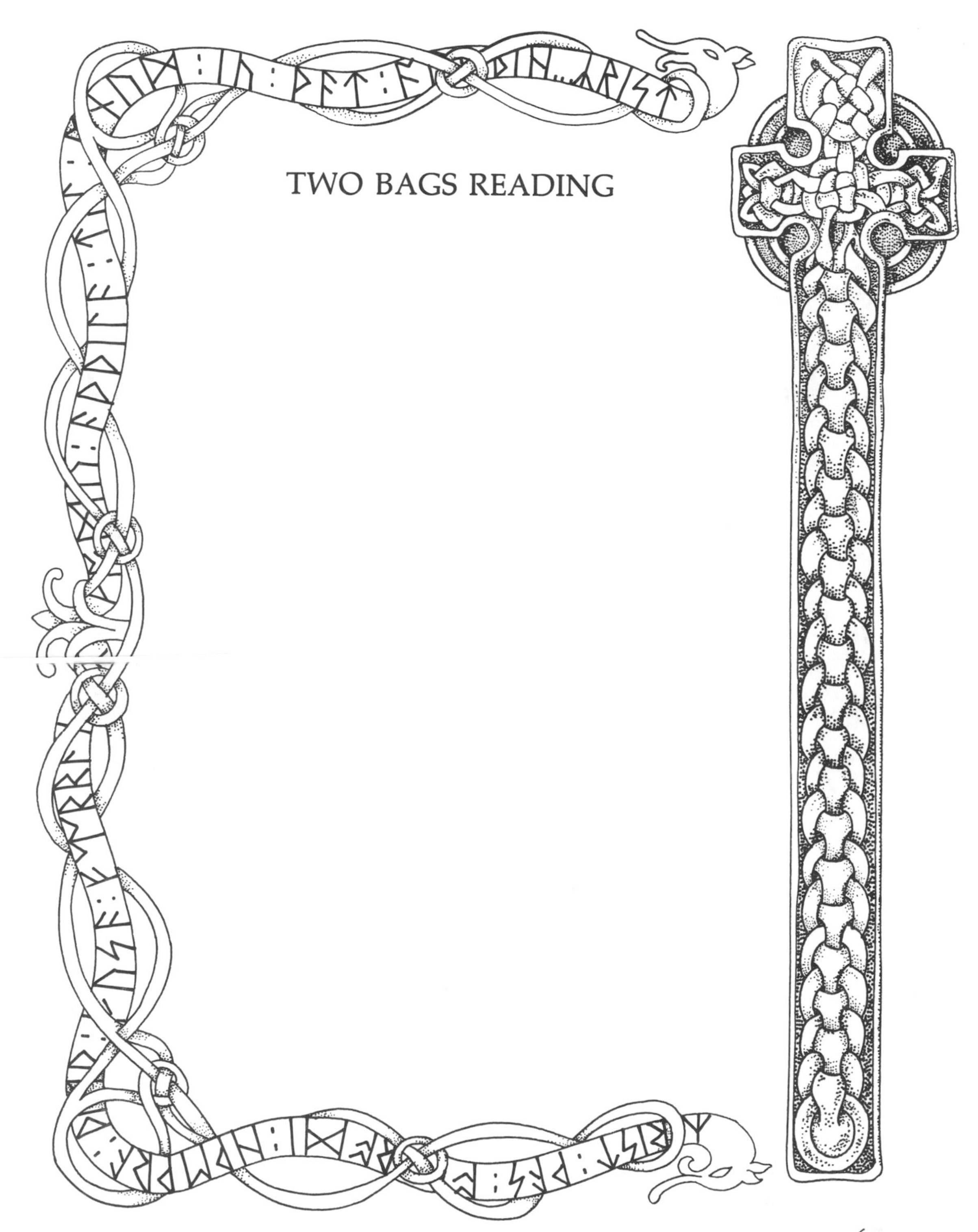

For the week of ____________

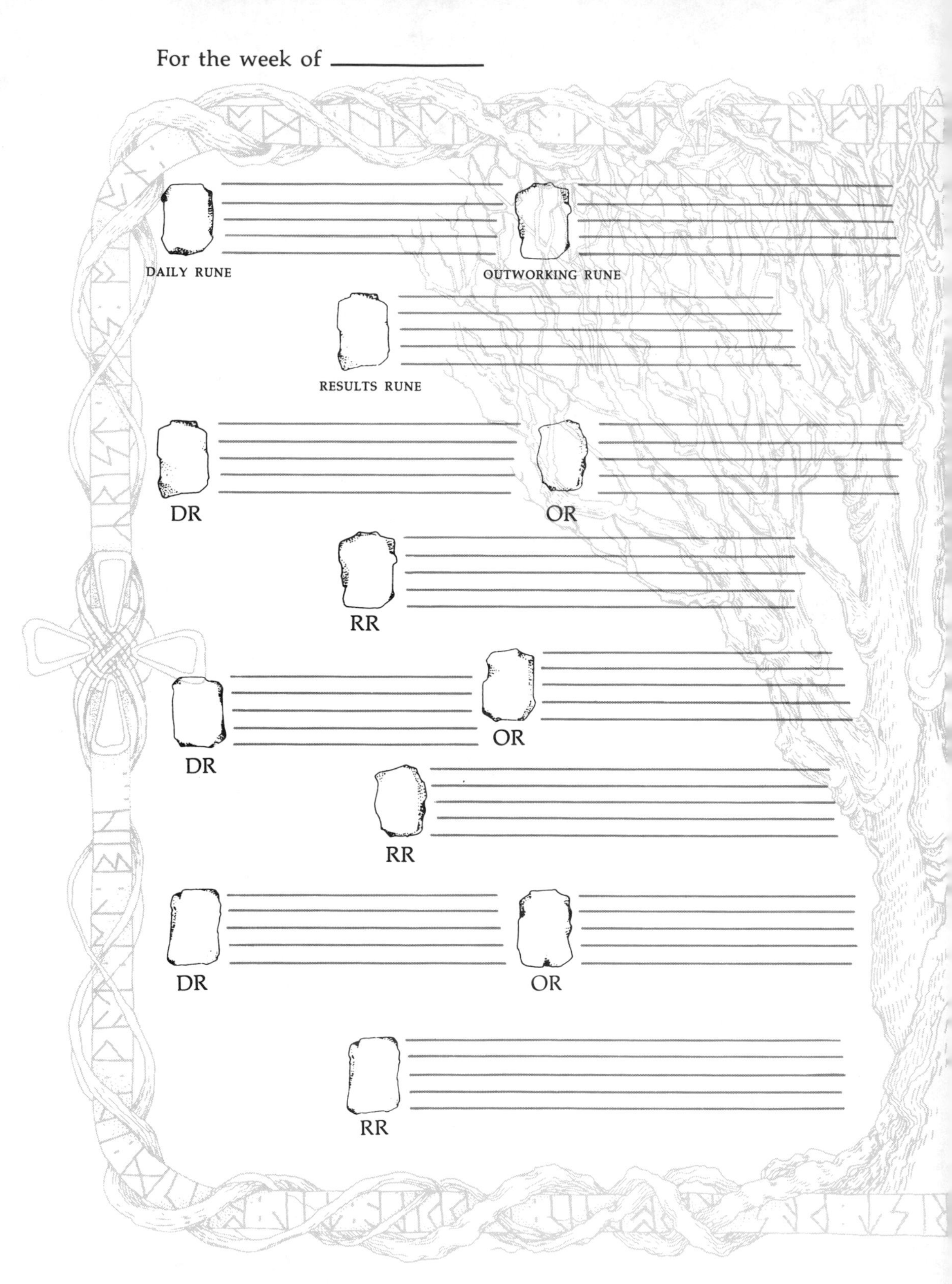

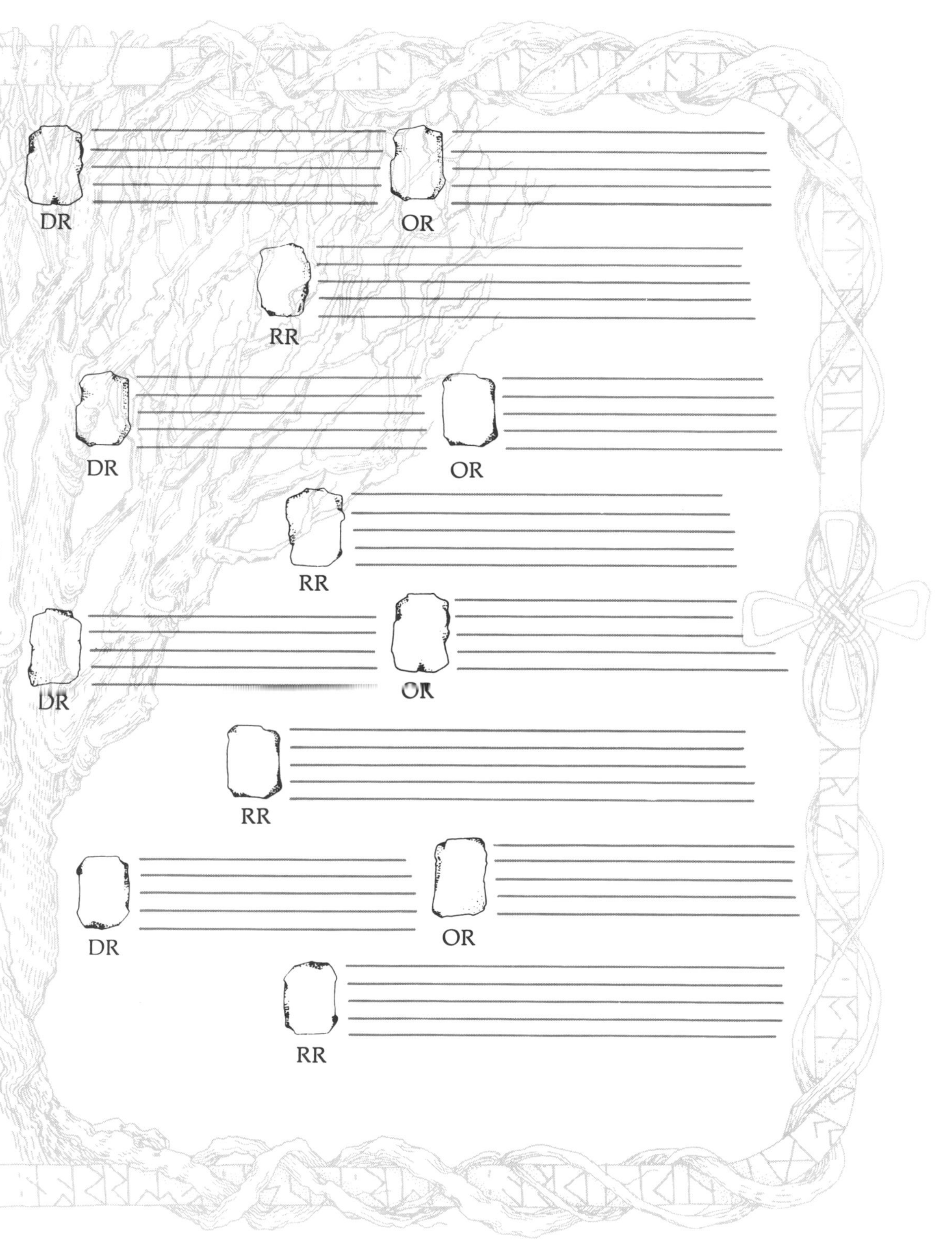
DR
OR
RR
DR
OR
RR
DR
OR
RR
DR
OR
RR

For the week of ____________

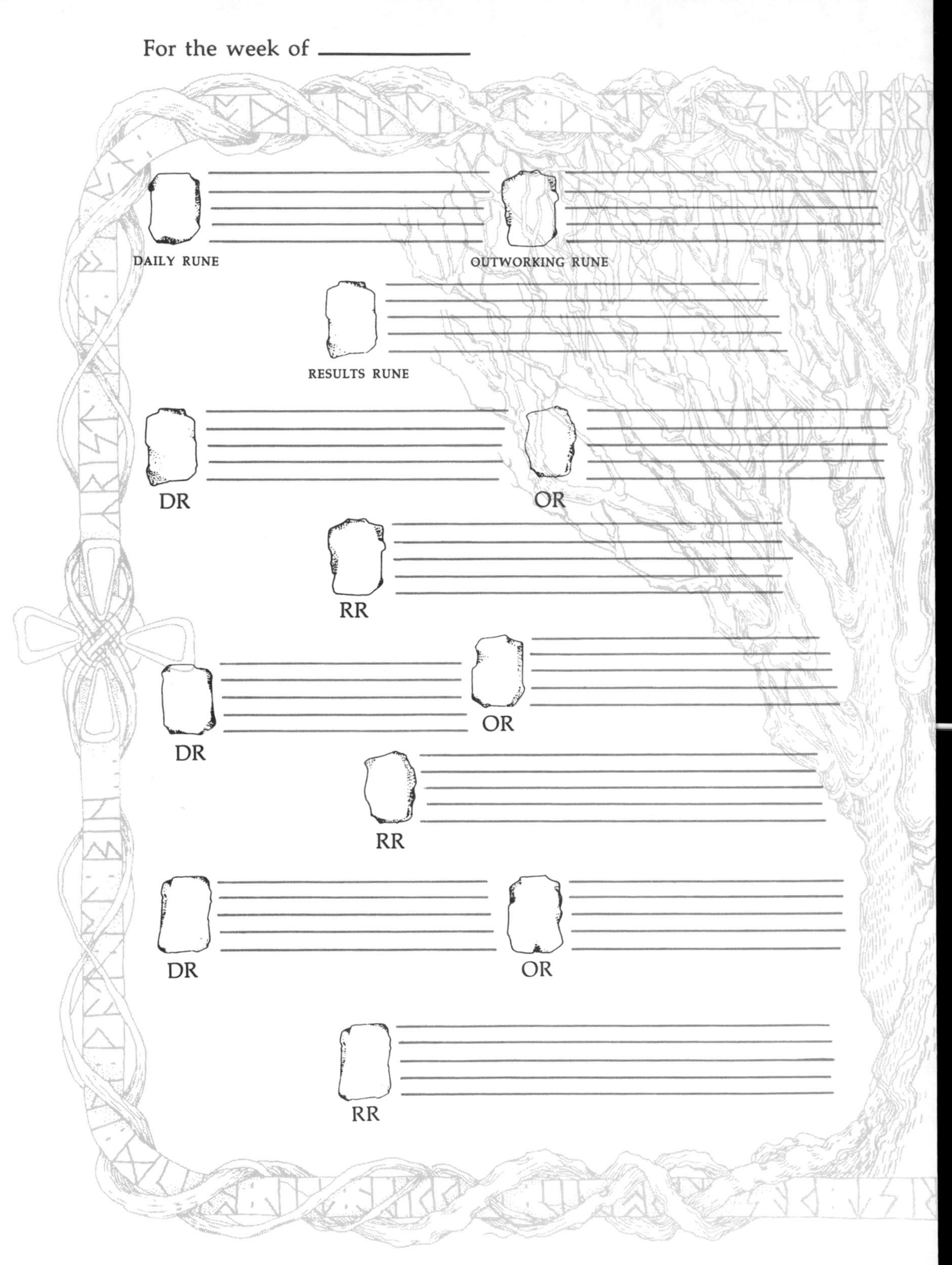

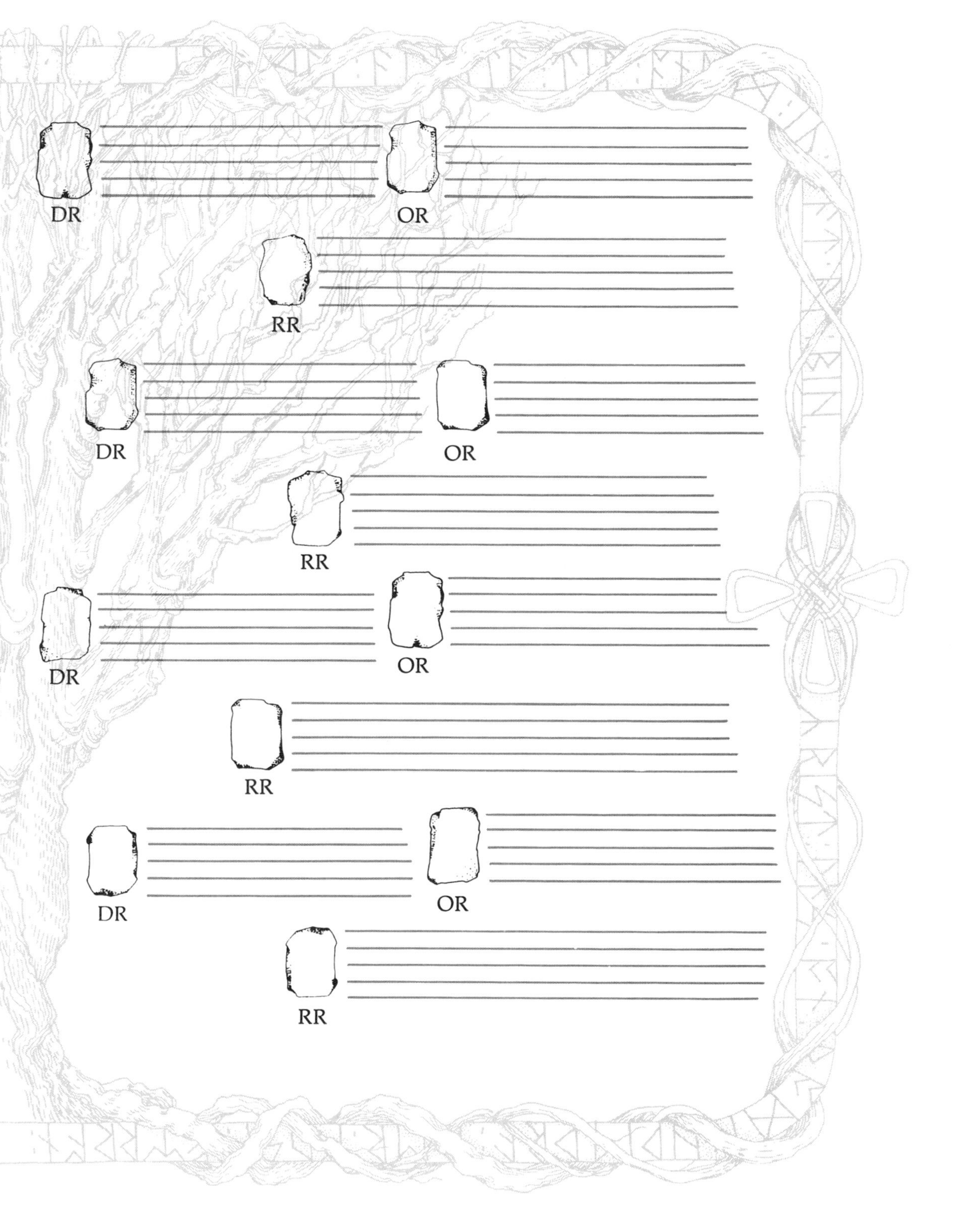
DR
OR
RR
DR
OR
RR
DR
OR
RR
DR
OR
RR

For the week of ____________

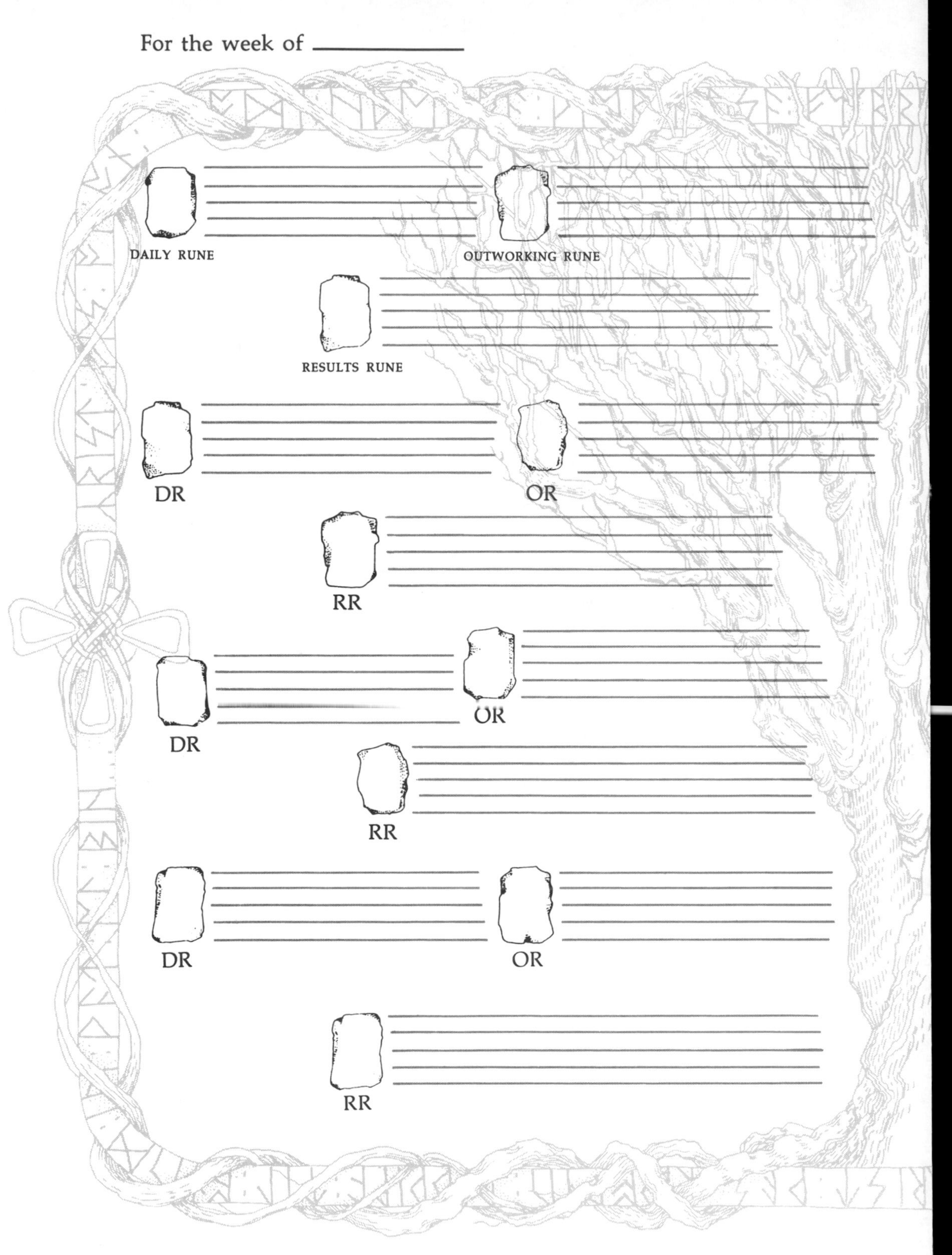

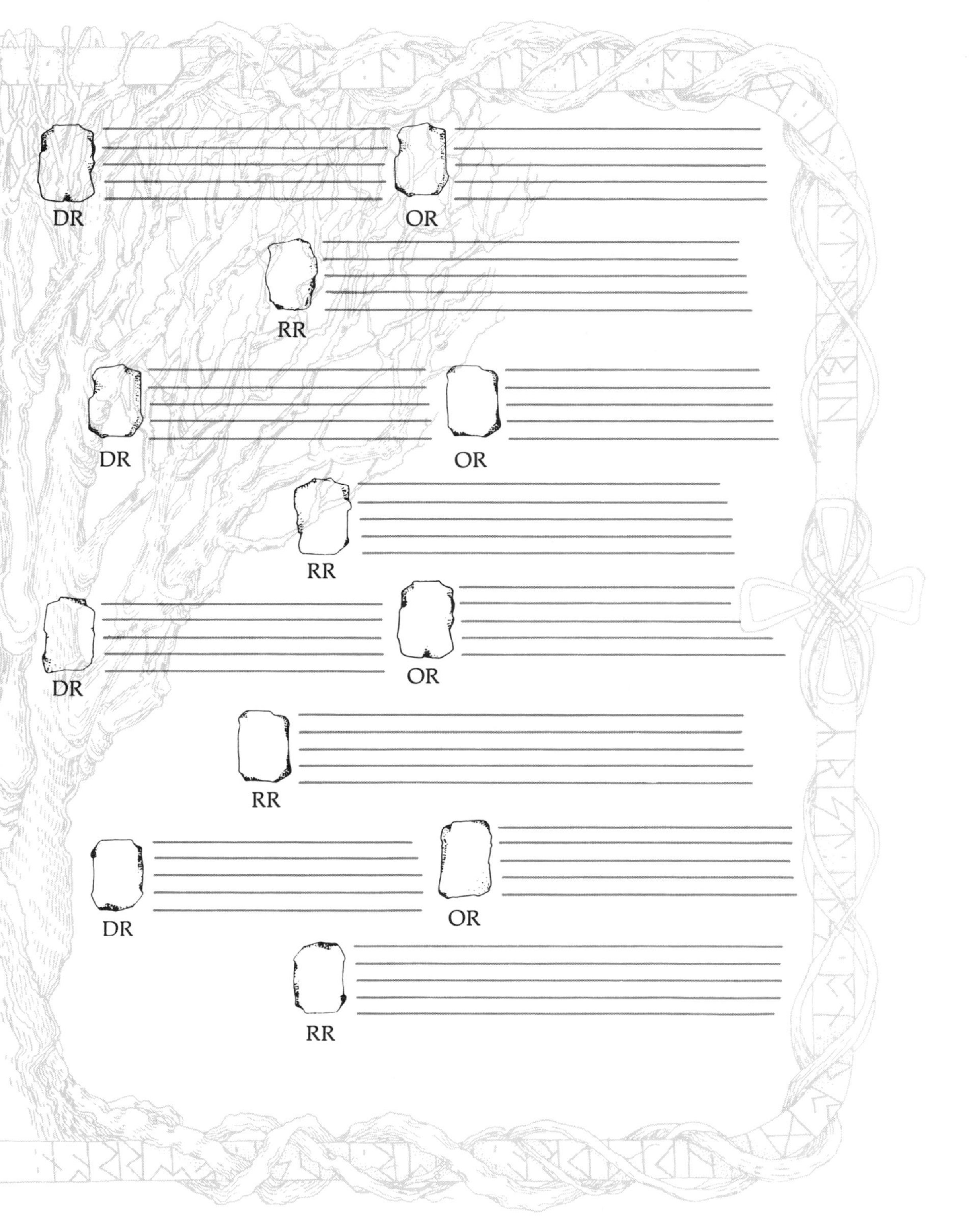
DR
OR
RR
DR
OR
RR
DR
OR
RR
DR
OR
RR

For the week of ______________

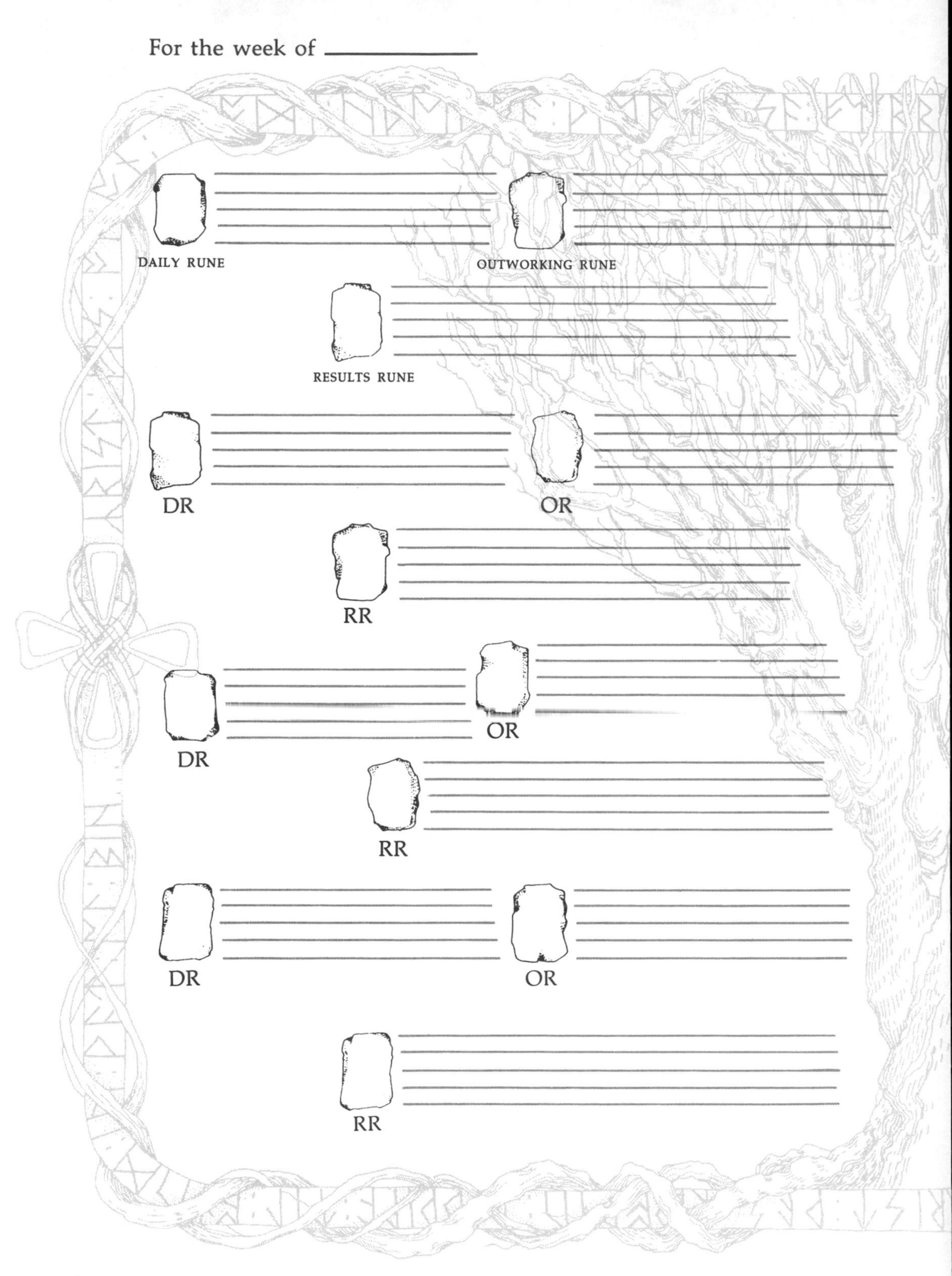

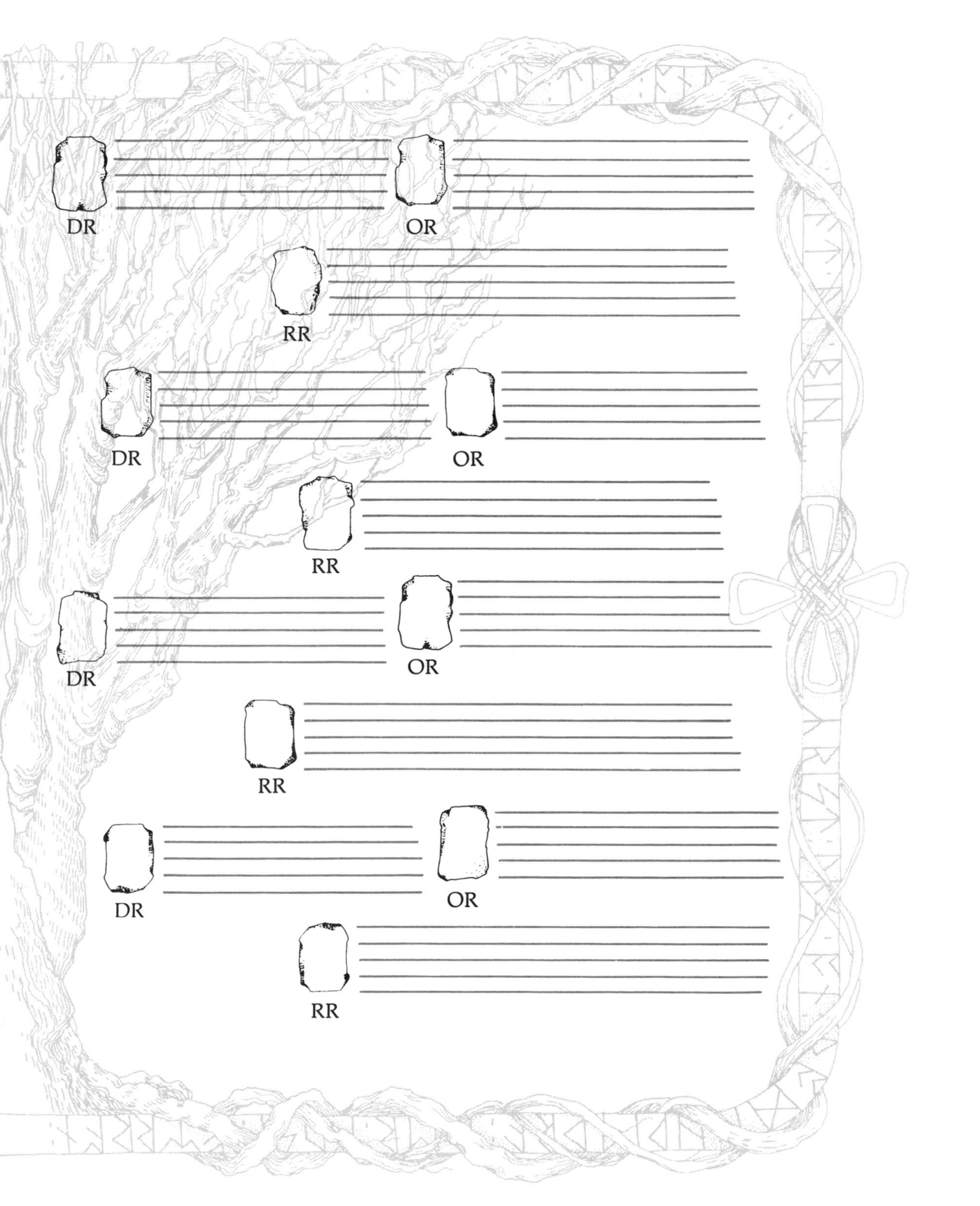
DR
OR
RR
DR
OR
RR
DR
OR
RR
DR
OR
RR

For the week of ______________

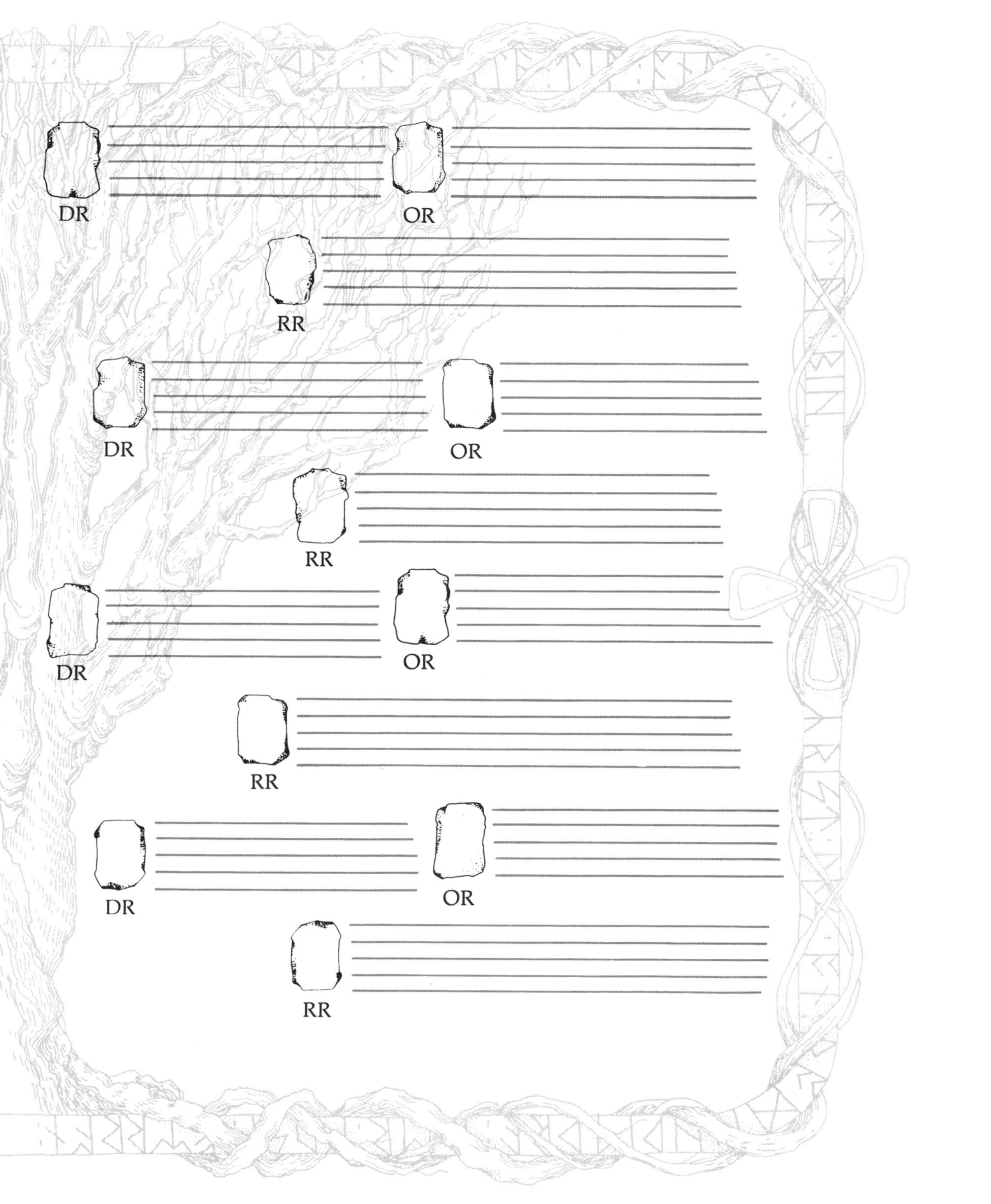
DR
OR
RR
DR
OR
RR
DR
OR
RR
DR
OR
RR

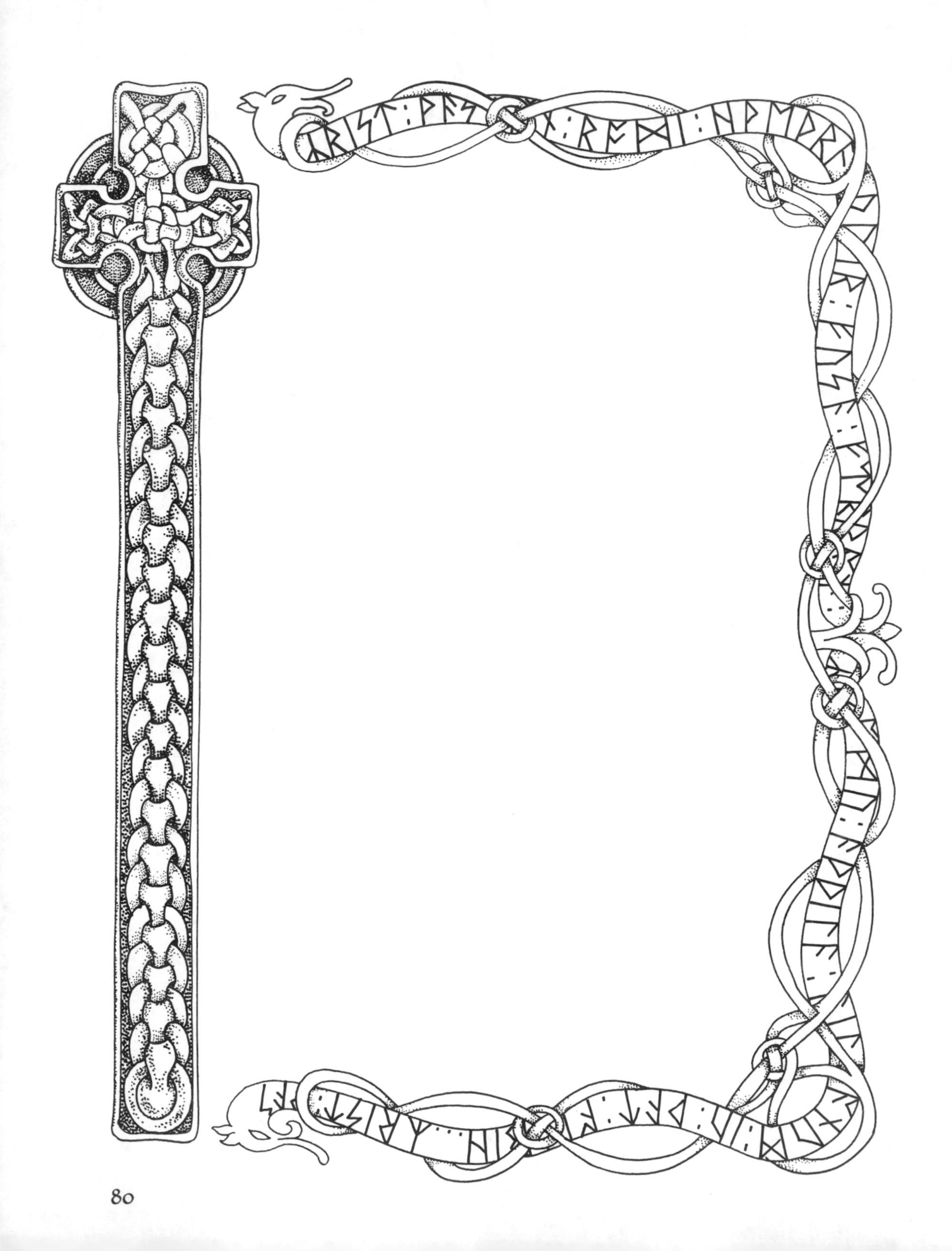

The Primstave Reading

rimstaff, or primstave, was a marking device found in Scandinavia—a tray, a board, or more often, a stick—into which had been cut pictures and symbols which enabled the owner to keep track of special event days in the calendar year. In its way of relating events to the course of the year, a primstave could be called an events calendar. The spread of Rune stones used in the *Primstave Reading* breaks out the distinctive features of a situation that holds us in thrall by its magnitude of complexity or uncertainty. When your initial or eventual reaction is "I can't cope with this," it's a fair sign that what is called for is a Primstave Reading.

Since there are 41 Runic possibilities contained in a bag of 25 stones (by virtue of 16 glyphs which can be read upright or reversed, according to how drawn from the bag), the odds are 41:1 on choosing a particular Rune regarding your issue. Using the Primstave Reading, in which five Runes are drawn from the bag, the odds against this particular combination of Runes occurring in a spread, in this particular order, soar to 3,000,000:1. That the Primstave Reading is highly personal and specific is evidenced by such odds.

Clearly formulate your issue. Then draw five stones from the bag, one at a time, and place them one below the other, like a totem pole building from the top down. It is your choice as to whether you prefer placing the glyph side up or, to avoid temptation, glyph side down and then turn them over one by one. In descending order, let the Runes stand for:

(1) Overview of the Situation
(2) The Challenge
(3) Course of Action Called For
(4) The Sacrifice
(5) Evolved Situation

As it is used in the fourth position, the term "Sacrifice" has a meaning akin to the "peeling away" called for in ᛟ, *Othila,* the Rune of Inheritance, Separation, Retreat, the Rune of separating paths. Originally a bonding of two Latin words *(sacrificium* and *facere)* that conjointly carry the meaning "to make sacred," the concept of sacrifice has, over time, come to be associated primarily with pain and loss. But as used in the Primstave Reading, sacrifice refers to that which has to be peeled away, shed, discarded, in order for a new wholeness to be accomplished.

Test out the Primstave Reading during your next life crisis.

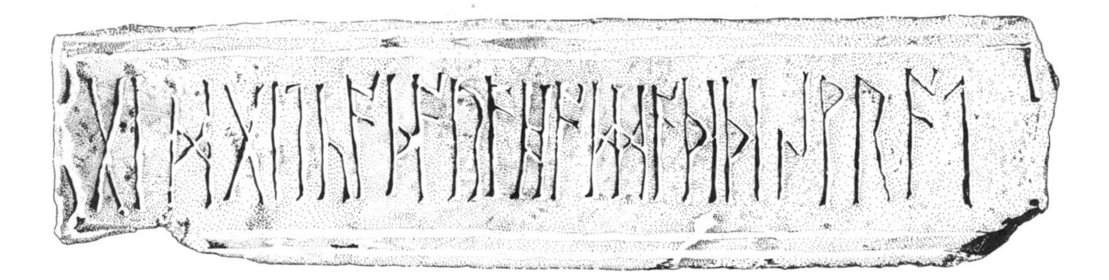

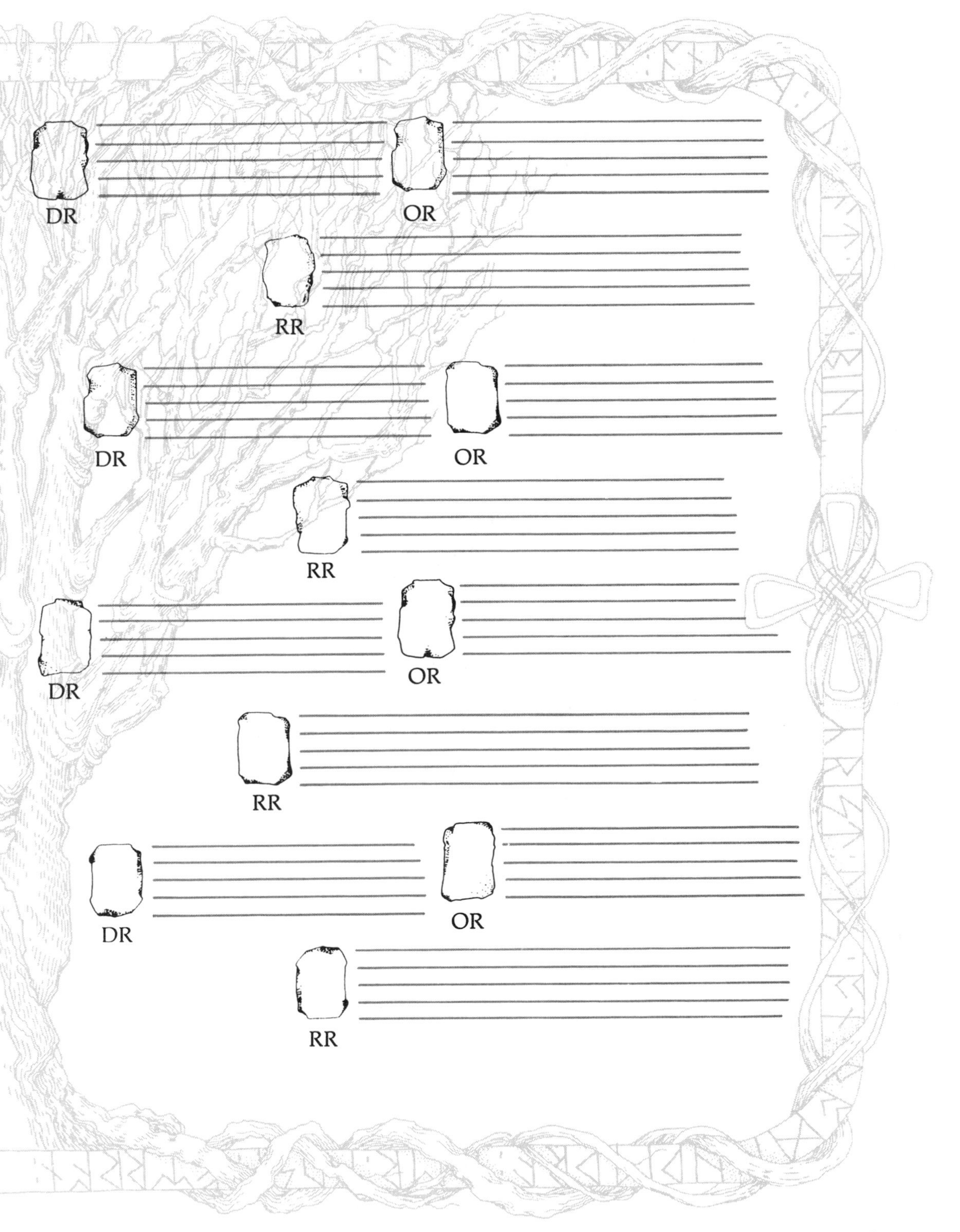
DR
OR
RR
DR
OR
RR
DR
OR
RR
DR
OR
RR

For the week of ______________

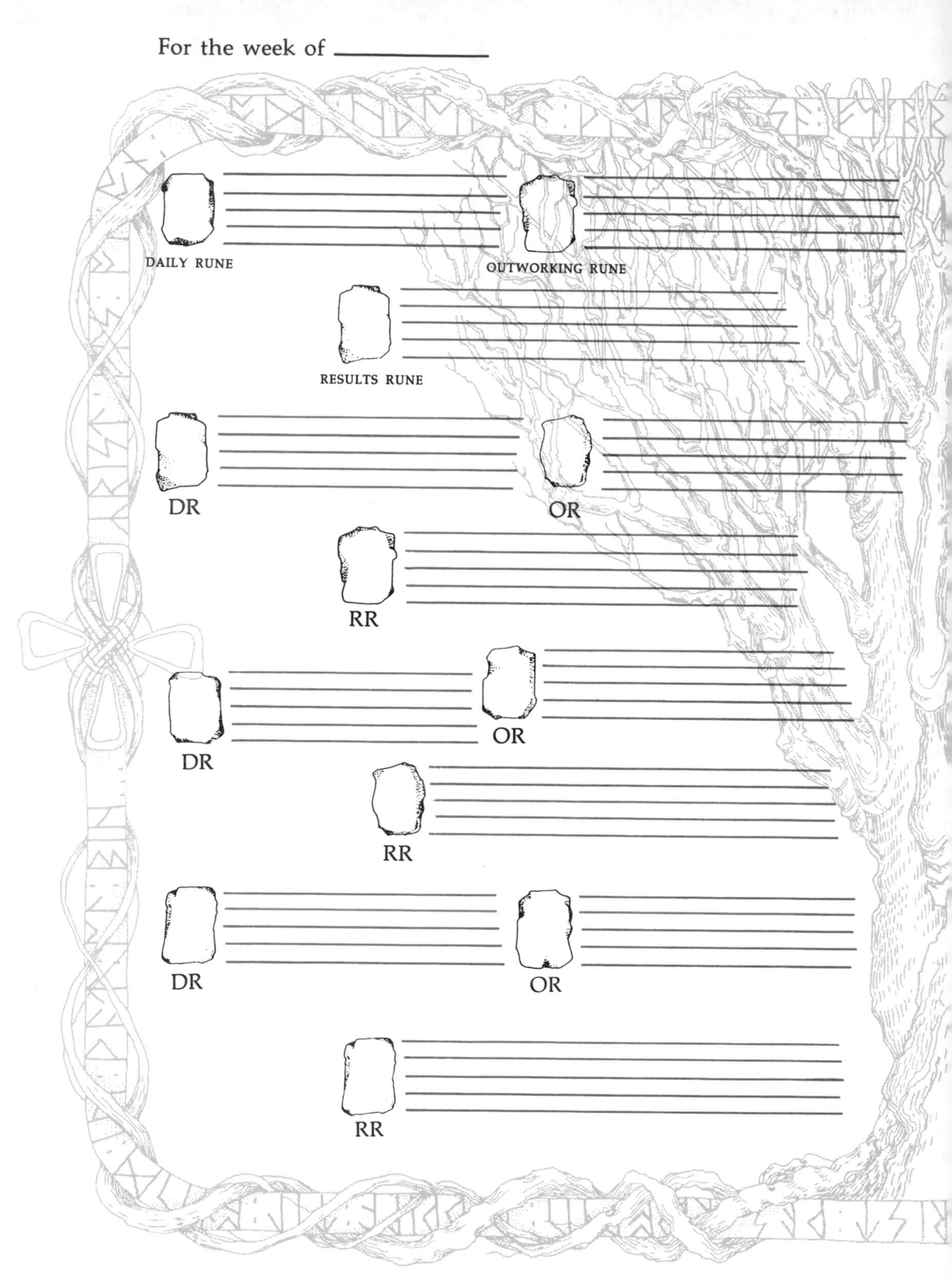

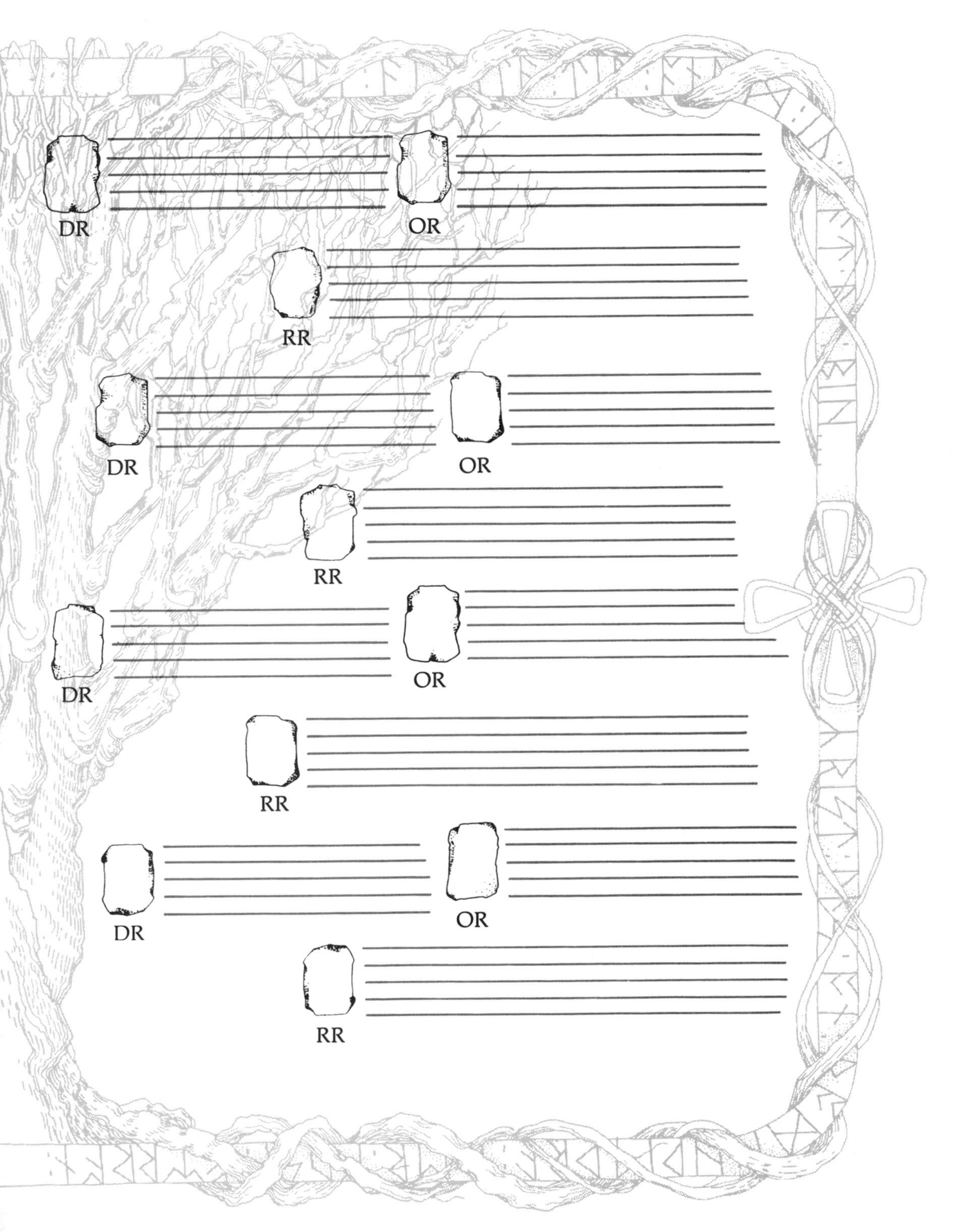
DR
OR
RR
DR
OR
RR
DR
OR
RR
DR
OR
RR

For the week of ____________

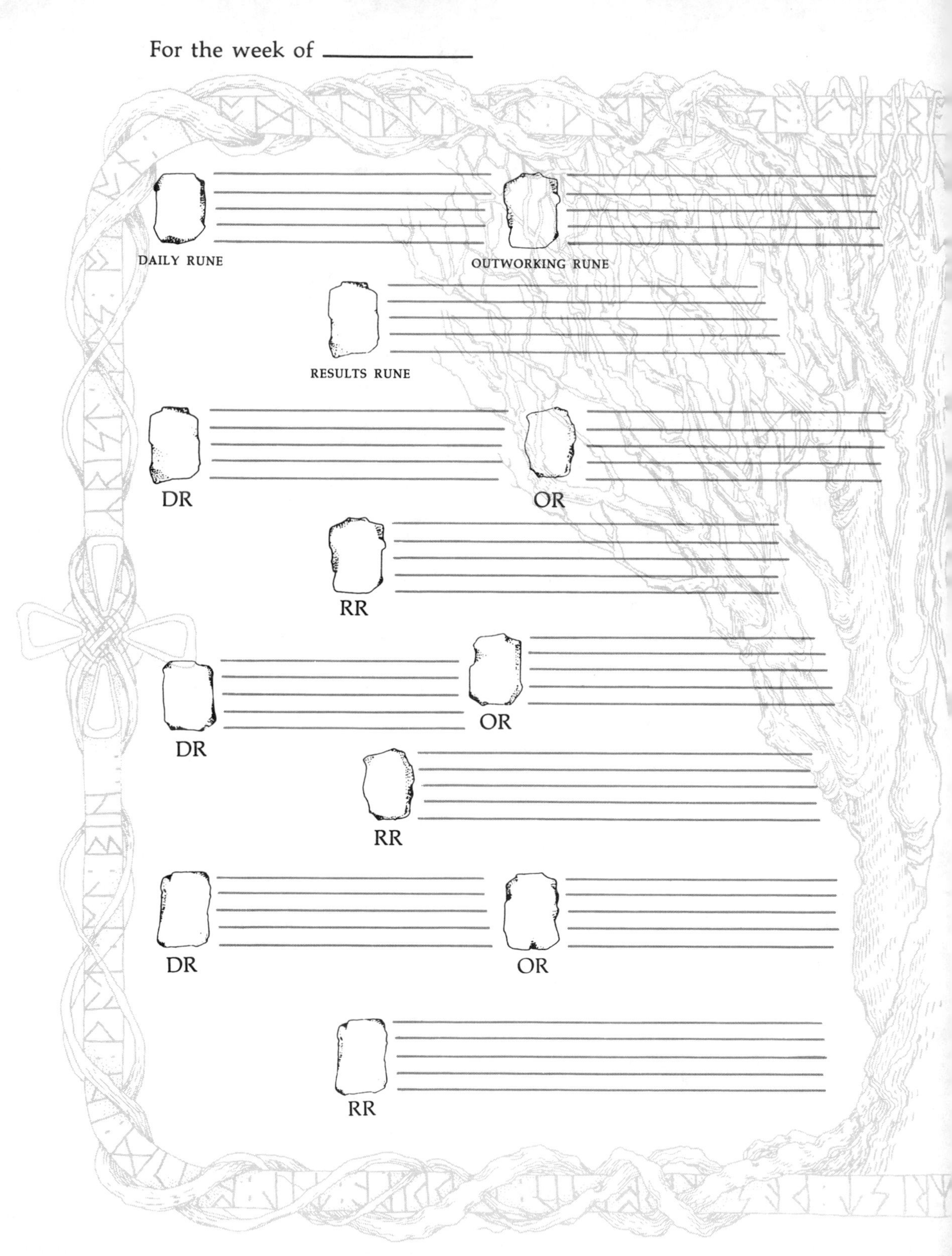

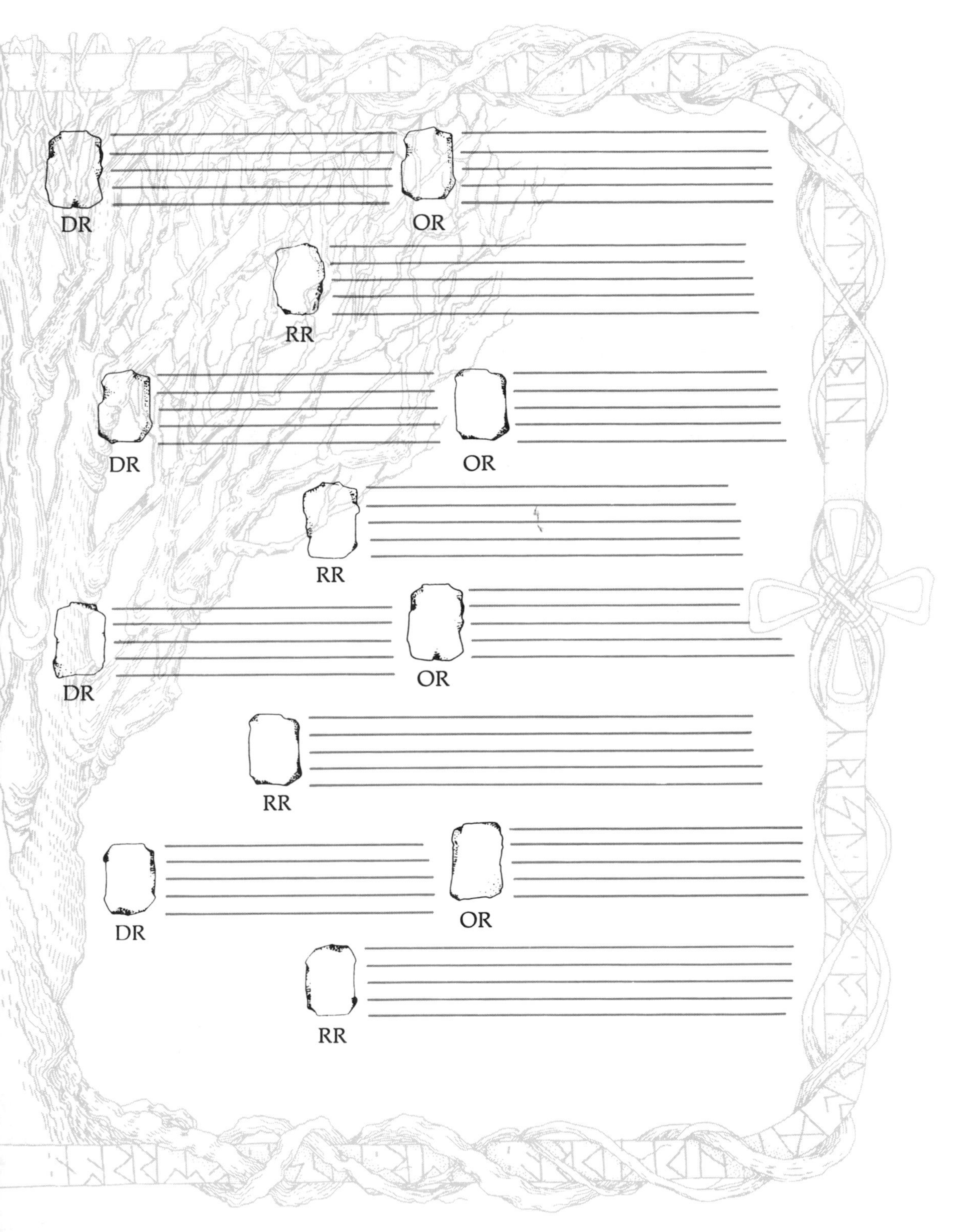
DR
OR
RR
DR
OR
RR
DR
OR
RR
DR
OR
RR

SPRING

Doing Ing

Ing at first was seen by folk
Among the East Danes, till afterwards he
Went over the waves, followed his wagon.
Thus the Heardings named this hero.

"The Old English Rune Poem"
Translation by Marijane Osborn

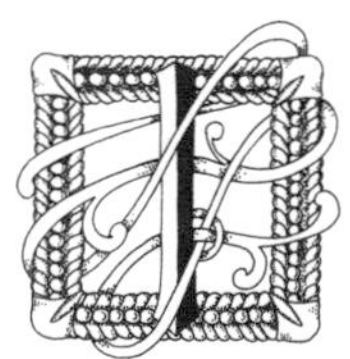

nguz—Ing to the Anglo-Saxon world—is a splendid archetype: a male fertility figure who, by his passage, transforms and prepares us for what is to come. In *Rune Games* it is explained this way:

> The progress of a god and his wagon formed an ancient fertility rite, performed to release the creative power locked up in the soil over the winter. . . . Ing is the key which releases the creative aspects of the psyche.*

A Rune of emergence, *Inguz* can also serve in time of emergency. This Rune is a wand to be waved over the soil of our nature, thereby releasing what is blocked. The energies freed up from the winter of the spiritual life are signaled in *The Book of Runes* as "emergence from a closed, chrysalis state." It is the emergence from the seed, an old habit or relationship with others or with your self. *Doing Ing* is a remedy for the divided self.

Eight people are required for Doing Ing: Co-workers gather to consider the way a project is working, or not working; members of a spiritual fellowship meet to consider the most efficacious ways to utilize their energies; a civic

*Marijane Osborn and Stella Longland, *Rune Games* (London: Routledge & Kegan Paul, 1982), pp. 48–49.

group sets out to establish priorities. Almost any group can benefit from Doing Ing. Therapists, teachers, householders, business entities, members of any nuclear or extended family who are ready to confront characteristics or conduct they no longer consider appropriate—all can be served by Doing Ing.

Let the god Ing come into your midst following his wagon. See the figure trudging along. Be in touch with his centers of power: Head, Heart, Groin, Feet. These four centers correlate with the Thought, Feeling, Core Energy, and Grounding of the condition or challenge that has brought you together.

The following illustration shows you how the elements of this spread are arranged:

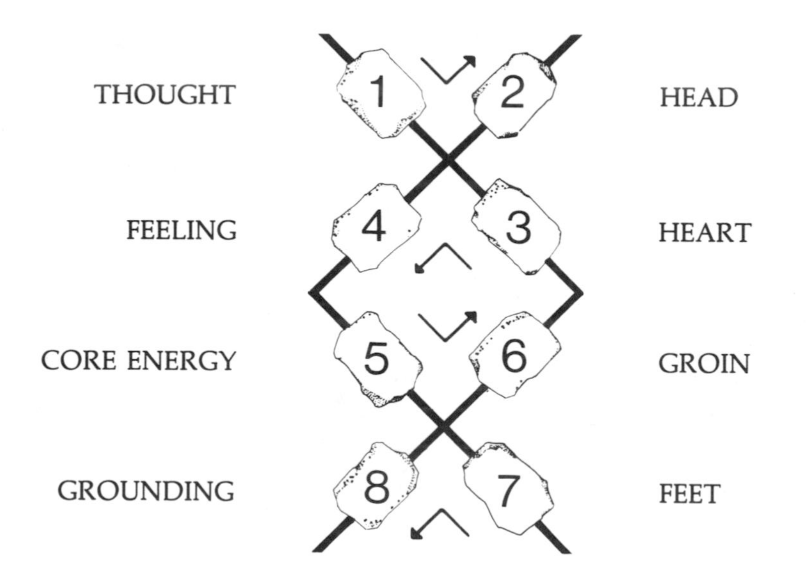

The numbers represent the order in which the reading will unfold. They indicate the path your venture must take in order to remedy the divided self and achieve wholeness. Begin by drawing the design. It can be small (on a single piece of paper), or it can be large (drawn out on a blackboard). Write the numbers 1 through 8 on eight slips of paper, put them in a hat, then have each person choose a number. Next, have each of the participants draw a Rune and place it, glyph side down, on the spread so that it corresponds to their number. You may, if it is convenient, align yourselves right and left on both sides of a long table. Turn the glyphs right side up and you are ready to begin.

EXAMPLE OF A GROUP *DOING ING*

A men's support group has come together to decide whether to open the group to newcomers. Several members feel that, if they do so, they will have to start all over again in order to build the trust that comes from shared experience. Others believe that new members would add to the group by bringing in new energy, new perspectives. This faction feels that things are getting stale. Unable to resolve this division through discussion, the group decides to play Doing Ing.

The following represents their spread with the Runes in place:

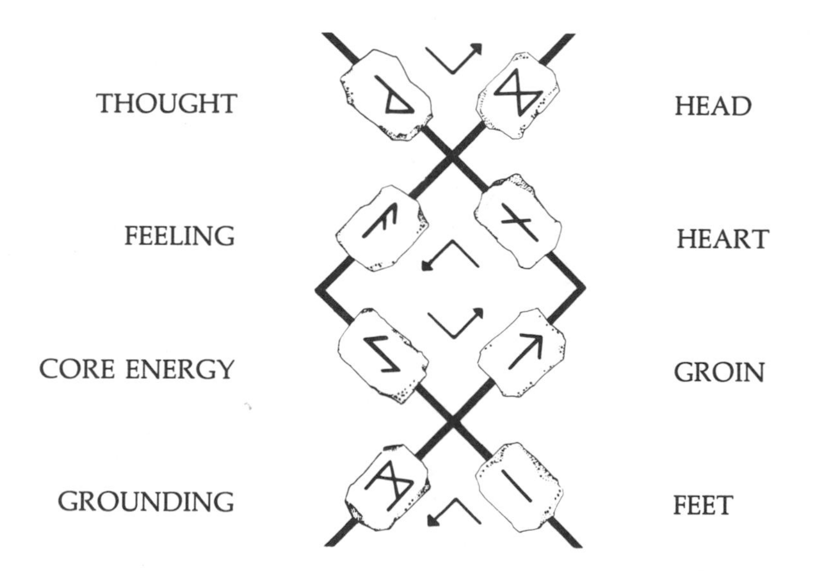

(1) HEAD (left side): , *Wunjo,* Joy, Light, *Reversed.*

The person who drew *Wunjo* feels that he is nearing a breakthrough. He doesn't want the group cohesion diluted, and yet he recognizes the importance of the opening up for other members of the group. This situation is a challenge for him to meet joyfully. Ultimately he will accept the challenge of an enlarged group.

(2) HEAD (right side): , *Dagaz,* Transformation.

Number two is sitting on the fence, looking for evidence that will sway him in one direction or the other. , *Dagaz* calls for a complete transformation in attitude, a 180-degree turn to achieve a new level of expanded integration. Radical trust is called for here

> because the timing is right, the outcome is assured although not, from the present vantage point, predictable.

This gives him the evidence he needs to support expanding the group. Both sides of the thinking energy are in alignment. Having heard from the head, the heart must be heard from next.

(3) HEART (right side): ᚾ, *Nauthiz,* Necessity, Constraint, and Pain, *Reversed.*
This person is having a temper tantrum over the mere possibility of bringing "strangers" into this family. ᚾ tells him in the most literal way that a cleansing is required of him. "When something within us is disowned, that which is disowned wreaks havoc." He is put on notice that his will is in disrepair, he's instructed to control his anger and impulses, and to practice modesty and good temper. Even though he does not like what he hears, Number Three sits and ponders the lessons of *Nauthiz.*

(4) HEART (left side): ᚨ, *Ansuz,* The Rune of Signals, Messenger Rune.
Opening up the group was the founder's idea. He looks to his Rune as a test of appropriateness for expanding the number of members. ᚨ speaks to new life unfolding, new connections, and "a new sense of family solidarity."
A dissonance is revealed here between the right & left elements of Feeling, i.e., the left side doesn't really "have his heart in it." Later, in discussion, a reconciliation will need to take place.

(5) GROIN (left side): ᛇ, *Eihwaz,* Defense, Avertive Powers.
Number Five is just beginning to feel comfortable in the group—this is the first time he has ever shared his intimate feelings with a group of men. He's afraid he will revert to his former shyness if new members come into the group. This Rune is telling him that he is strong enough to meet tests and even undergo defeat and still continue growing in the process. It is advising him that he is strong enough to give up his comfort. He will decide in favor of opening up the group.

(6) GROIN (right side): ᛏ, *Teiwaz,* the Rune of Warrior Energy.

This person is the energizer of the expansionist faction, the young buck keen to confront new challenges. ᛏ speaks to the need for self-conquest and all it involves. He is reminded especially in this case to be unattached to outcomes. The Rune points out his responsibility for spiritualizing the core energy of the group, keeping in touch with its highest goal, which means taking into account the needs of those who oppose expanding the group. This causes him to assume a more moderate attitude toward the "vital importance" of bringing in new members. He is being instructed in the necessity for balance.

The core energy is not far out of alignment. Both are powerful men. Both are dealing with balance: one by backing off, the other by stepping forward. This becomes clear to them during the discussion period.

(7) FEET (right side): ᛁ, *Isa,* the Rune of Standstill.

Number Seven is the group diplomat. Sensitive to the temperament of the others, he is the observer, the witness, the one who needs to see the whole before making a decision so that any obstructions can be first cleared away. ᛁ calls for standstill until the release of the old has occurred for everyone. This Rune reminds him "to be patient, for this is the period of gestation that precedes a rebirth."

(8) FEET (left side): ᛗ, *Mannaz,* the Self.

He is the last member to have joined the group and is prepared to see it change—as it changed when it accepted him. But he will not support the shift unless they can all reach agreement. ᛗ reminds him that rectification, setting things right, must come before progress. He takes his counsel from the Rune to be "yielding, devoted, and moderate."

Standstill is appropriate before the birth of a new group self. The two aspects of grounding are in harmony.

In the discussion that followed, the two elements of the heart were, to a degree, reconciled, but a general decision was taken to defer opening up the group at that time. Six weeks later the matter was brought up for reconsideration by Number Three (temper tantrum) and Number Five (shy person), both of whom had friends they wanted to introduce into the group.

The following lines were written down after another group of men and women experienced the passage of the god Ing through their midst.

DOING ING

The man doing Ing
Has architecture in his heart,
And in his hands, some magic wand.
Now watch him do this thing.
We are the arches of the Ing.

The woman doing Ing
Has feather grass in her hands
And the Rule of Love in her heart.
She comes to us like spring.
We are the arches of the Ing.

The One doing Ing
Has empty hands,
A listening mind,
A lifted heart
From which It starts to sing.
We are the arches of the Ing.

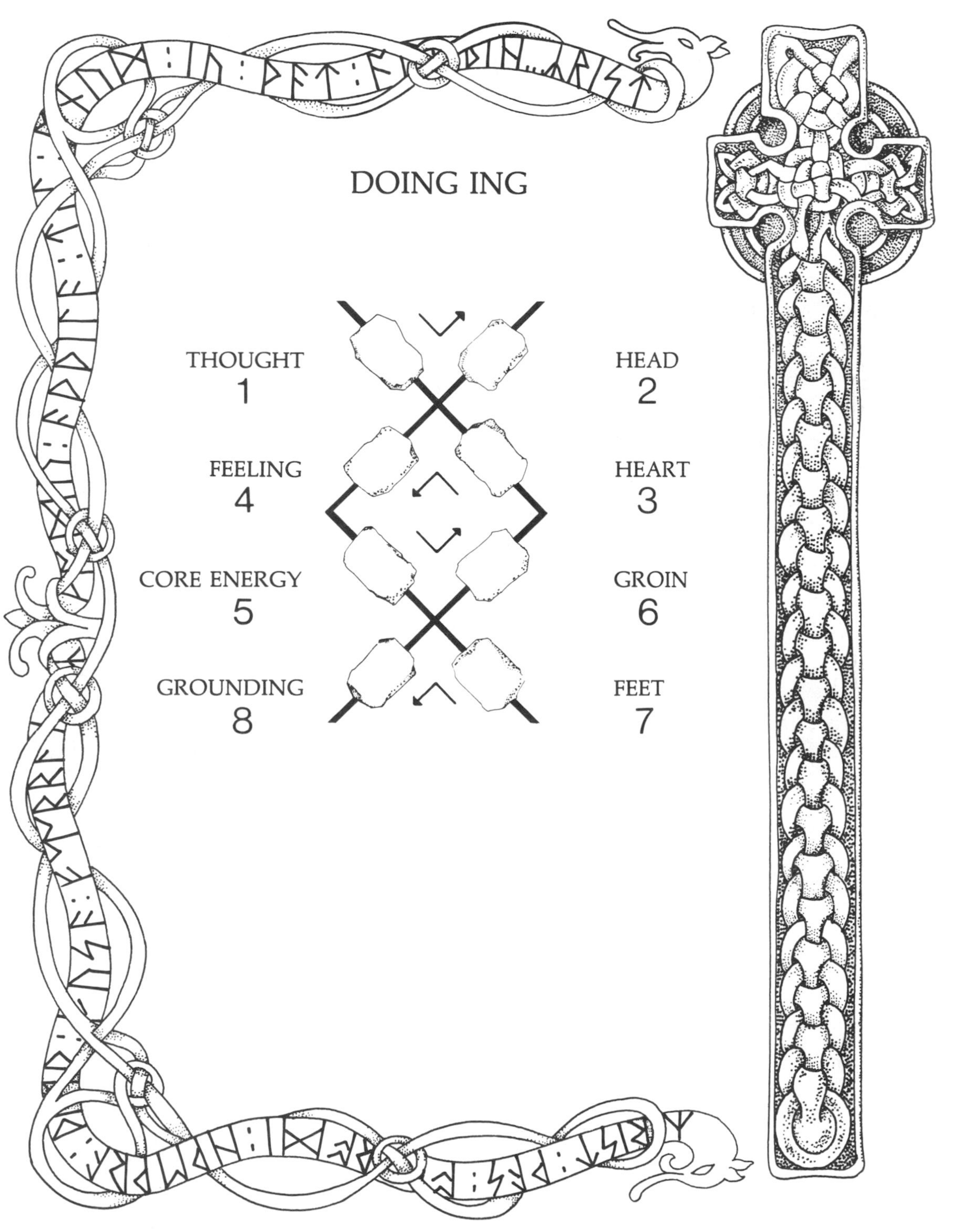
DOING ING
THOUGHT
1
HEAD
2
FEELING
4
HEART
3
CORE ENERGY
5
GROIN
6
GROUNDING
8
FEET
7

For the week of ____________

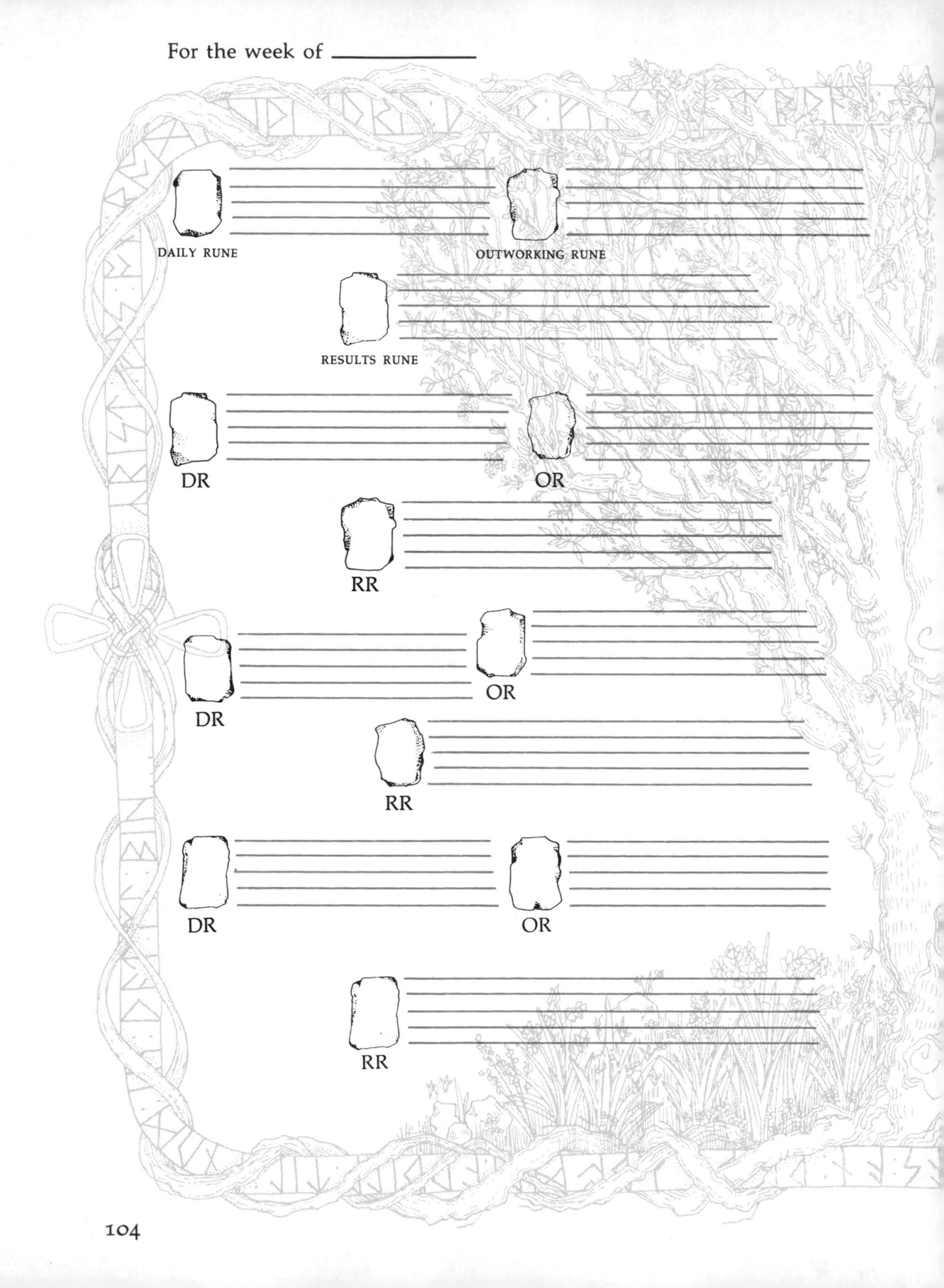

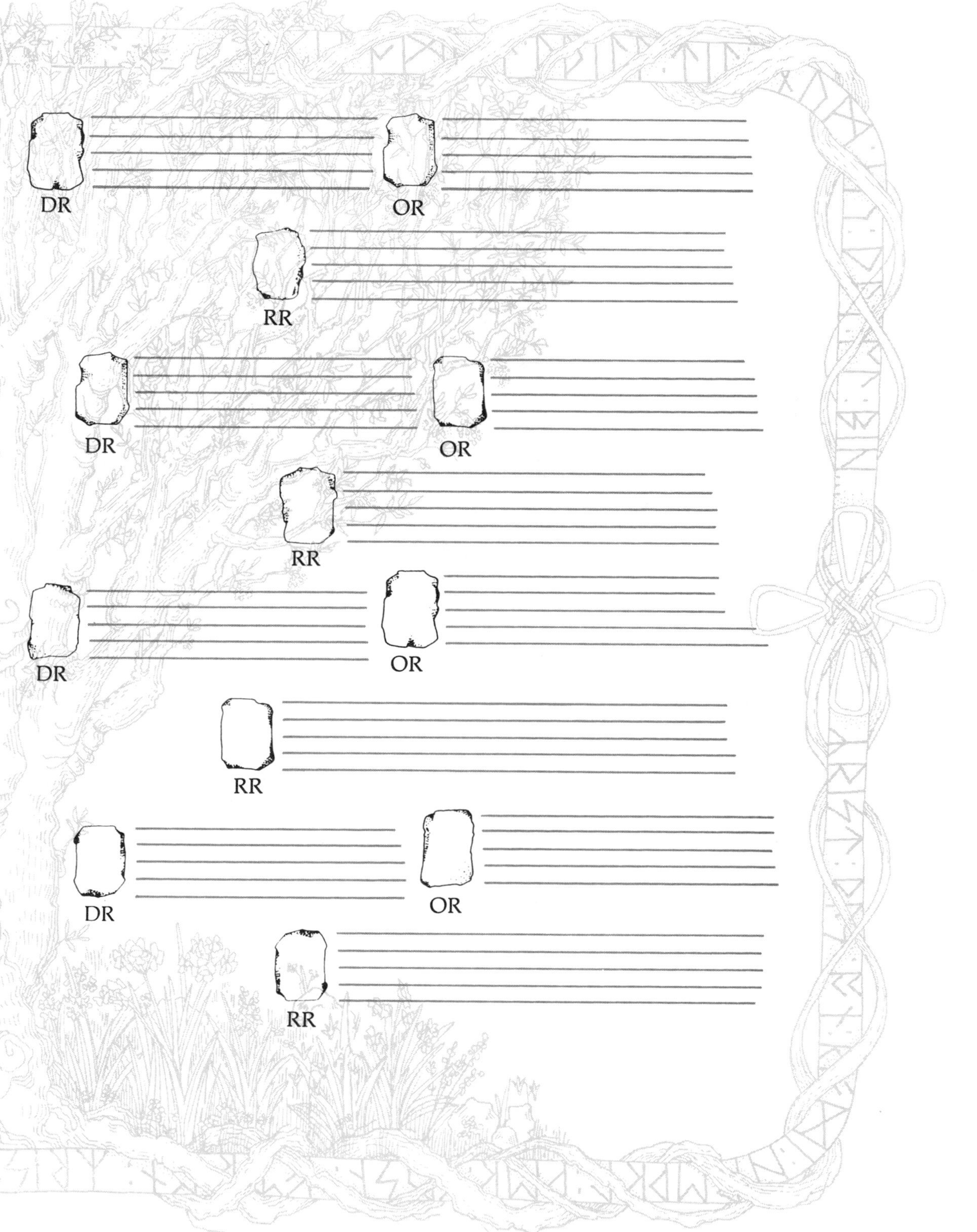
DR
OR
RR
DR
OR
RR
DR
OR
RR
DR
OR
RR

For the week of ___________

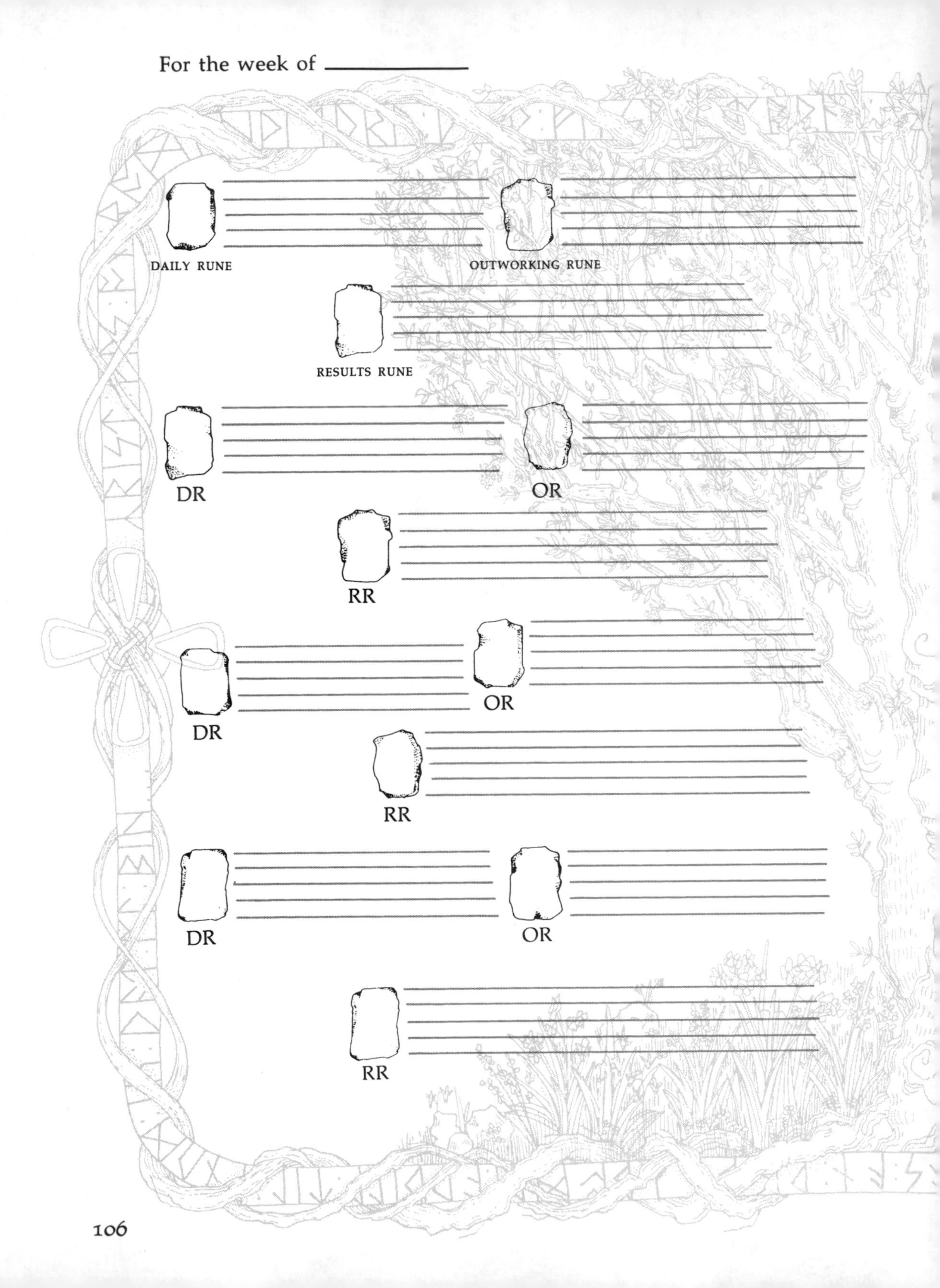

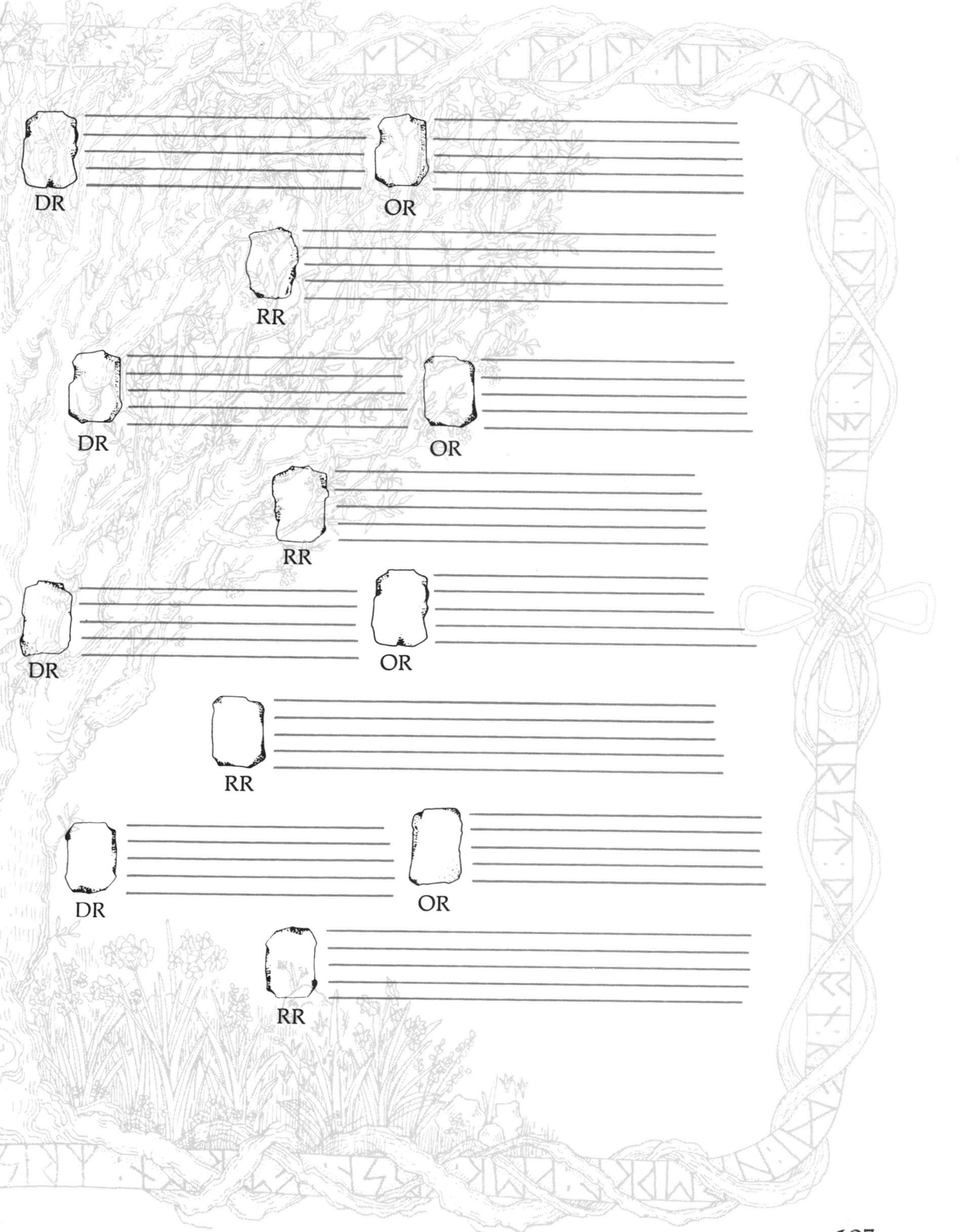
DR
OR
RR
DR
OR
RR
DR
OR
RR
DR
OR
RR

For the week of ______________

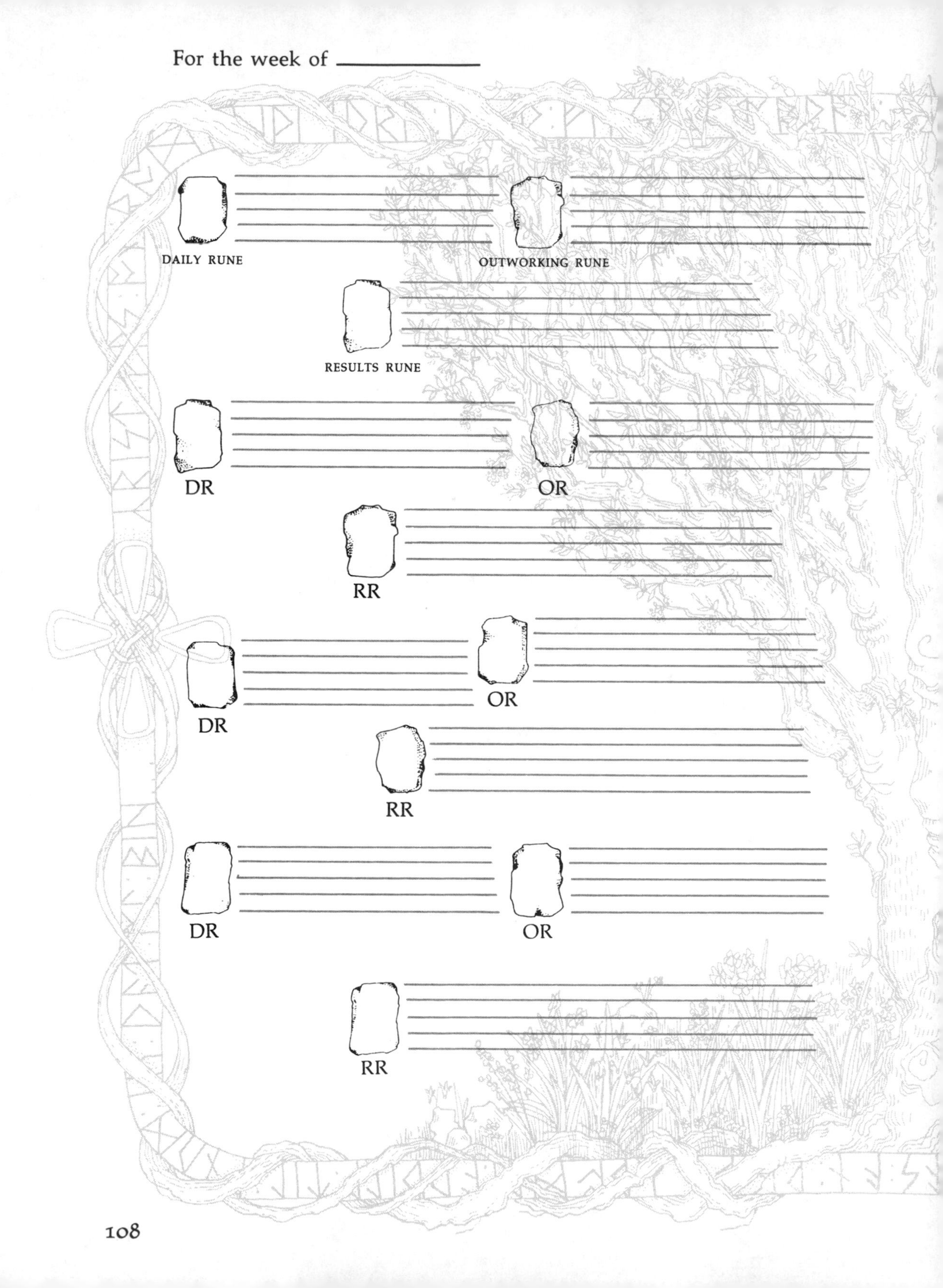

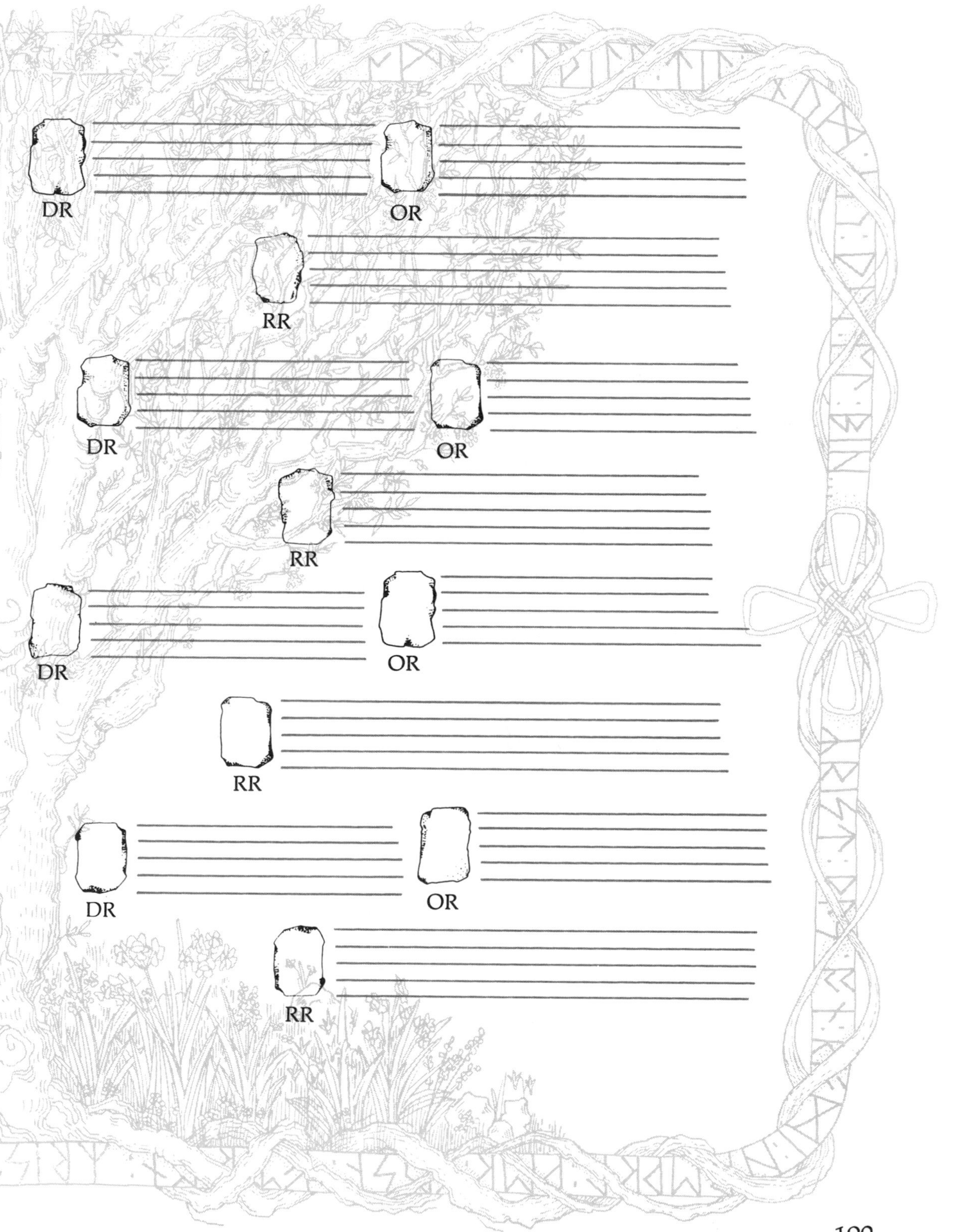
DR
OR
RR
DR
OR
RR
DR
OR
RR
DR
OR
RR

For the week of ____________

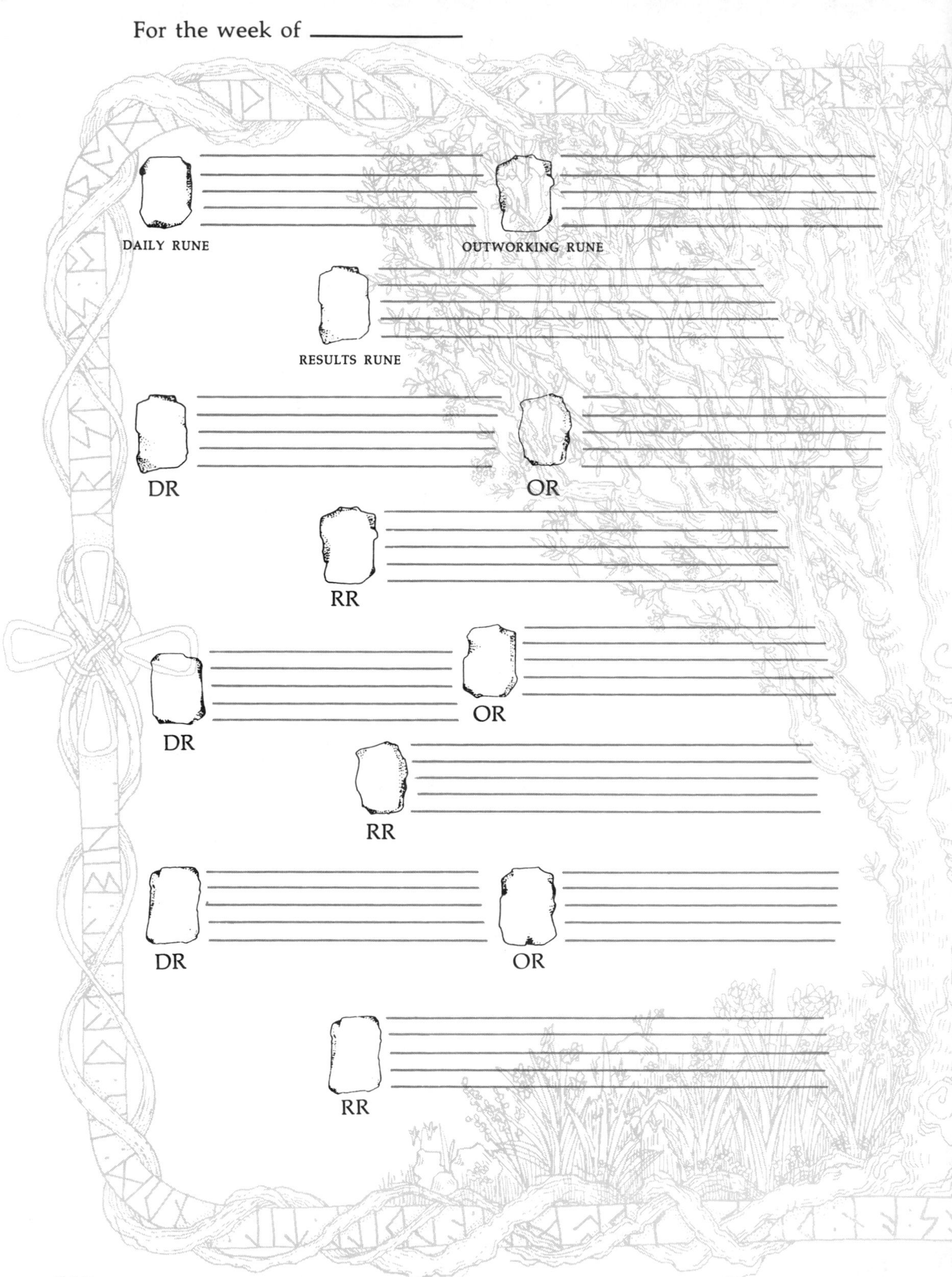

DR
OR
RR
DR
OR
RR
DR
OR
RR
DR
OR
RR

For the week of ____________

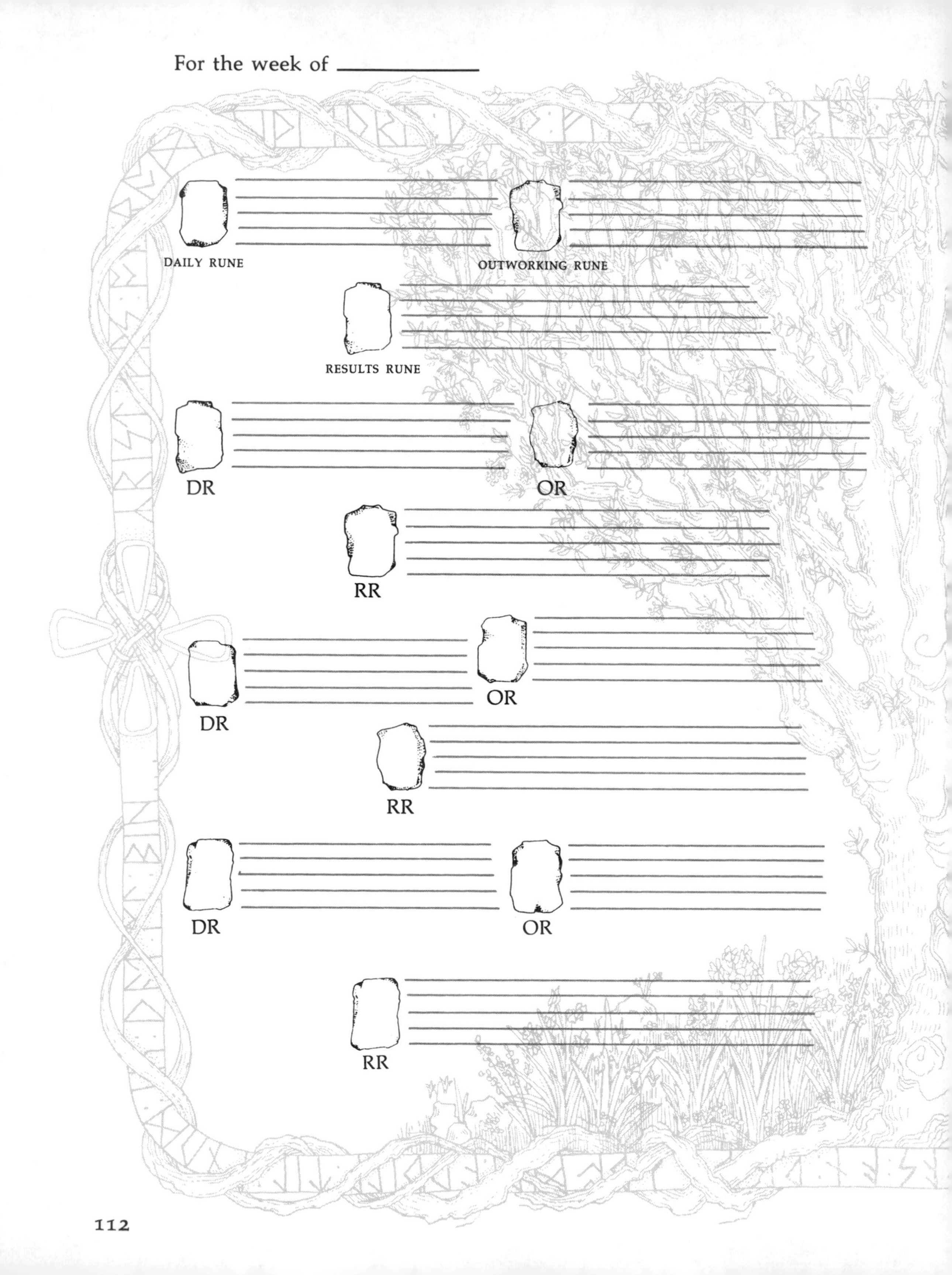

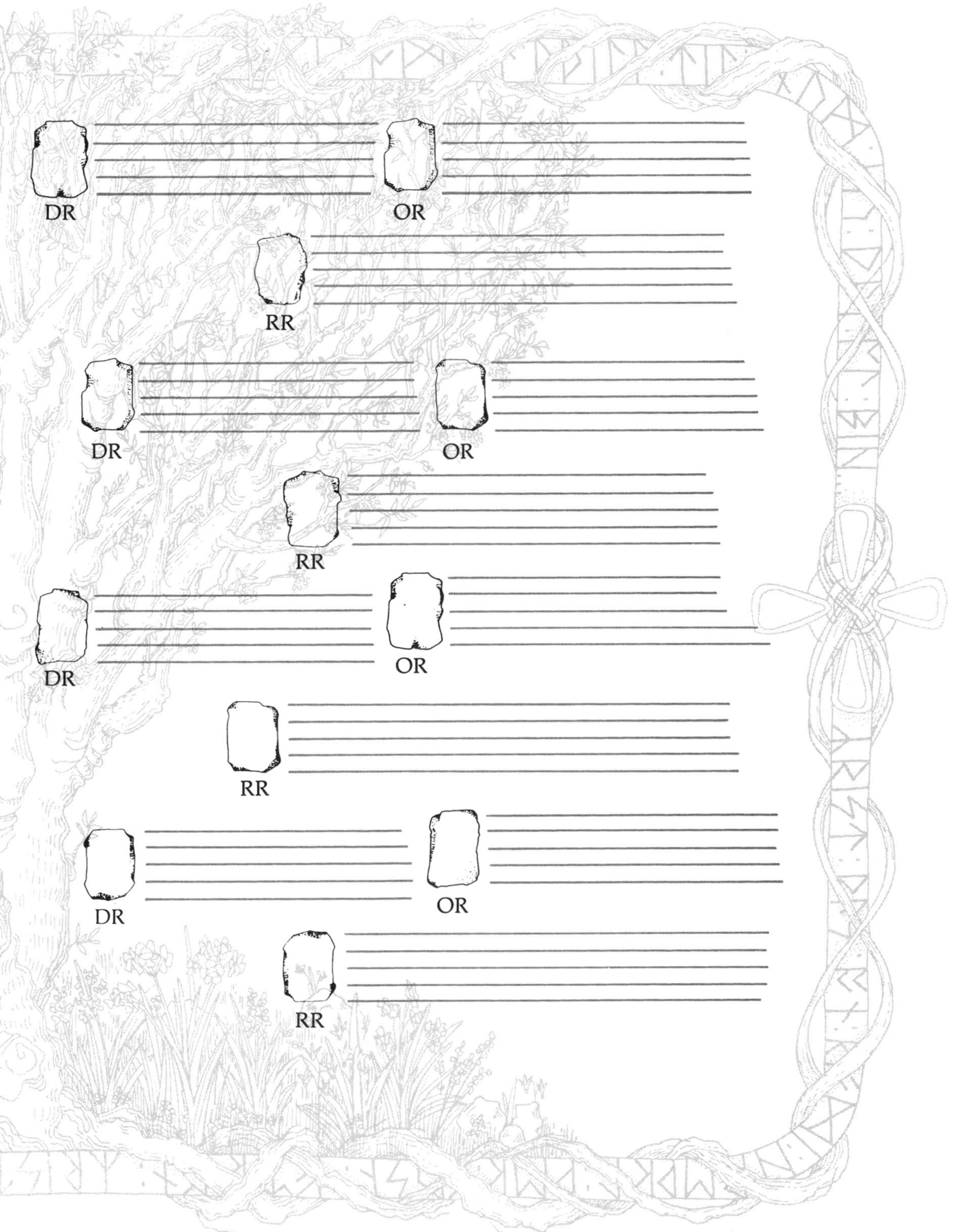
DR
OR
RR
DR
OR
RR
DR
OR
RR
DR
OR
RR

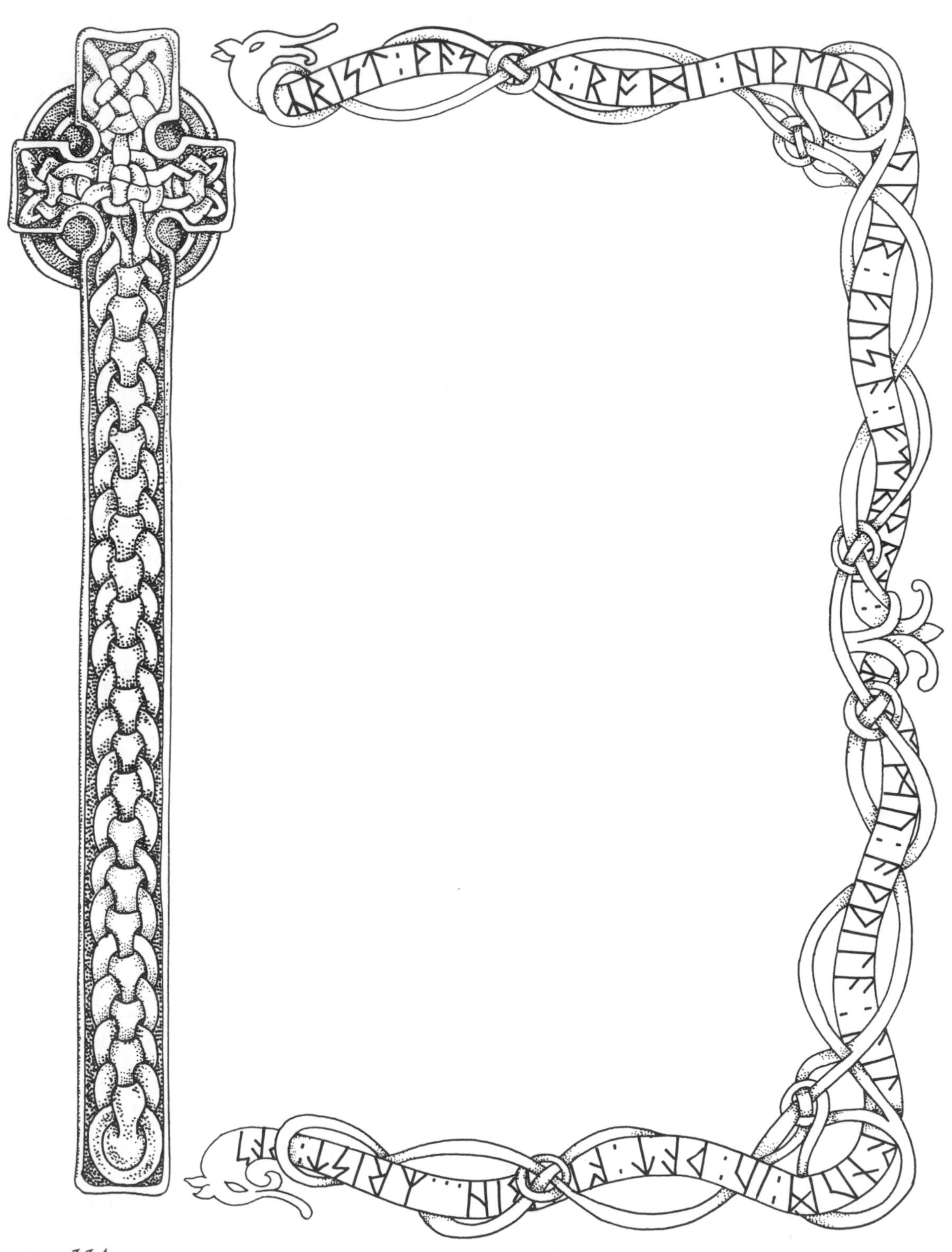

Night Runes

arious schools of thought exist as to what is going on while we sleep. Dream interpretation is a passion for some of us, while others leave the dreaming to itself, acknowledging that dreams may be one valuable means of "taking out the garbage." Runes have various uses to the dreamer and you are the one to choose or create the method most appropriate to your needs.

Some people pick a Rune to determine what in their life requires work during the night. Some look at the Rune they choose, others don't. Some practitioners of Runecraft write that they place the Rune under their pillow. A few see fit to hold it in their hand as they fall asleep. Occasionally, the Rune is still clenched in their fingers come morning, although more often it is to be found among the bedclothes. If the Rune you chose for the day was *Gebo* X, Partnership, you might decide to hold that Rune as you fall off to sleep, thereby carrying forward the work you have been doing on yourself during the day.

Before sleep, it is a good practice to pray for instruction during the night. Sometimes understanding will come in the form of a dream. At other times you won't remember your dreams but will have received instruction during the night that will affect your behavior the following day.

Note that you can ask for instruction without resorting to drawing a Rune. *Prayer alone is always sufficient.* However, if you want to focus on a particular issue that is important to your life right now, you may wish to pick *Night Runes* when asking for instruction, healing, or whatever else you feel is timely to your nature. Picking a *Night Rune* brings other energies into play and, at the same time, affirms that you are entrusting your care, nourishment, and growth to the Higher Self and to Holy Spirit.

Remain mindful that Runecraft is not intended as a substitute for prayers, but rather as a companion activity to the outworking of the Divine Plan for you in your life.

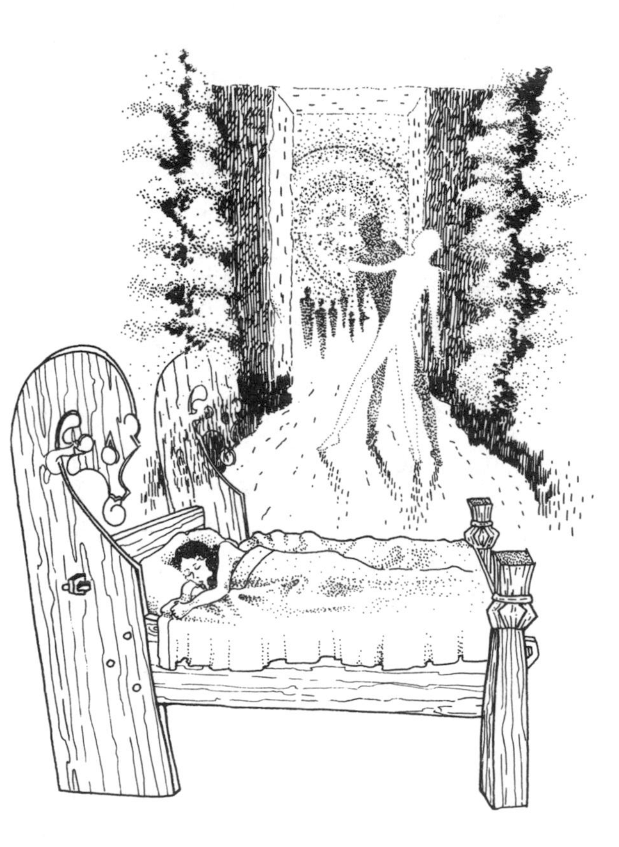

NIGHT RUNES

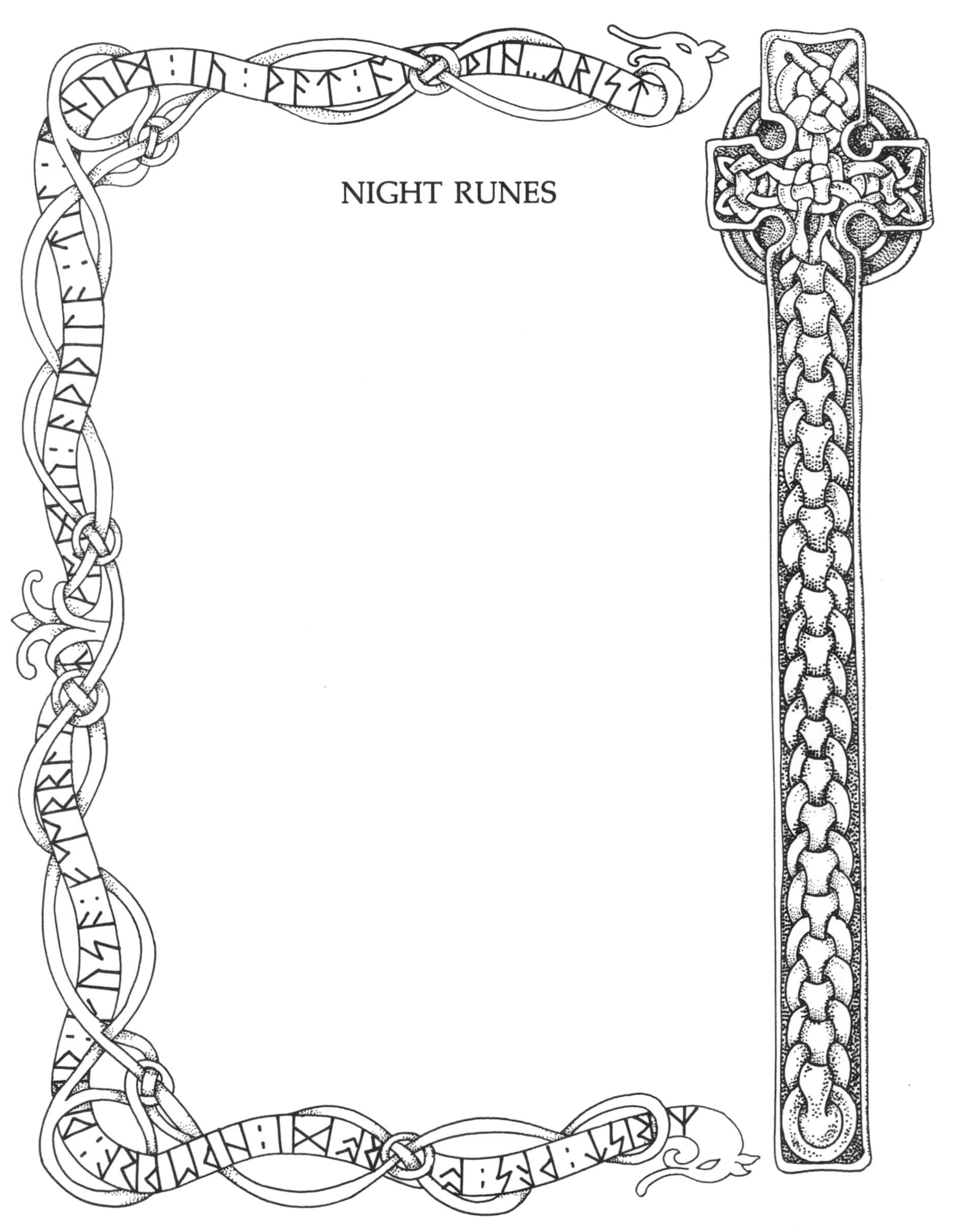

For the week of ____________

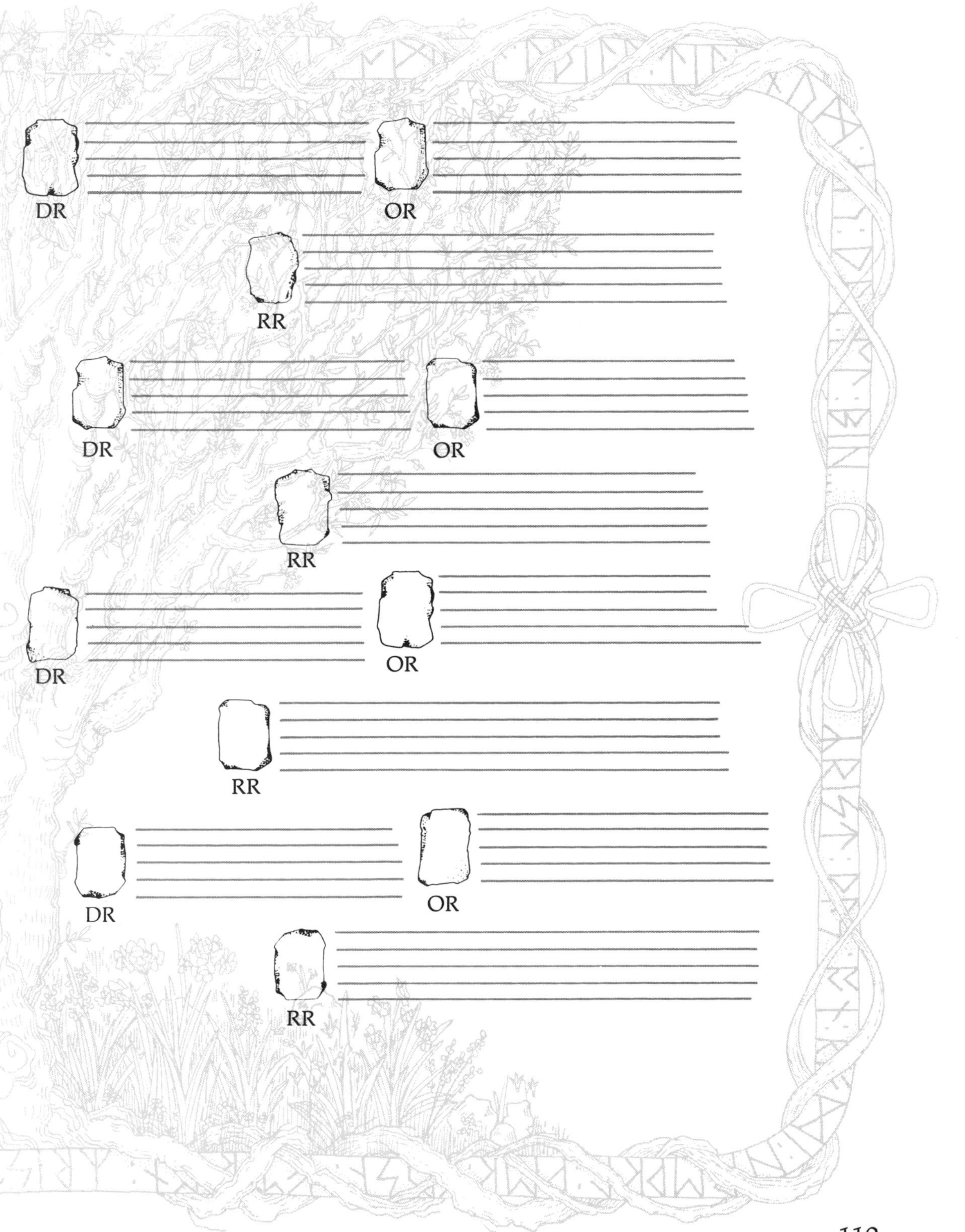
DR
OR
RR
DR
OR
RR
DR
OR
RR
DR
OR
RR

For the week of ____________

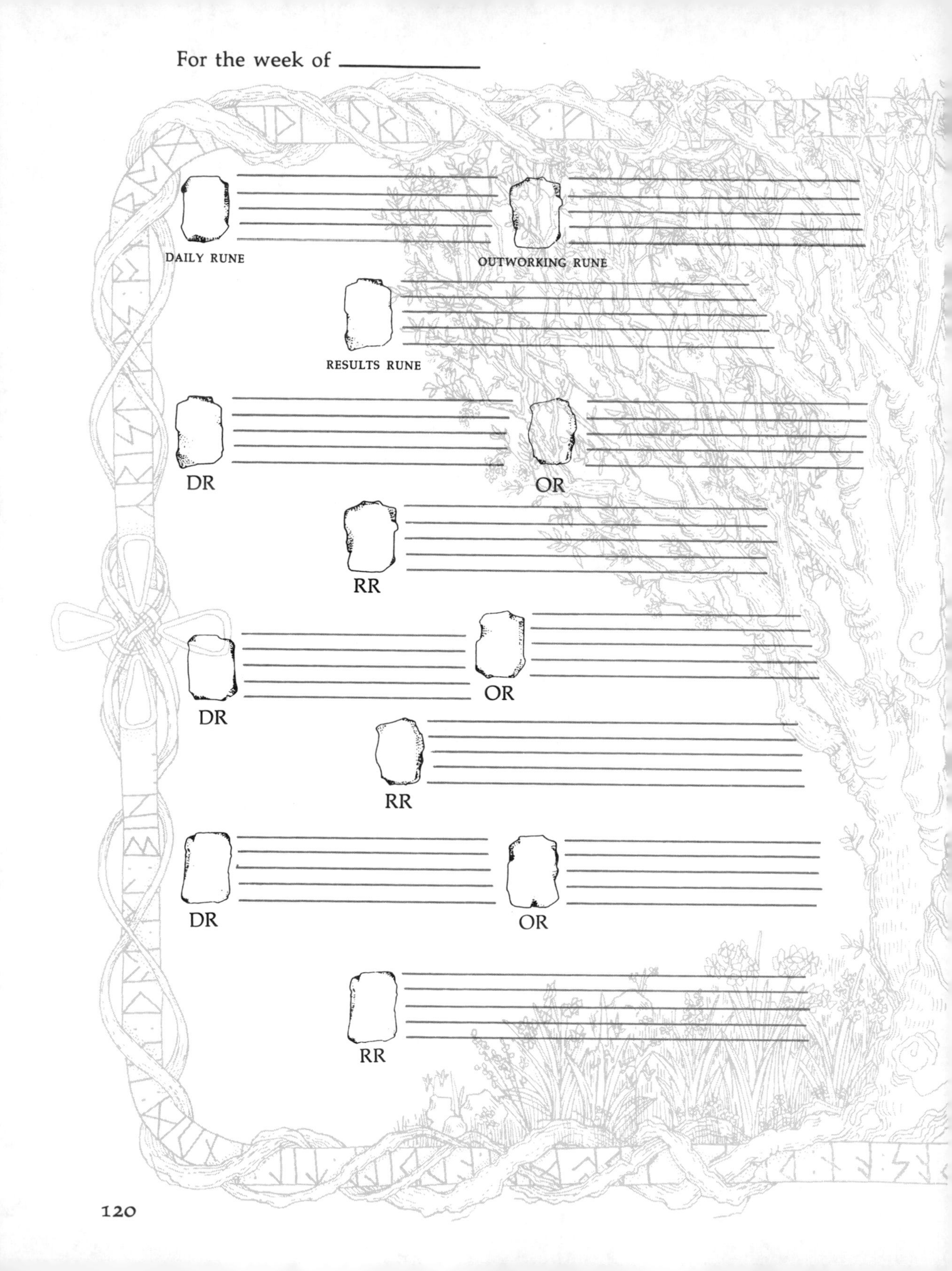

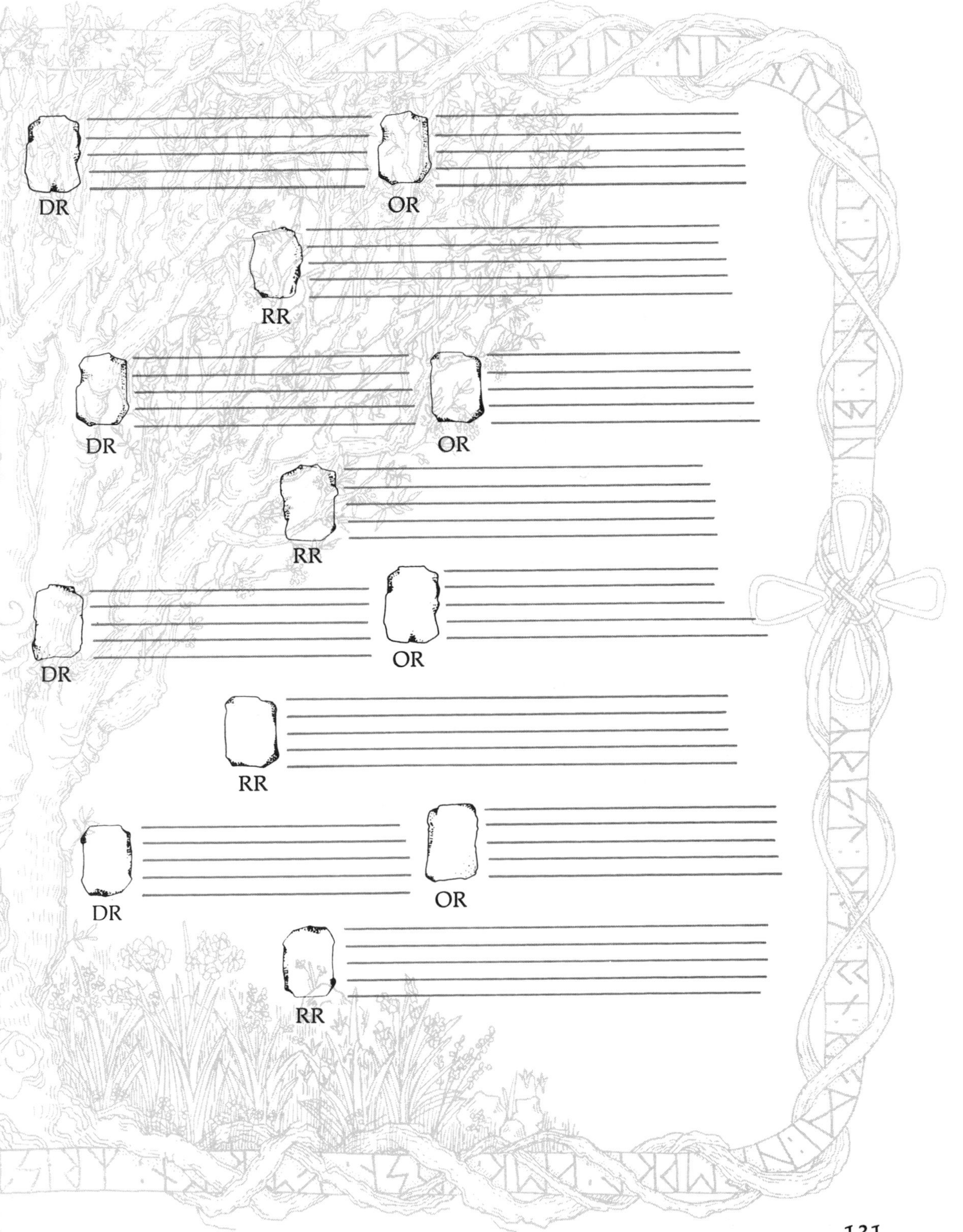
DR
OR
RR
DR
OR
RR
DR
OR
RR
DR
OR
RR

For the week of ____________

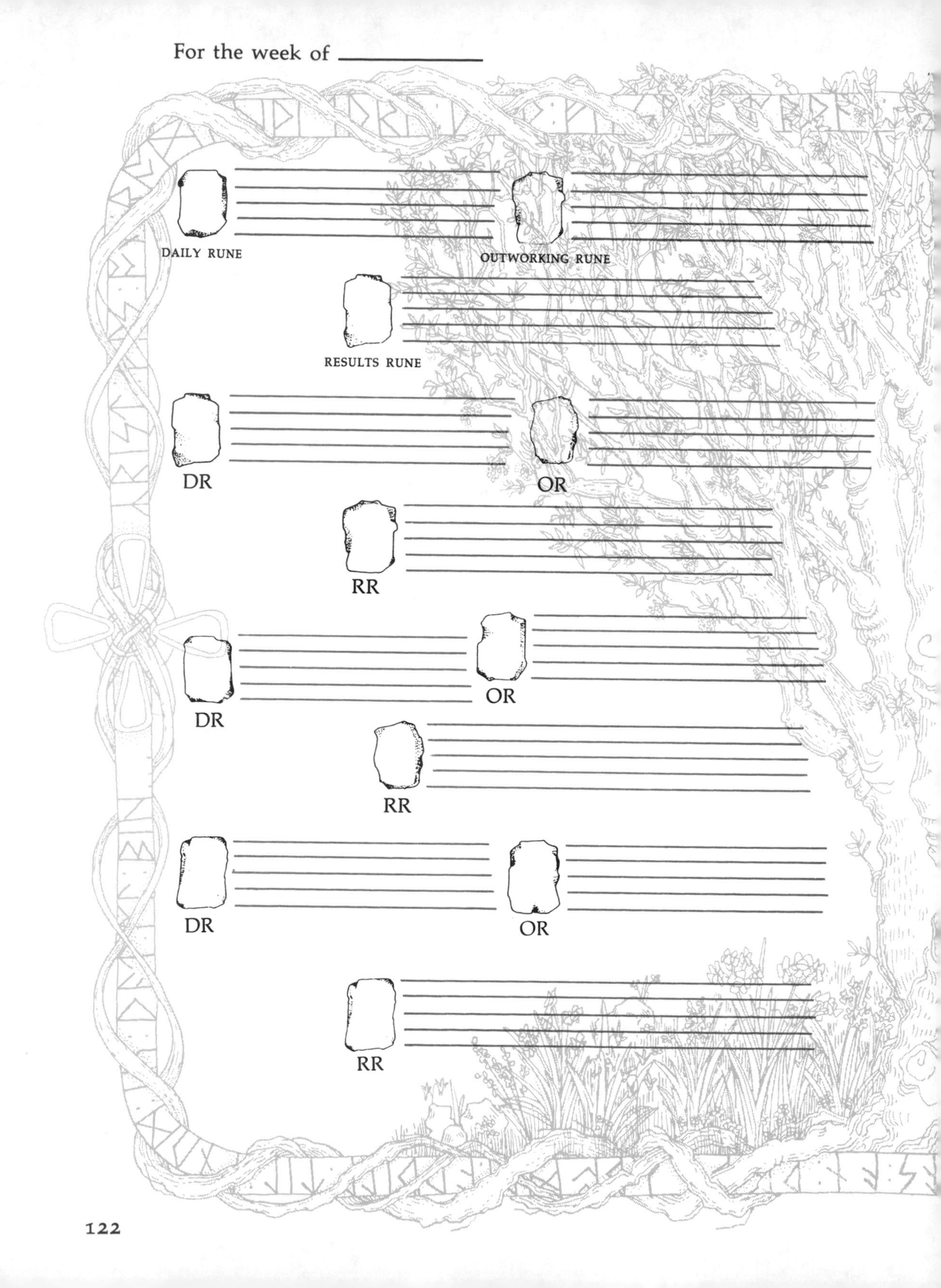

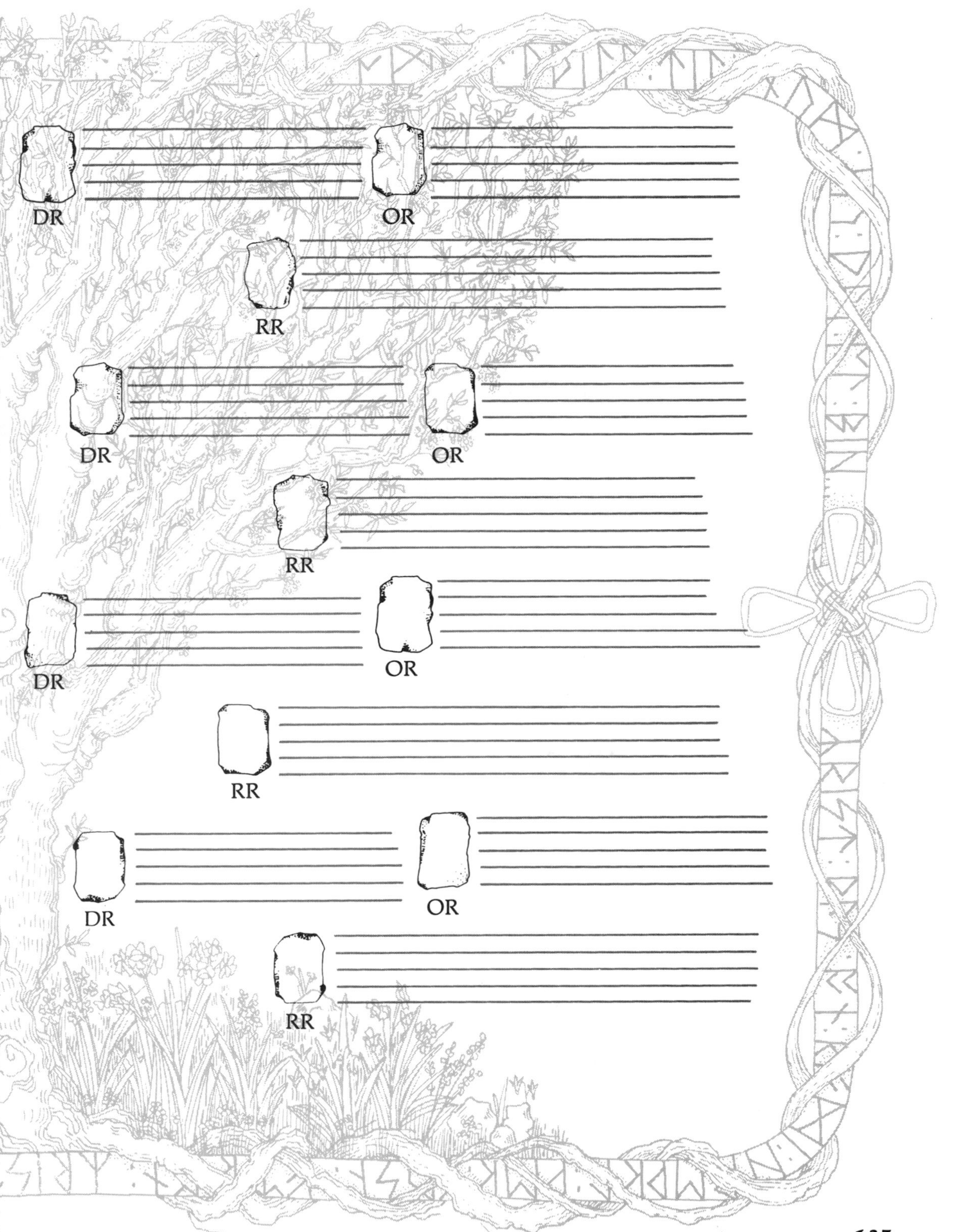
DR
OR
RR
DR
OR
RR
DR
OR
RR
DR
OR
RR

For the week of ____________

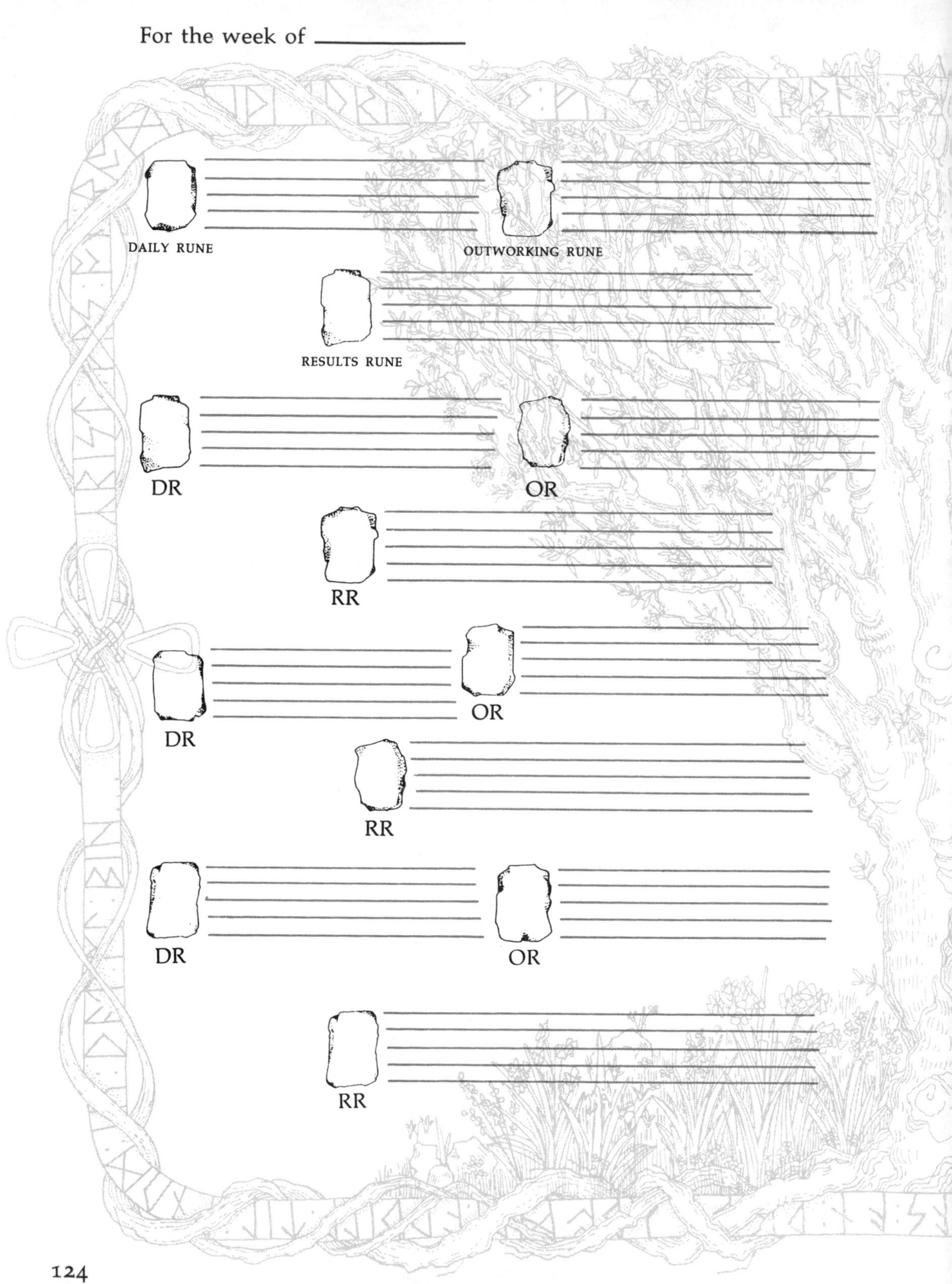

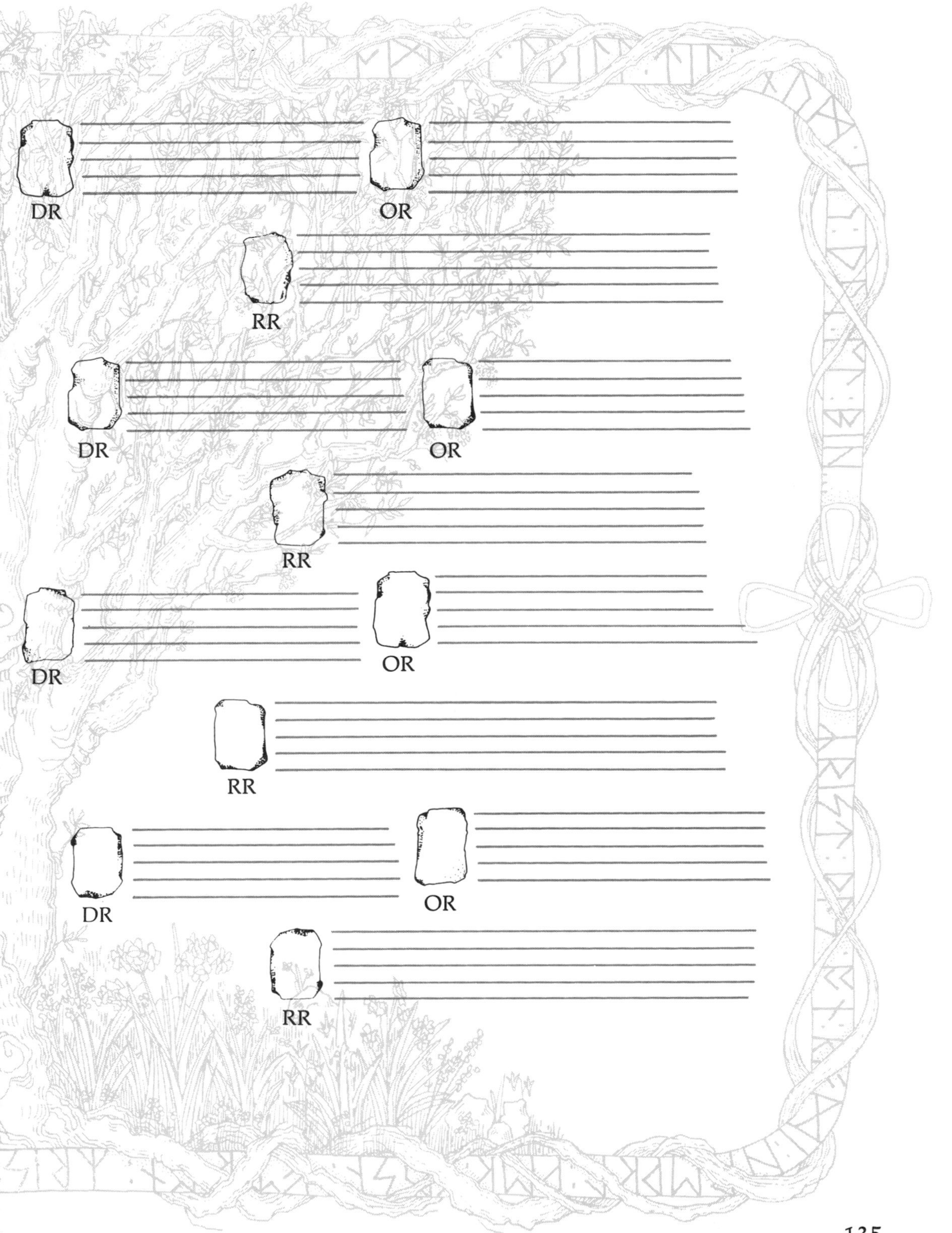
DR
OR
RR
DR
OR
RR
DR
OR
RR
DR
OR
RR

For the week of ____________

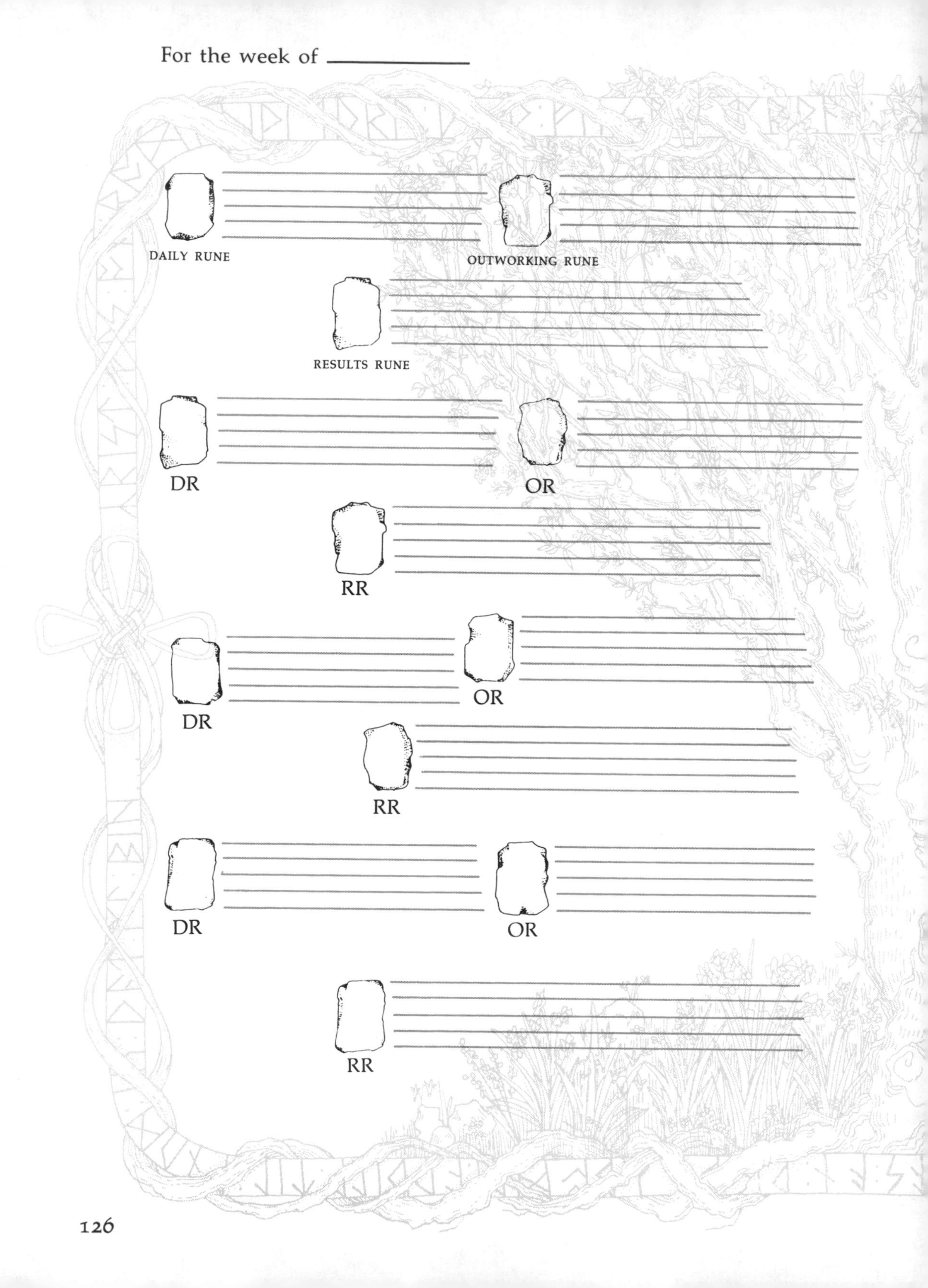

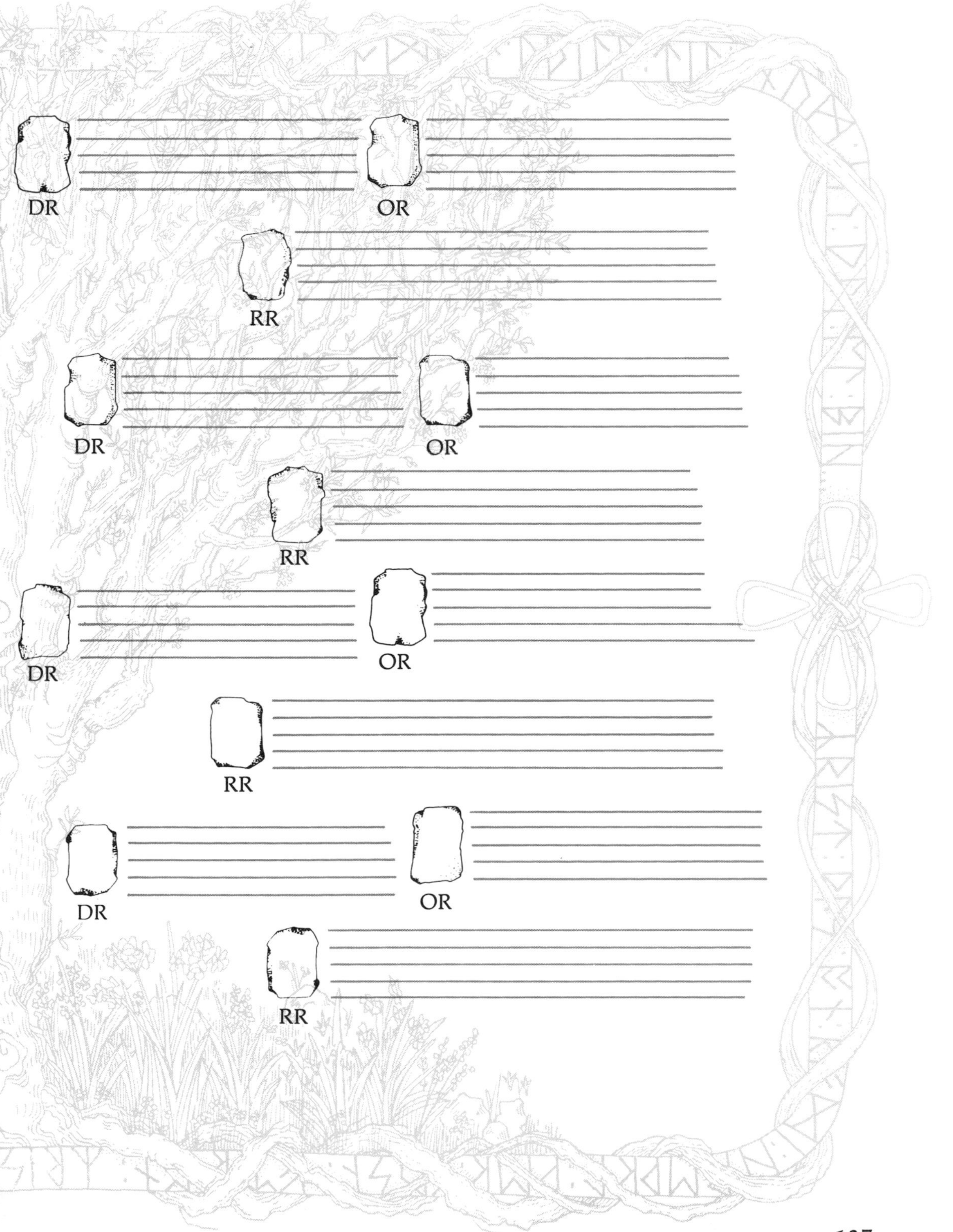
DR
OR
RR
DR
OR
RR
DR
OR
RR
DR
OR
RR

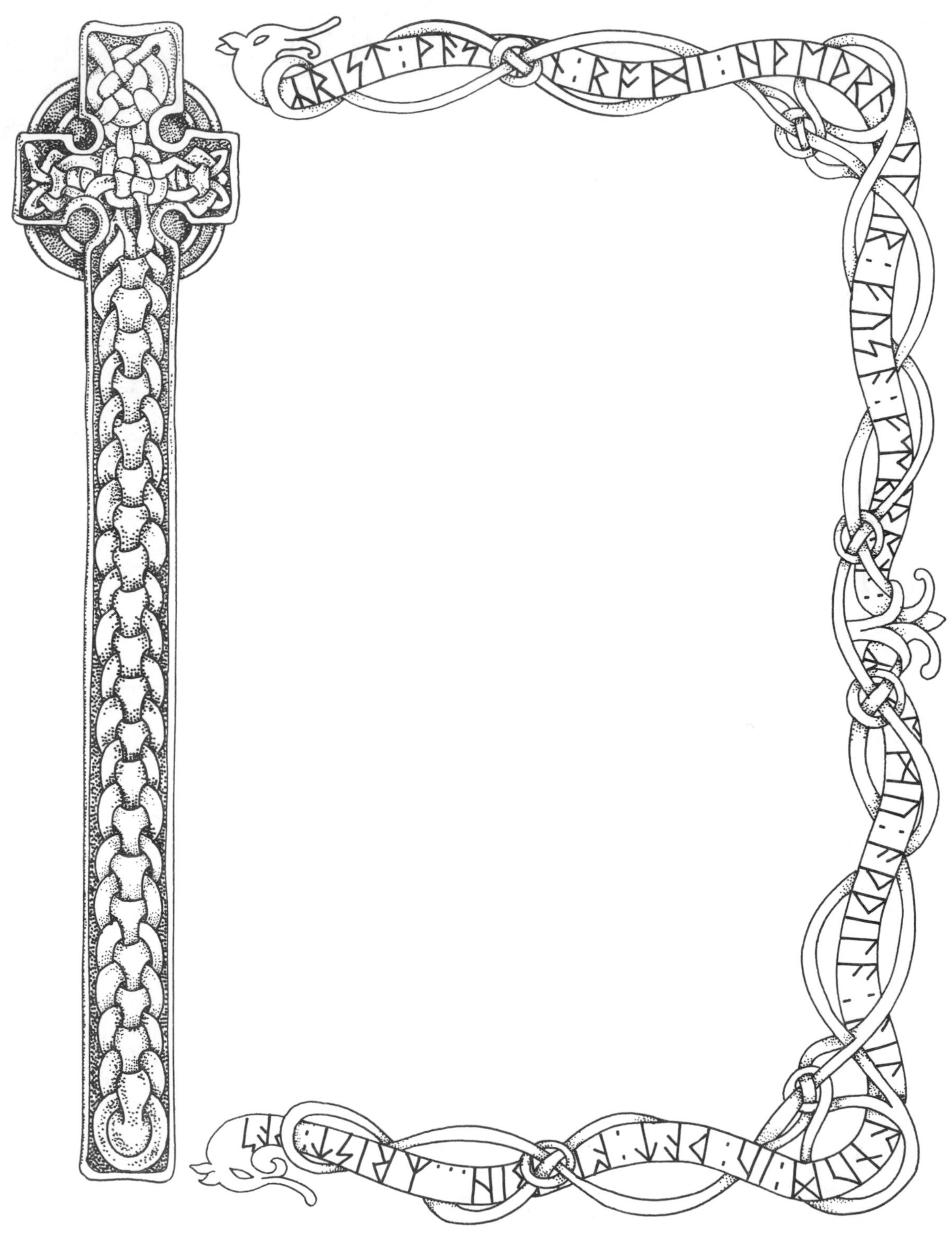

Runes of Rectification

rectify **1.** to put or set right; correct; amend; **2.** to adjust, as in movement or balance . . .

Webster's New World Dictionary
of the American Language

This is a technique for those times when things are not going smoothly between co-workers, friends, lovers, and all others who collaborate across boundaries of understanding and temperament.

As quickly as is convenient after something happens that causes dissension or blockage, come together with the intention of bringing Light to the situation. The procedure here is reversed from the usual, in that the Rune casting comes at the end of the process. The core of the process is the asking and answering of five questions. They are:

(1) What happened?
(2) How did that make you feel?
(3) How would you do it differently next time?
(4) What results would you like to see?
(5) What insight have you gained from what happened?

First, put aside time enough for all participants to answer each question, remembering to allow time for discussion and the drawing of Runes for further clarification. Close the door, unplug the telephone, and set your intention to bring insight to the situation.

One person may elect to take notes while each person speaks. All of the participants should respond to each question before going on to the next question. Cross-talk or responding to someone while they are speaking is to be discouraged. Statements of *how you feel* (hurt, angry, self-conscious, afraid) rather than statements of "what you did to me" or "what you did wrong," will help to keep the question period from dissolving into speeches of self-justification. During this process, agree willingly to suspend judgment for the sake of better understanding. Keep it light. Keep it clear.

Finally, after everyone has had the opportunity to express their feelings regarding each question, allow any of the participants who still require clarification on a particular issue to pick a Rune. One of you might be disturbed and confused about feelings you experienced that seem disproportionately magnified in answer to question #2, "How did that make you feel?" Perhaps there is disagreement among the participants as to what really took place. If so, an overview of the key events can be provided by selecting a Rune for question #1, "What happened?" It will be up to each of you to bring up elements where you are still dissatisfied, uncomfortable, or unclear.

When all is said and done, one of the group may wish to draw a final Rune to comment on the essence of the matter in the Light of the process of rectification.

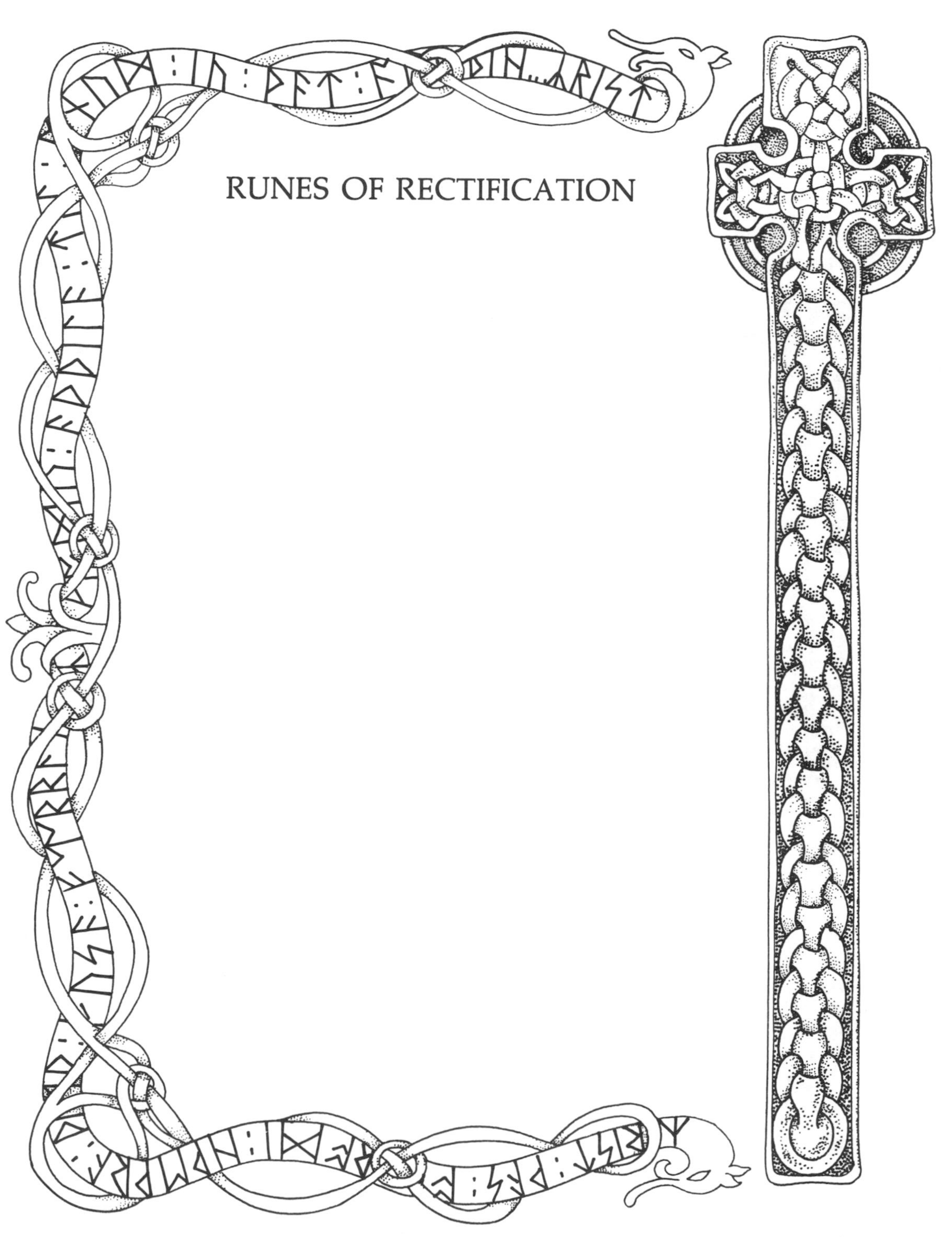

RUNES OF RECTIFICATION

For the week of ____________

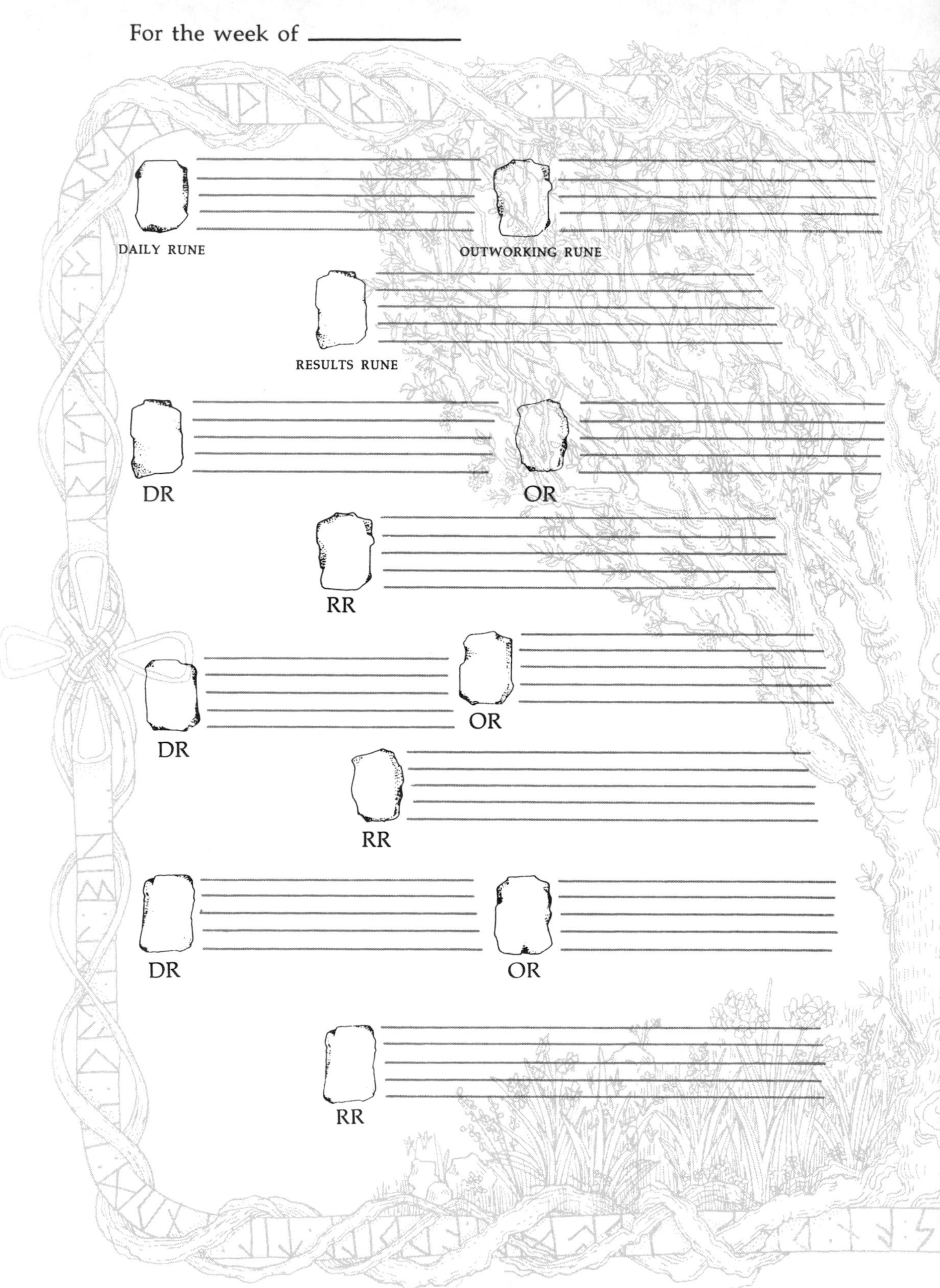

DR
OR
RR
DR
OR
RR
DR
OR
RR
DR
OR
RR

For the week of ______________

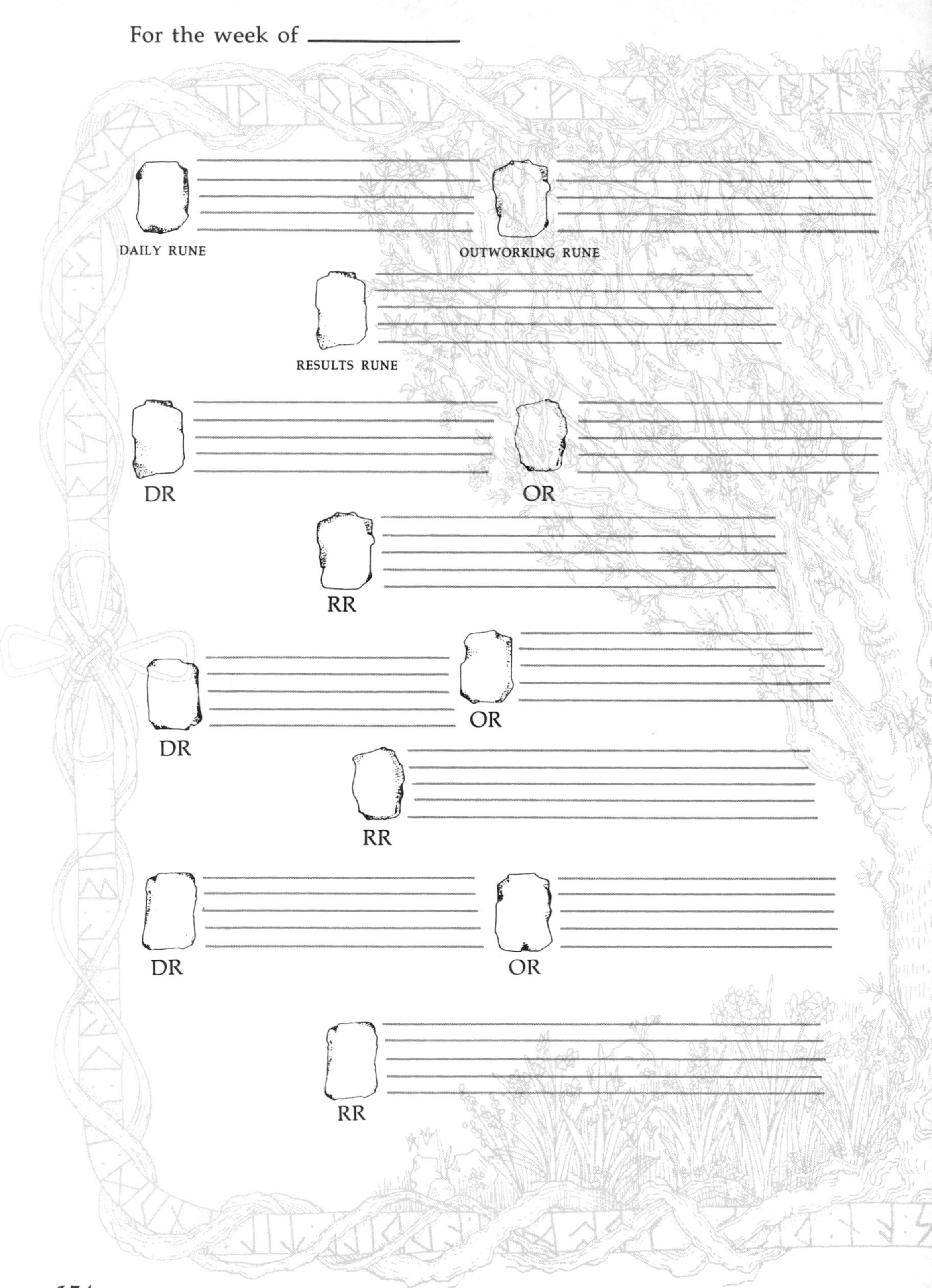

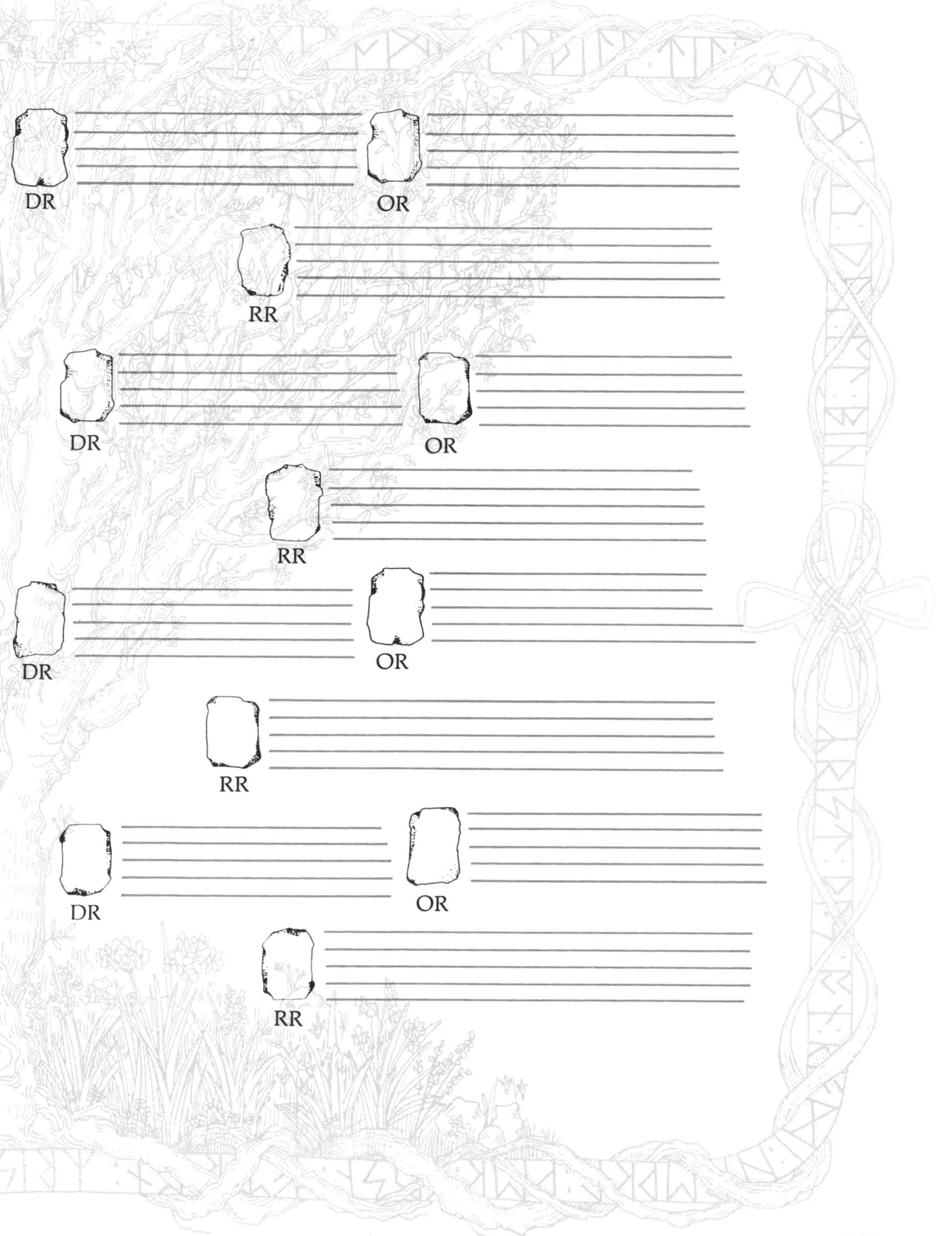
DR
OR
RR
DR
OR
RR
DR
OR
RR
DR
OR
RR

For the week of ______________

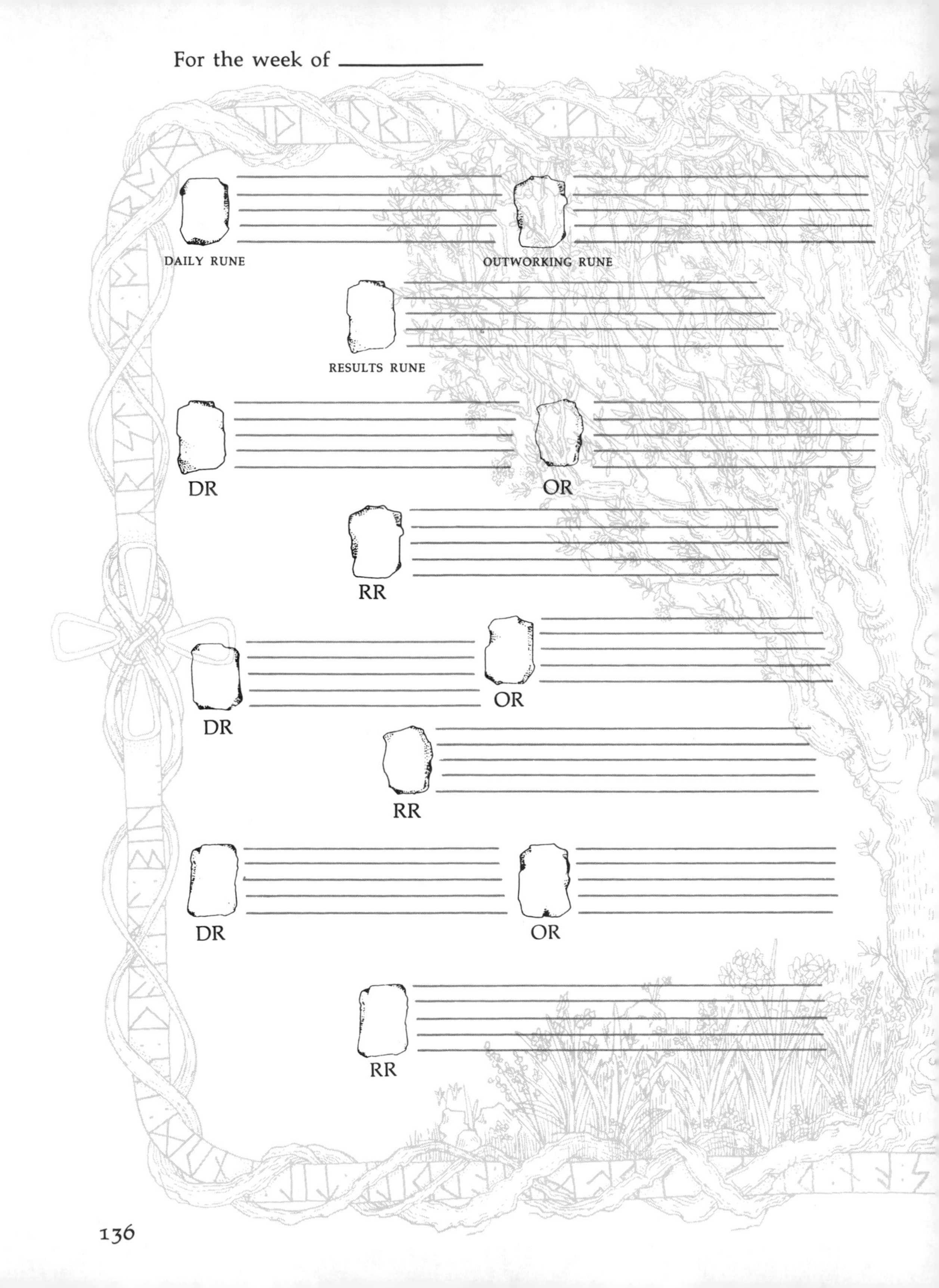

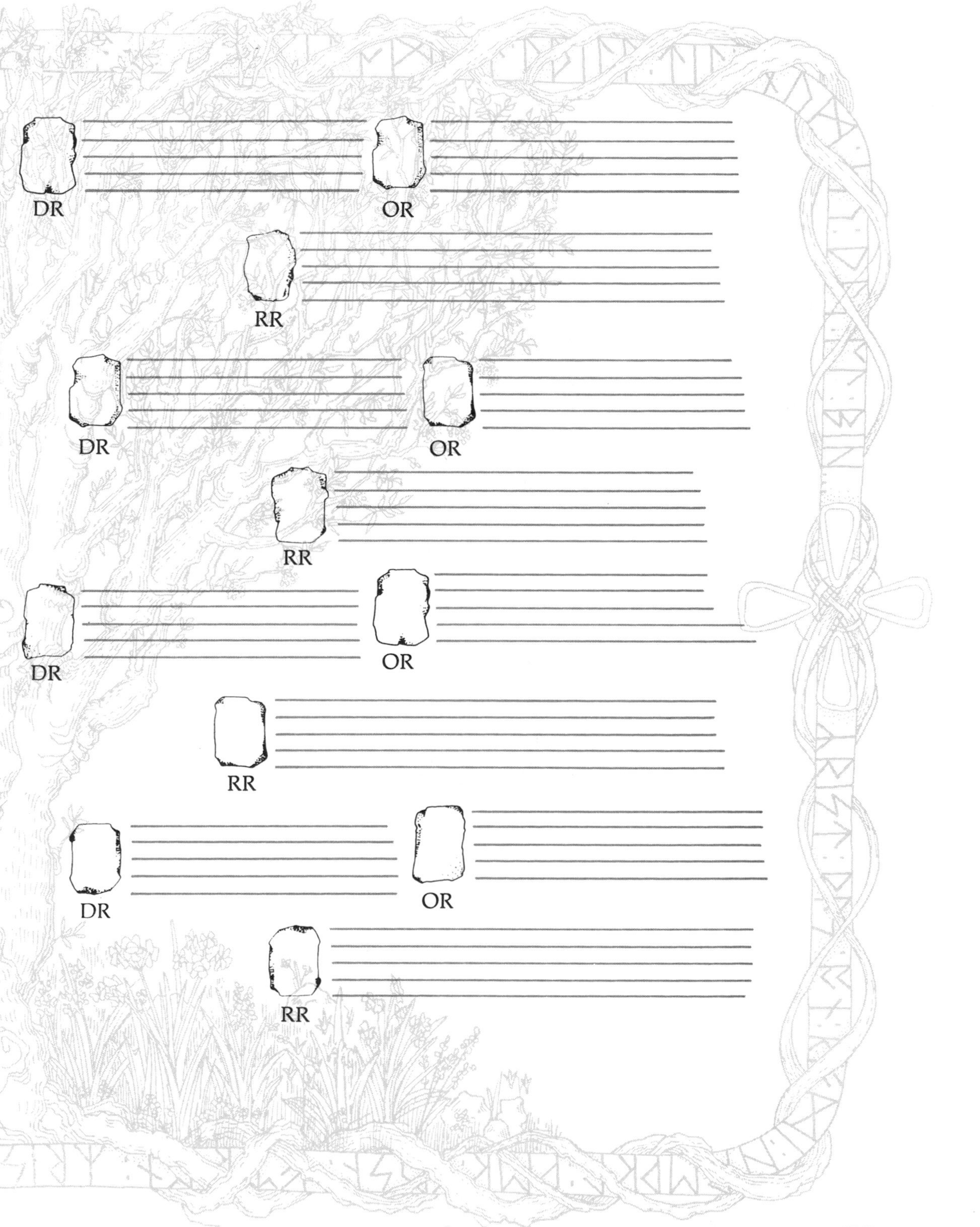
DR
OR
RR
DR
OR
RR
DR
OR
RR
DR
OR
RR

For the week of ____________

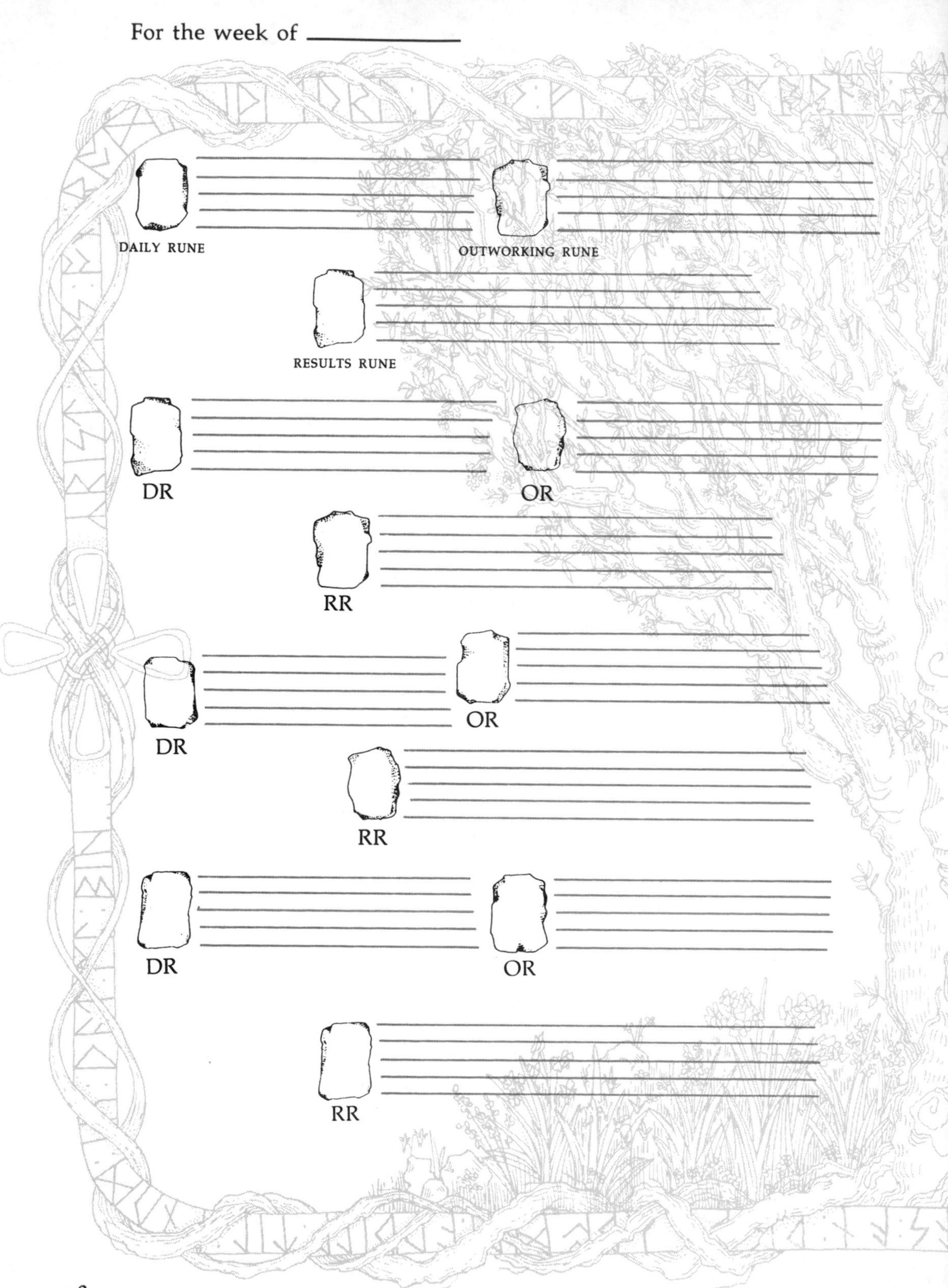

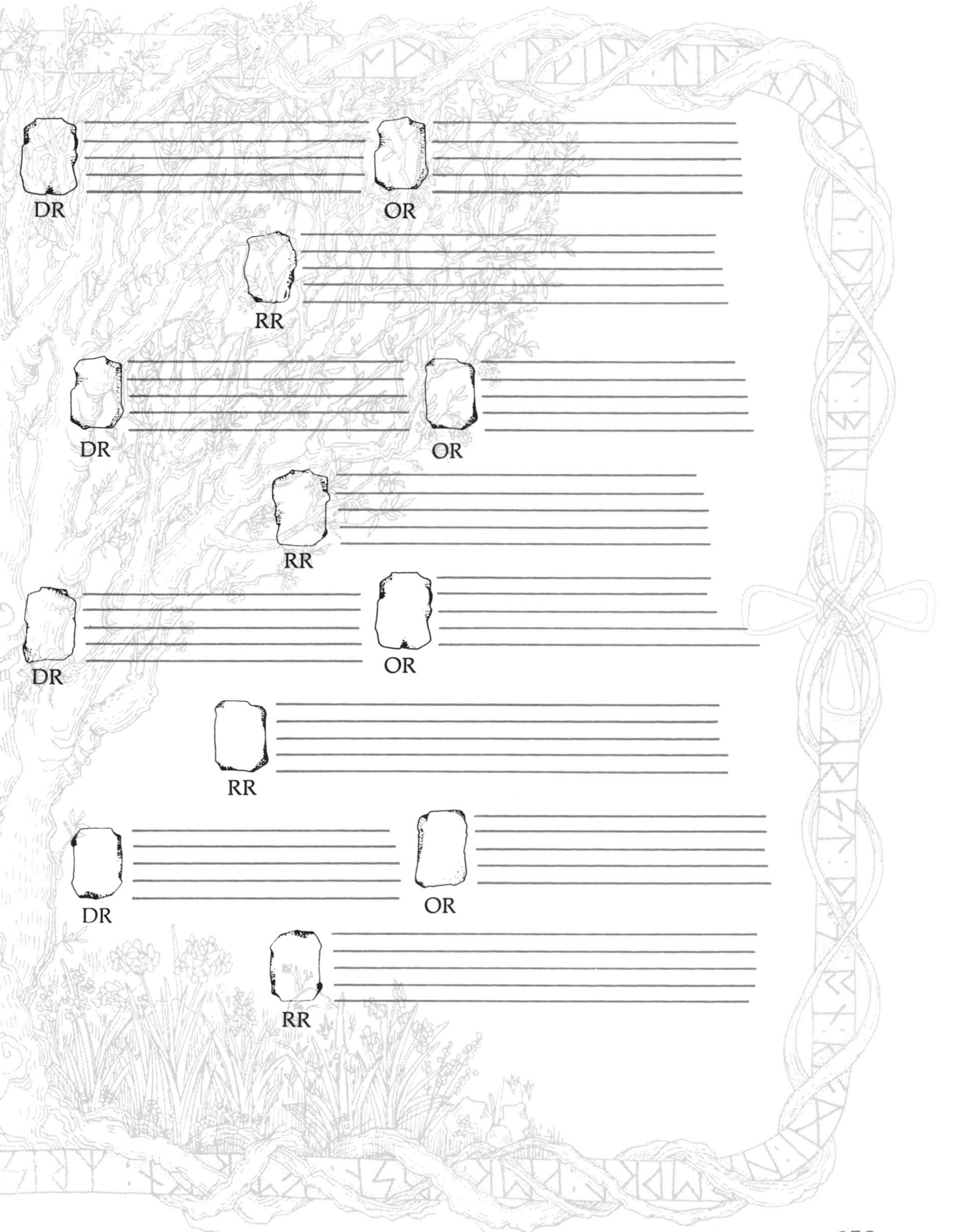
DR
OR
RR
DR
OR
RR
DR
OR
RR
DR
OR
RR

For the week of ____________

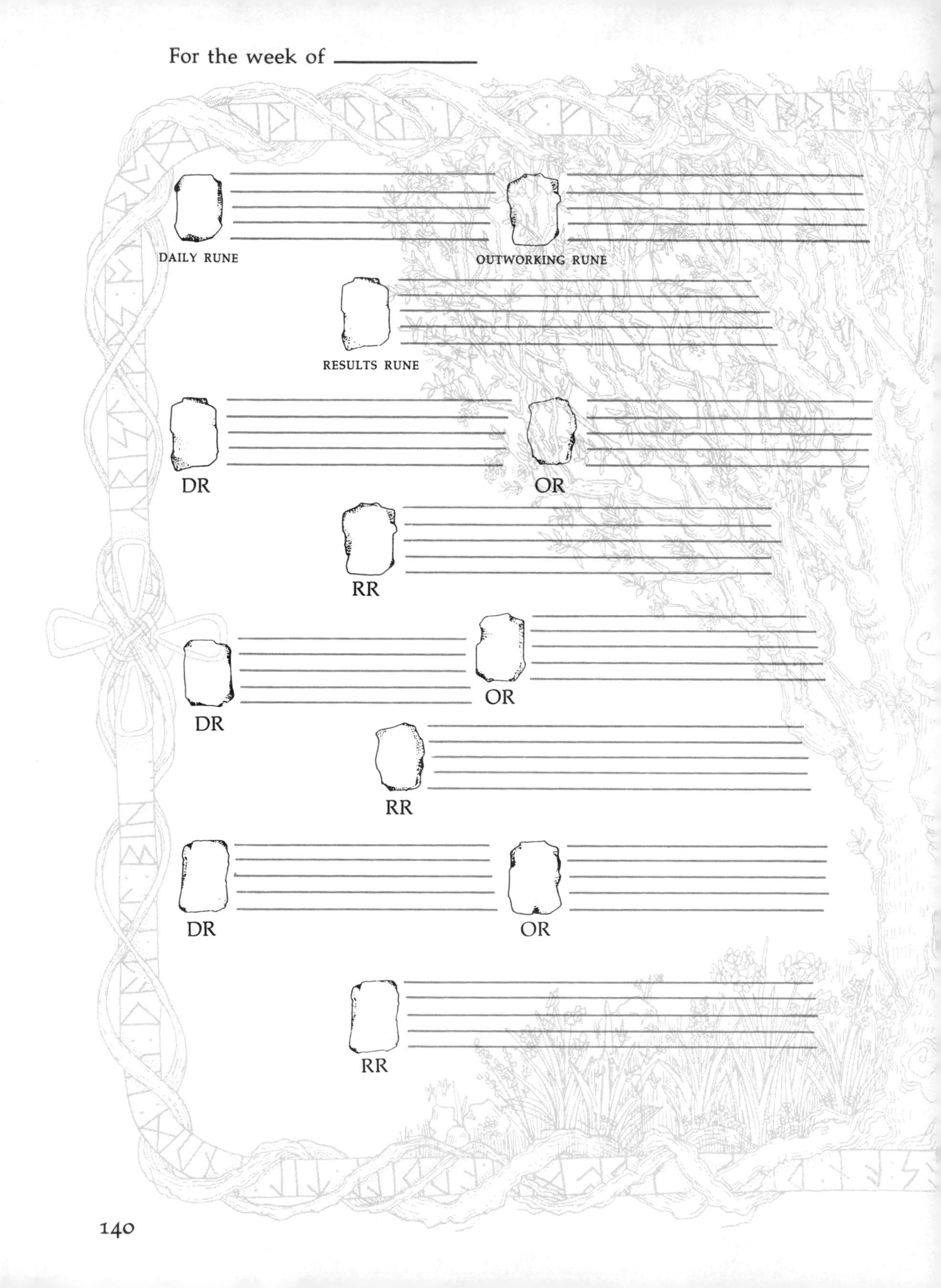

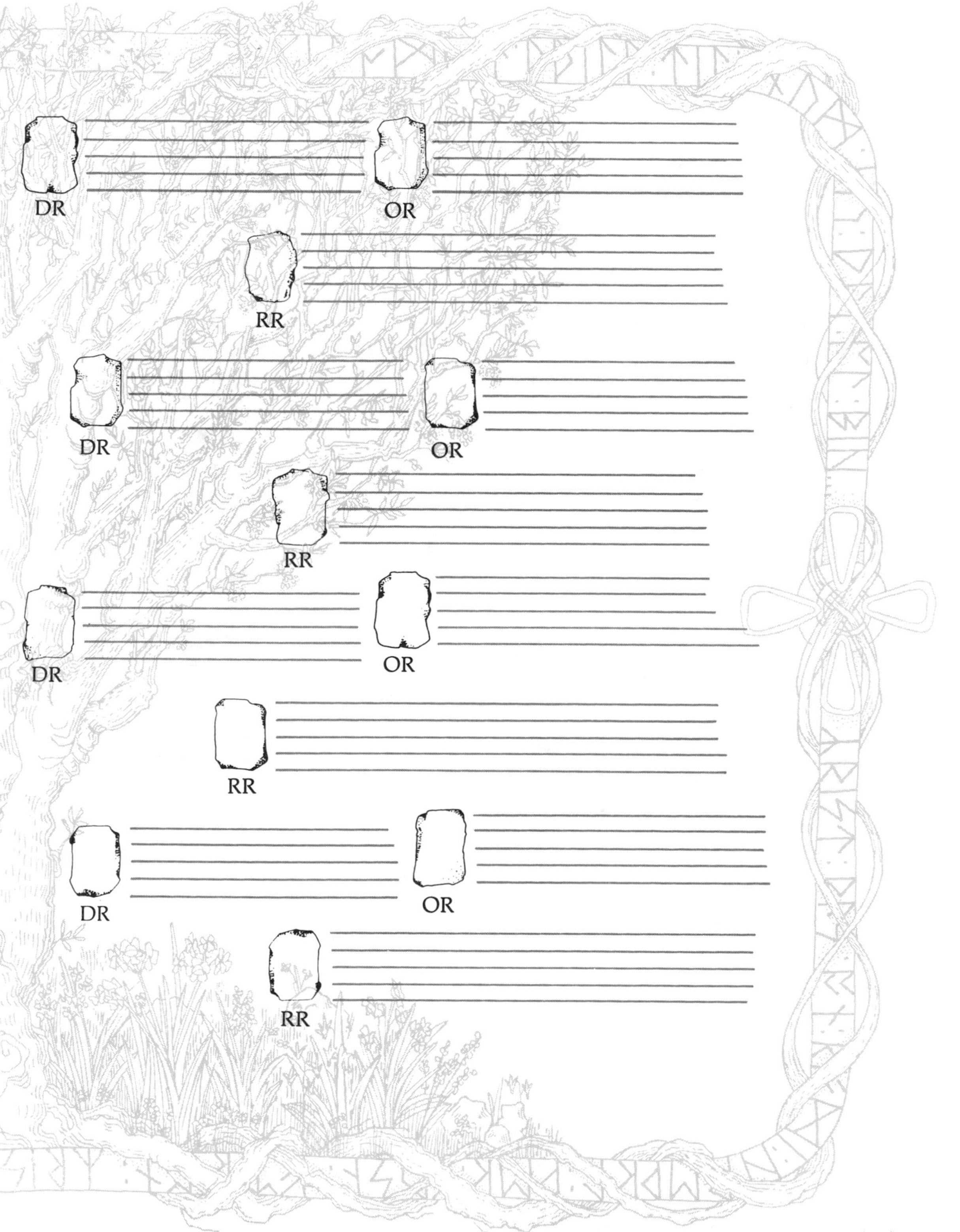
DR
OR
RR
DR
OR
RR
DR
OR
RR
DR
OR
RR

SUMMER

A Destiny Profile

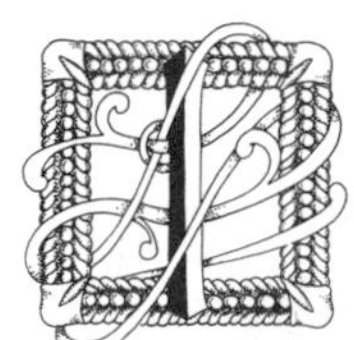

In undertaking the work of self-change, we are asked to delve down to the foundations of our life. This may prove hard and painful for many of us but there is no other way. We hear it said in many camps, by spiritual teachers of all persuasions, that we are to "discover the teacher within." What one really wants now are some useful techniques for listening to oneself. And, as Margaret Mead put it, "You don't need an appointment to see your Runes."

One such technique was devised by Dr. Allan W. Anderson for use with the *I Ching,* the Chinese *Book of Changes.* He calls it *A Destiny Profile.* The Profile, which consists of six questions, comprises a grid within which a human life can be framed.

The Destiny Profile adapts itself wonderfully to use with the Viking Runes. However, there is a seriousness about this spread that sets the Destiny Profile apart from other Runic exercises. According to Dr. Anderson, the six questions that make up the Profile shall be asked *only once* in the course of one's lifetime. That restriction has about it something awesome, especially in our "try, try again" culture. We don't *like* limitation. And yet, the "gift" the Destiny Profile conveys is the *creative essence of limitation.*

Asked "What are we to be made conscious of through the Destiny Profile?" the Runes replied with ᛚ, *Laguz,* the Rune of Water, Flow, That

Which Conducts—but *Reversed.* The reading is precisely in praise of limitation:

> A warning against overreach, excessive striving, a counsel against trying to exceed your own strength or operate beyond the power you have funded to date in your life.
>
> *Laguz, Reversed,* often indicates a failure to draw upon the wisdom of instinct. As a result, the intuitive side of your Nature may be languishing, leaving you out of balance. What is called for now is to go within, to honor the receptive side of your Warrior Nature.

You may wish to defer casting the Runes for the Destiny Profile until you have lived with the idea for a while—until your own consciousness tells you that the time and the place and your awareness are right for the undertaking. When the moment arrives, when you have familiarized yourself with the meaning of each question, begin. *Draw one Rune for the first question. Then replace it in your bag. Each question must be posed with all 25 Runes in the bag.* Perhaps you will want to ask the first question, receive the answer, then live with that for a time before you go on to the second question. Or, you may elect to ask all six questions at one sitting, but study them one at a time over an extended period. Let the receptive side of your Warrior Nature be your guide.

As you change and grow, your understanding of the six answers will change and grow—grow even perhaps to include an appreciation that "only once" was enough.

Here are the six questions that comprise the Destiny Profile, each followed by a sample reading for that question.

(1) WHAT IS MY NATURE?

In asking the question *"What is my Nature?"* you are concerning yourself with the underlying principle, the material cause, of your Nature. Your Nature is the "fixings," the stuff you were born with, what you "came in" with. It is a cluster, a constellation of possibilities, *and* it is surrounded and circumscribed by numerous impossibilities.

So start by examining your limitations: You come from a certain background, you have lived your life in a certain way, you have a heart condition, you can't have children, whatever it might be. As your limitations become clearer to you, you will begin to see that many notions you hold about yourself are *not* supported by the reality of your life. As your Nature is "limited" by what you can't do or be, it is also *specified* by what you *can;* it is through this process of limiting and specifying that your view of yourself will become clearer and more simple. As you simplify, you fund the power to work with your Nature, to work with that out of which your Destiny is to be realized.

Sample Rune Drawing: WHAT IS MY NATURE?

[ᛗ], *Ehwaz,* the Rune of Movement, Progress, *Reversed.* "Movement that appears to block" speaks to your inability to consider what is and what is not timely to your nature. The feeling that you are so often "missing out" will always be your wrong perception; the challenge will be to avoid action until it is timely. First, work on yourself to strengthen the interior life; when that is strong enough, what needs to be done will flow out from you. But if you insist on forging ahead unstrengthened, you will fail to find the support you require. The conditions simply will not be right, and you will make no contribution. Your Nature won't permit it. Your Nature will turn against everything you do that is premature. Destiny cannot be humbugged, wheedled, or influenced. There is an old saying, "What is for you will not pass by you." Or, as *Ehwaz* puts it, "As I cultivate my own nature, all else follows."

(2) WHY WAS I BORN?

According to Dr. Anderson, the meaning of the question is this: "What is the lack or privation with which I have come into the world, whose satisfaction will empower my continuing growth and self-change in keeping with the will of the Divine?" In other words, *What is Heaven's mandate for me?* In addressing this question, you are preparing to discover what is missing in your makeup that you are here to acquire—patience, strength in the face of adversity, or any other underdeveloped aspect of the self, the acquiring of which will enable you to navigate your ideal passage through this life.

Sample Rune Drawing: WHY WAS I BORN?

[ᛊ], *Sowelu,* the Rune of Wholeness, stands for "that which our Nature requires. It embodies the impulse toward self-realization and indicates the path you must follow, not from ulterior motives but from the core of your individuality." Your quest as a Spiritual Warrior is to seek after wholeness. Wholeness means bringing together that which requires unification. This Rune focuses on the ability to "retreat in strength." In timely retreat, allow the Light into that part of you which has been kept in darkness. Your privation, then, is centered on the *overcoming of self-alienation.* It is said that the mark of the Spiritual Warrior is "impeccability." All this really means is: Seek to be appropriate at all times. To this end, you are "required to face and vanquish your refusal to let right action flow through you." The result of your privation is the divided self, and timely right action will lead you to self-acceptance.

(3) WHAT IS MY VOCATION?

Vocation, as used here, does not mean what you do for a living. Drawing a Rune for Vocation will tell you how you are called to go through this life and what principles you must embody in your passage. If you conduct yourself properly, according to Vocation, you will satisfy the privation, the lack, described in the answer to the question *"Why was I Born?"* It is only through learning to relate correctly to severe privation that we grow in Spirit. That is why St. Paul says in Romans 4, "We rejoice in tribulations," since tribulations provide the occasions to meet privation courageously. In the process, you will grow in willpower and self-awareness. The principal goal of Vocation is to *come to one's self.*

Sample Rune Drawing: WHAT IS MY VOCATION?

ᛖ, *Ehwaz,* Movement, Progress, is the Rune that specifies that your Vocation lies in enabling "movement in the sense of improving or bettering any situation." Note that this Rune was also drawn *Reversed* in answer to the question *"What is my Nature?"* Drawing *Ehwaz* twice in the Profile lends emphasis to the understanding of movement as "gradual development and steady progress." Simply expressed, the principle is this: no acting needy, no lusting after outcomes.

There is a four-part exercise practiced by the Reverend Harry Haines that seems relevant to the work required of you. Whenever he is called upon to deal with an issue where clarity is lacking, he does four things: (i) Considers his needs; (ii) Considers the needs of others; (iii) Speaks with a "wiser Christian"; (iv) Waits for the peace that passes understanding. Only then does he

move. Learn how to wait. Learn how to ask. Learn how to go solitary through the world, not depending on its support systems. Then your Vocation, ᛗ, will agree with your Nature, ᚹ, and all movement will be in accord with the Will of Heaven.

(4) WHAT IS MY DESTINY?

Destiny, as used here, means our *ideal passage through this life, our ideal possibility.* There is no such thing as a "bad destiny," for our Destiny is the Divine's desire for our Highest Good. Our Destiny is our spiritual "destination." There is an energy that ceaselessly moves us to change well rather than ill, and that energy is the outworking of Divine Will in our lives.

At the same time, Destiny is confinement. Destiny is realized as the direct result of life's limitations. As the Runes tell us, "There are no missed opportunities; we have simply to recognize that not all opportunities are for us, that not all possibilities are open to us." If our limitations define what we may not do in the world, they also challenge us to accept ourselves and get on with what it is we can do.

Sample Rune Drawing: WHAT IS MY DESTINY?

ᛈ, *Perth,* the Rune of Initiation, *Reversed.* In drawing *Perth, Reversed,* you are reminded that "becoming whole, the means of it, is a profound secret. . . . *Nothing external matters here,* except as it shows you its inner reflection." Time after time in this life you will be asked to let go of the present (not to mention the past) while welcoming the future. By so doing, you will always possess a *true present,* which is the only time in which self-change can be realized. *Perth* has associations with the Phoenix, "the mystical bird that consumes itself in the fire and then rises from its own ashes." Again and again, the Oracle is saying, you will go through the flames. Treat each obstruction in your path as a challenge specific to the initiation you are presently undergoing. This is the Rune of questing: Live your life as initiation, for such is your sacred calling. The ongoing process of becoming completed by responding well to the Will of Heaven—that is your Destiny.

(5) WHAT IS MY CROSS?

The Cross stands for a condition that lasts a lifetime. It is your "ordeal" from birth to death. This question reveals the pattern of adversity you must undergo in order to grow in self-awareness and self-rule. Jesus said, "Take up thy cross and follow me." Your own Cross. Pick it up voluntarily. For in so doing you are declaring your willingness to undergo the pattern of adversity ordained for you by the Will of Heaven. As you grow in awareness, you will come to recognize that certain features of adversity are yours to work with for your lifetime. Many opportunities will be afforded you to meet the challenges represented by your Cross. As you change and grow, so too will your understanding of your Cross.

The Cross is the condition for wisdom. Christ on the Tree. Odin on the Tree. Each of us on the Tree. The Cross stands for that without which there can be no wisdom.

Sample Rune Drawing: WHAT IS MY CROSS?

ᛇ, *Eihwaz,* Avertive Powers, Defense. "As we are tested we fund the power to avert blockage and defeat. At the same time, we develop in ourselves an aversion to the conduct that creates stressful situations in our lives." Learn to see delays and blockages as potentially beneficial in that through inconvenience and discomfort growth is promoted.

There is a tendency in your nature to surpass the limits proper to that nature. This tendency—to push beyond where good can be achieved—calls for a Cross, a pattern of adversity, of being thwarted at every level every time your actions are inappropriate. All that is asked of you is to go through the world well.

(6) WHAT IS MY UNIFIED SELF?

In asking for the image of your Unified Self, ask for the quality that will emerge in the foreground of your life when intellect and will have begun to work in harmony with body and feelings. To act uncontrivedly and to act in a timely manner are the hallmarks of being in accord with one's Nature. By getting a sense of how you will be when you are whole and fully integrated —the things you will do then, the things you won't do then—you will achieve understanding not only of your Nature and Destiny, but also of the component forces you must work with in order to *come to yourself.*

Sample Rune Drawing: WHAT IS MY UNIFIED SELF?

ᚢ, *Uruz,* Strength, Manhood/Womanhood. The image of the Unified Self will emerge as "the old bonds are severed, when that which has outgrown its form can die, releasing its energy in a new birth, a new form." ᚢ is the Rune of "termination and new beginnings." It exemplifies the willingness to embrace change and to recognize that, in the life of the Spirit, you are always at the beginning.

In ancient times, *Uruz* was represented by the aurochs, the wild ox, a difficult animal to domesticate. Drawing ᚢ in response to the question *"What is my Unified Self?"* indicates that to achieve self-unification, you must undertake to harness the wild creature within. Gentle the wild creature, without breaking its spirit, by becoming one with it through your compassionate understanding of its nature and needs. Develop your will by setting a firm intention, by visualizing the new form your Unified Self will take. As you grow and change, that form will expand; as you embrace the image of the expanded form, that image will continue to evolve.

A beginning has been made. The elements of your Destiny are separated into manageable components. You can start to see how this Profile fits together. Through focusing on the correlation between "What is my Vocation?" (the occasion for acquiring strength) and "Why was I Born?" (the privation you were born with), you can begin to relate correctly to the undeveloped aspects of yourself. As your self-understanding grows, so will your self-acceptance, and you will experience the meaning and the joy of living your life in a *true present.*

The Destiny Profile, however comprehensive, is only a tool to be used as you persevere in the finest art of all, the art of self-change. Remember this: Self-change is never coerced; we are always free to resist. If there is one thing to bear in mind until the truth of its words eases the heart troubled by apparent loss, it is this: *The new life is always greater than the old.*

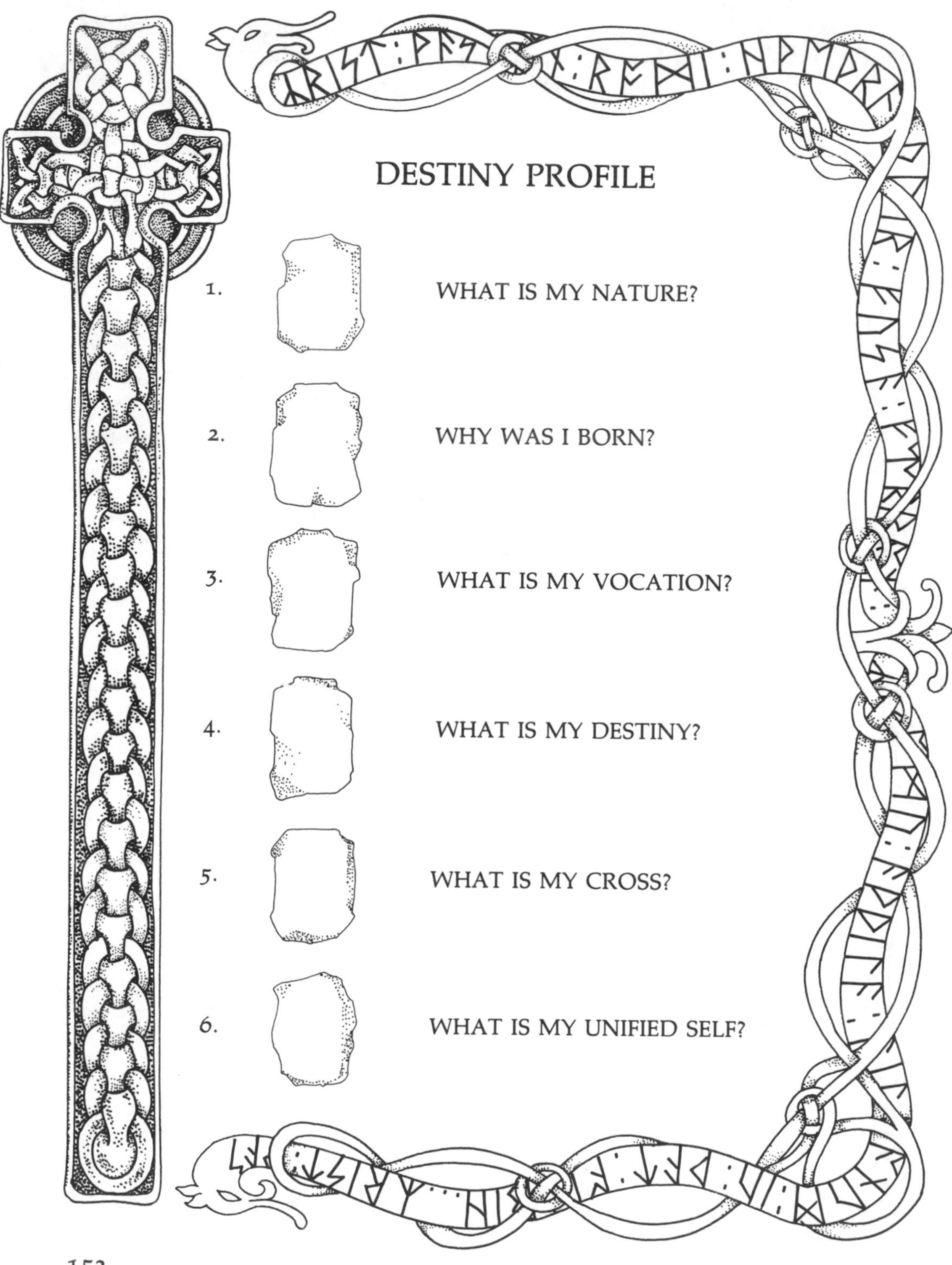
DESTINY PROFILE
1.
WHAT IS MY NATURE?
2.
WHY WAS I BORN?
3.
WHAT IS MY VOCATION?
4.
WHAT IS MY DESTINY?
5.
WHAT IS MY CROSS?
6.
WHAT IS MY UNIFIED SELF?

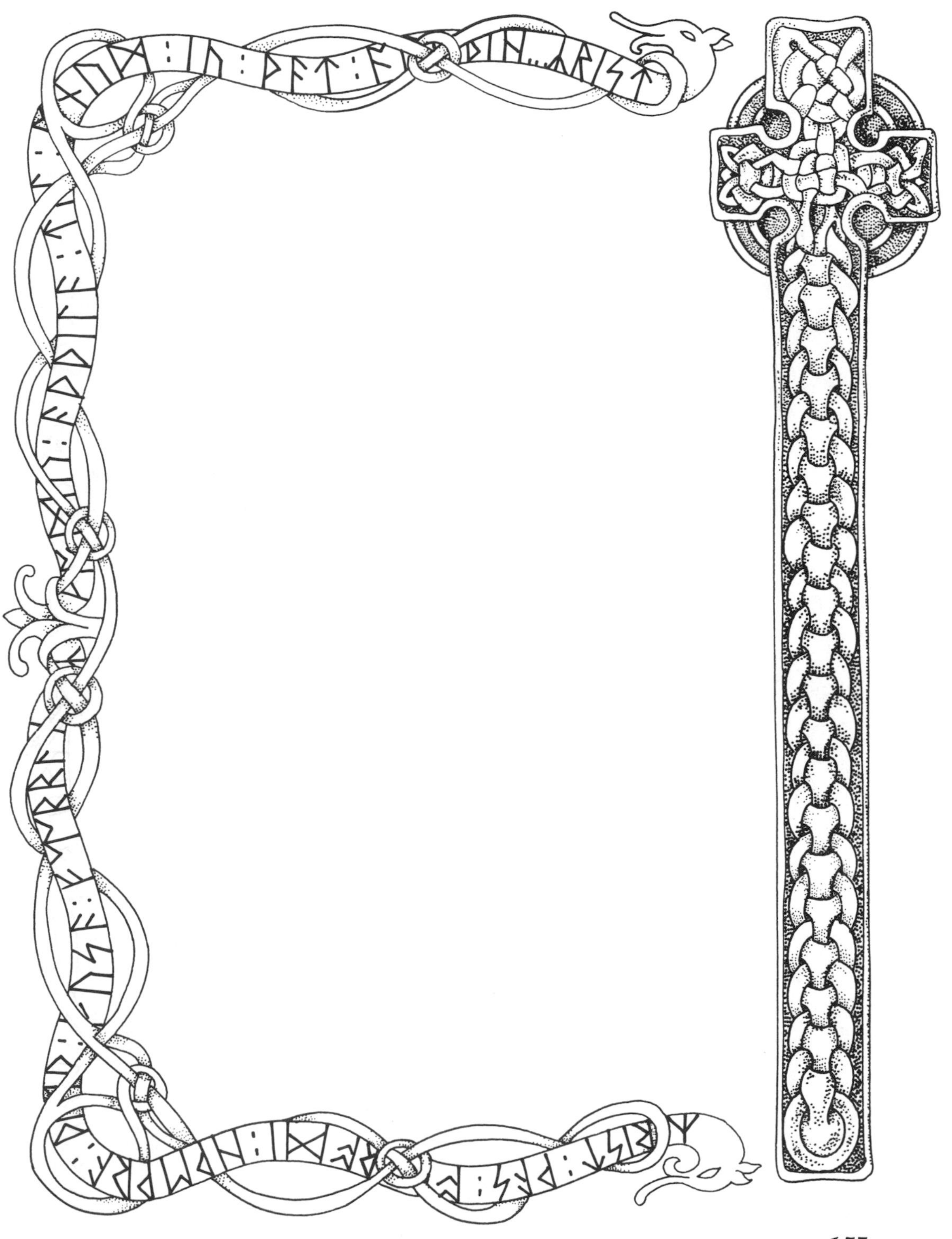

For the week of ______________

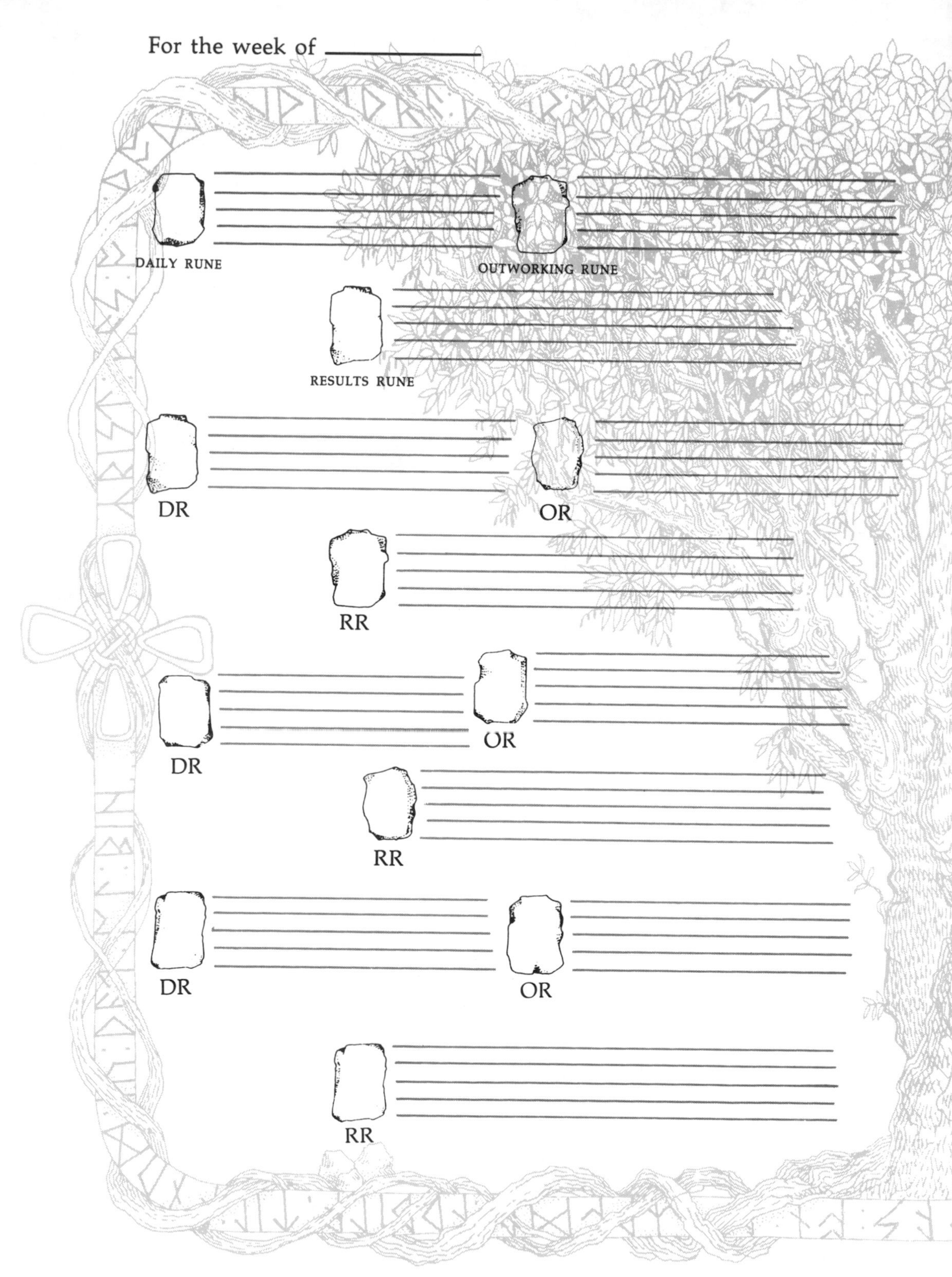

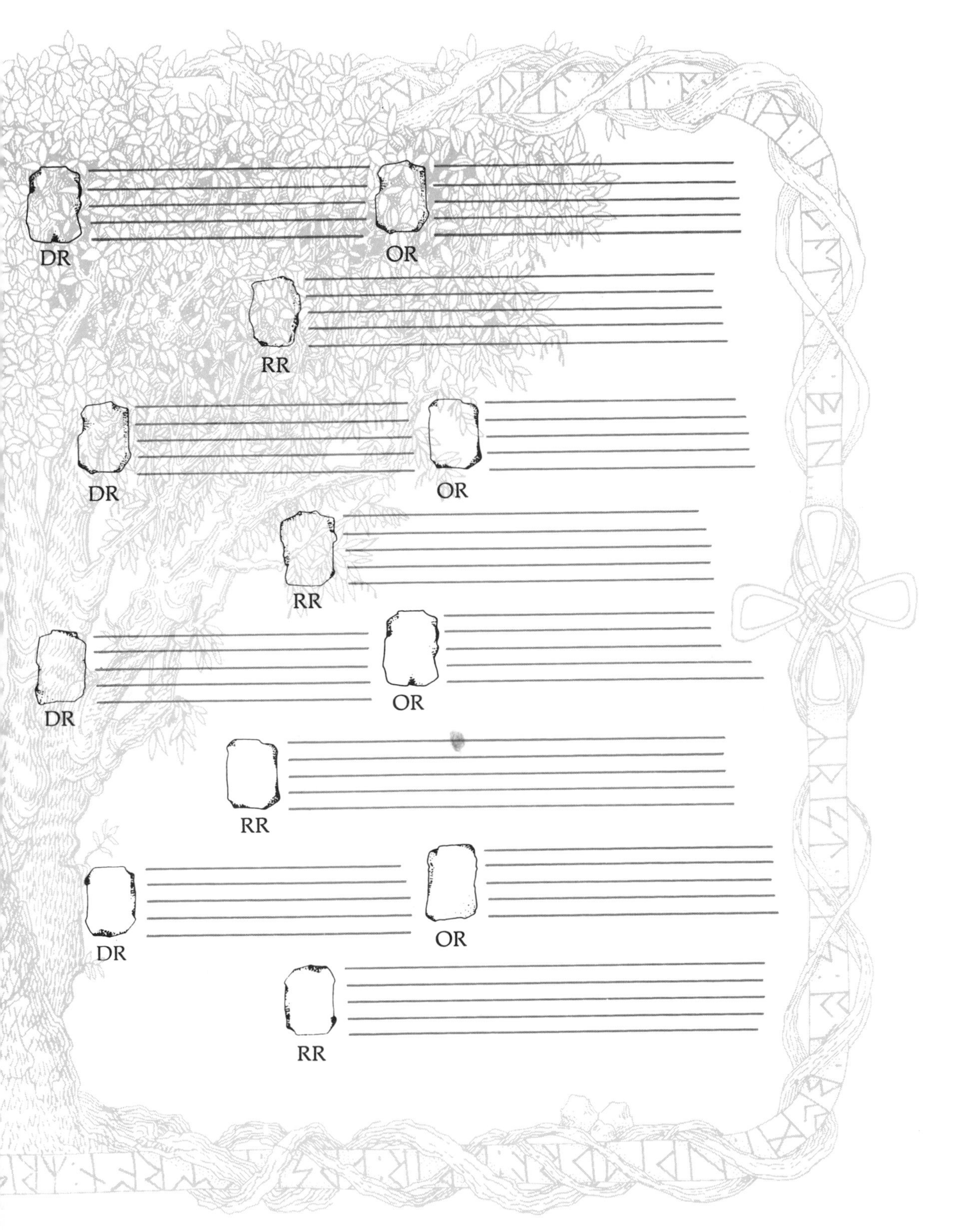
DR
OR
RR
DR
OR
RR
DR
OR
RR
DR
OR
RR

For the week of ____________

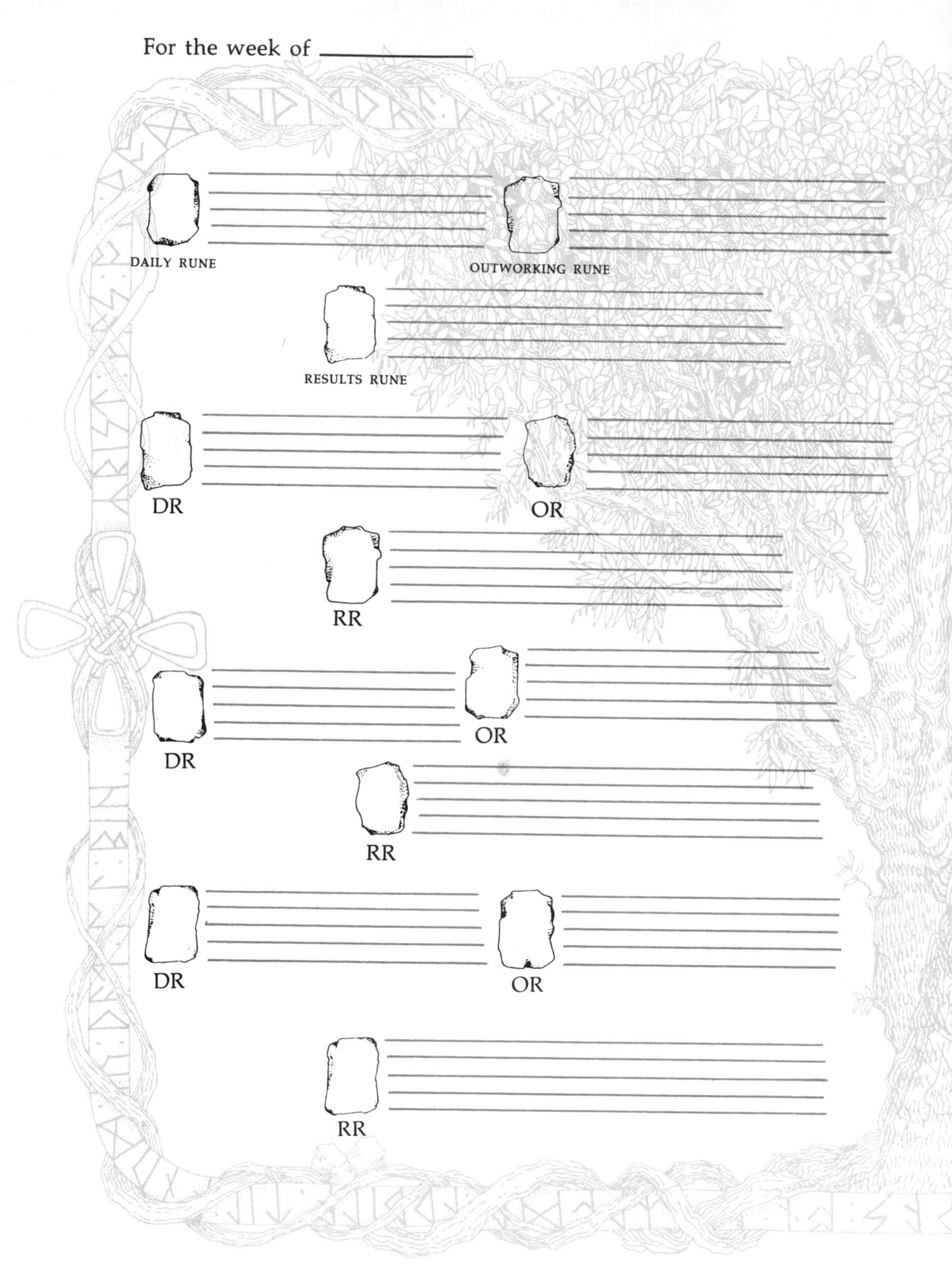

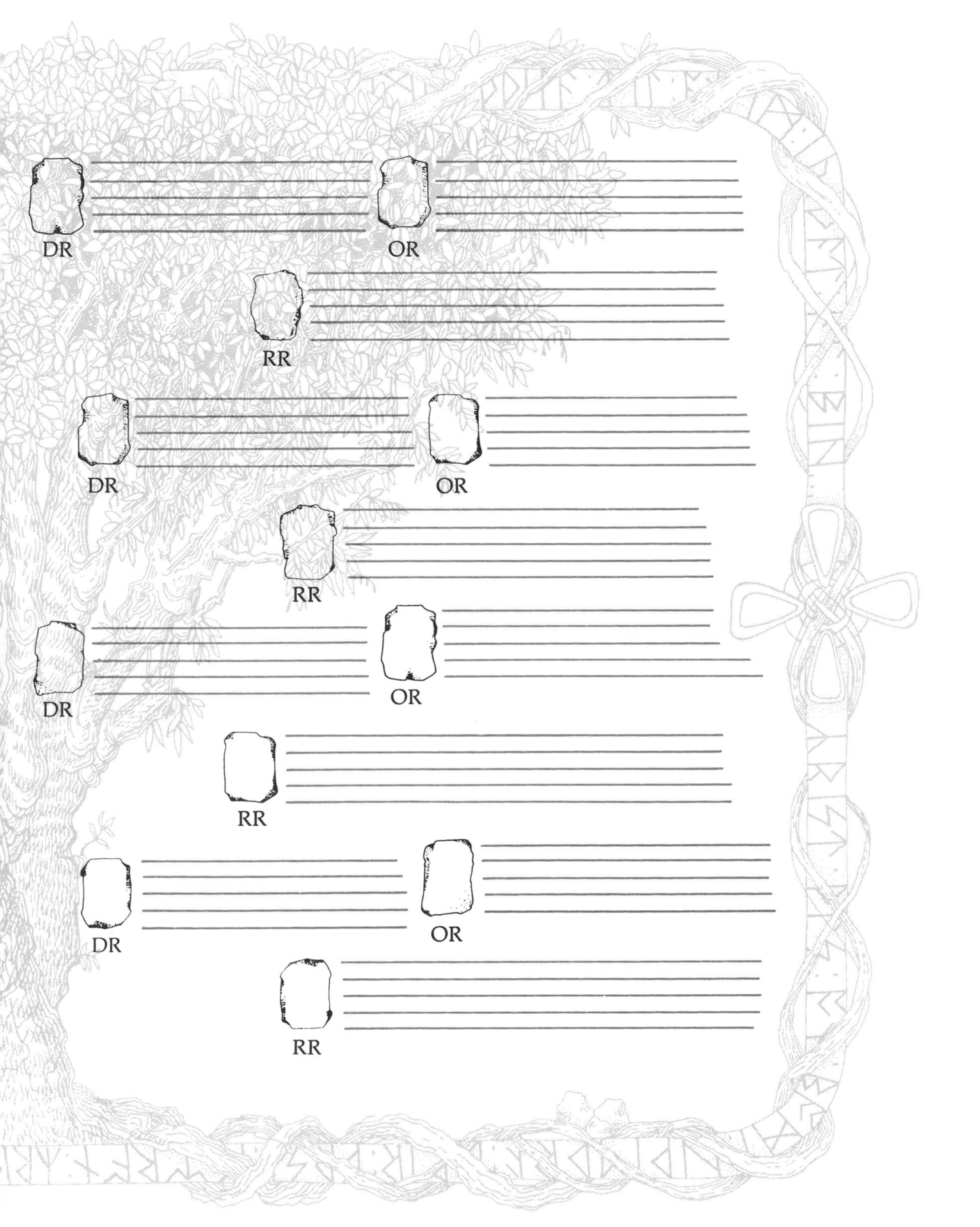
DR
OR
RR
DR
OR
RR
DR
OR
RR
DR
OR
RR

For the week of ____________

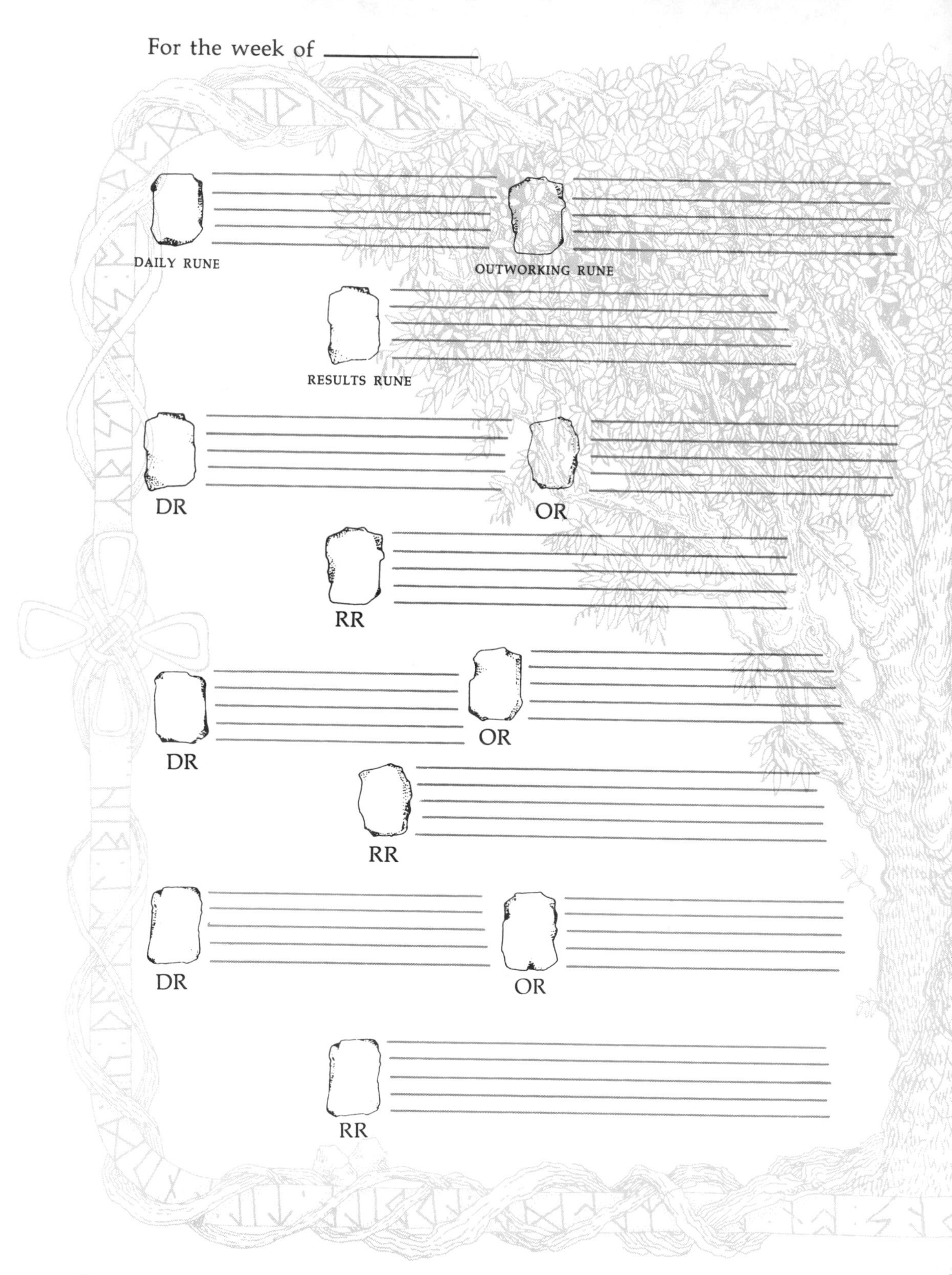

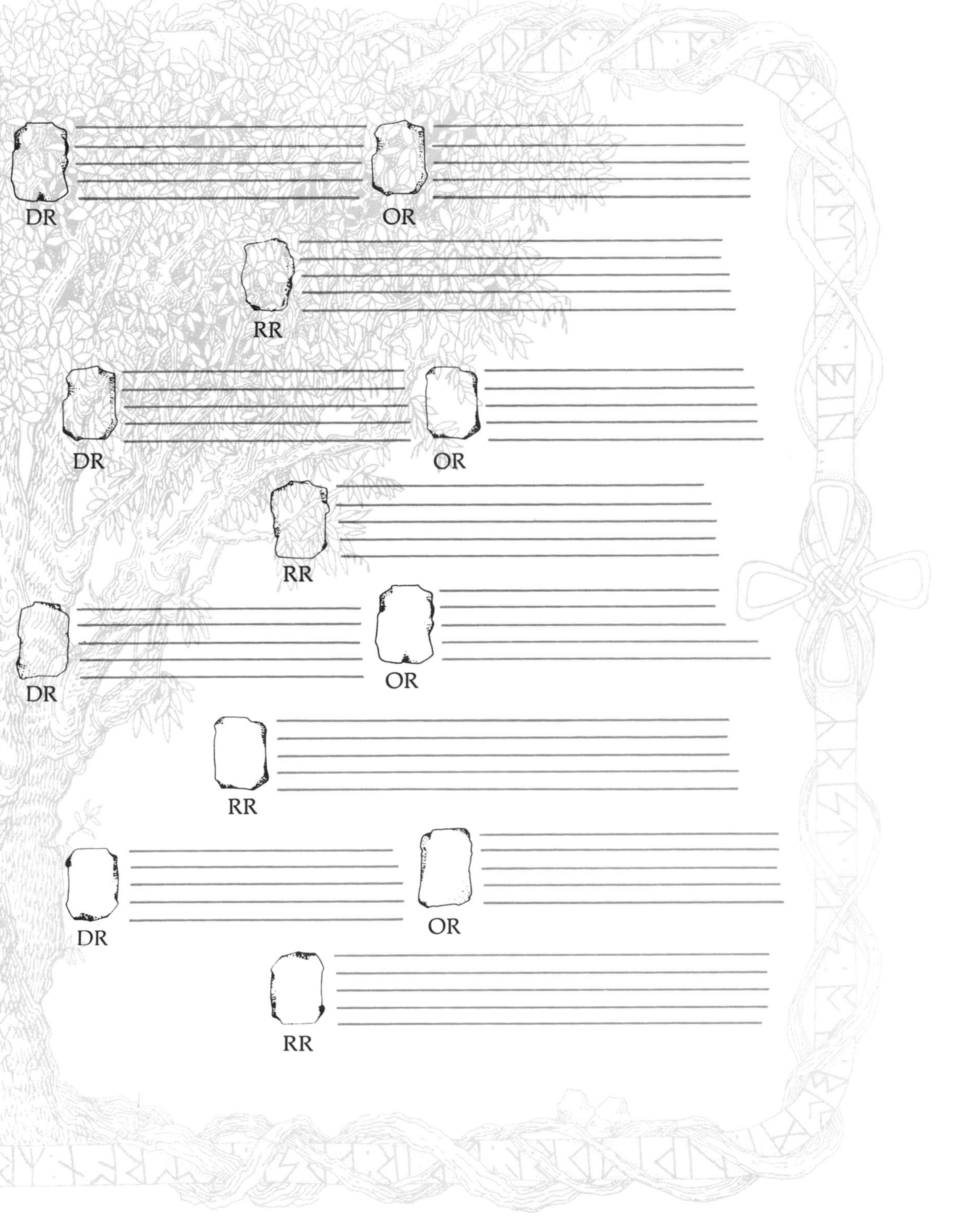
DR
OR
RR
DR
OR
RR
DR
OR
RR
DR
OR
RR

For the week of ____________

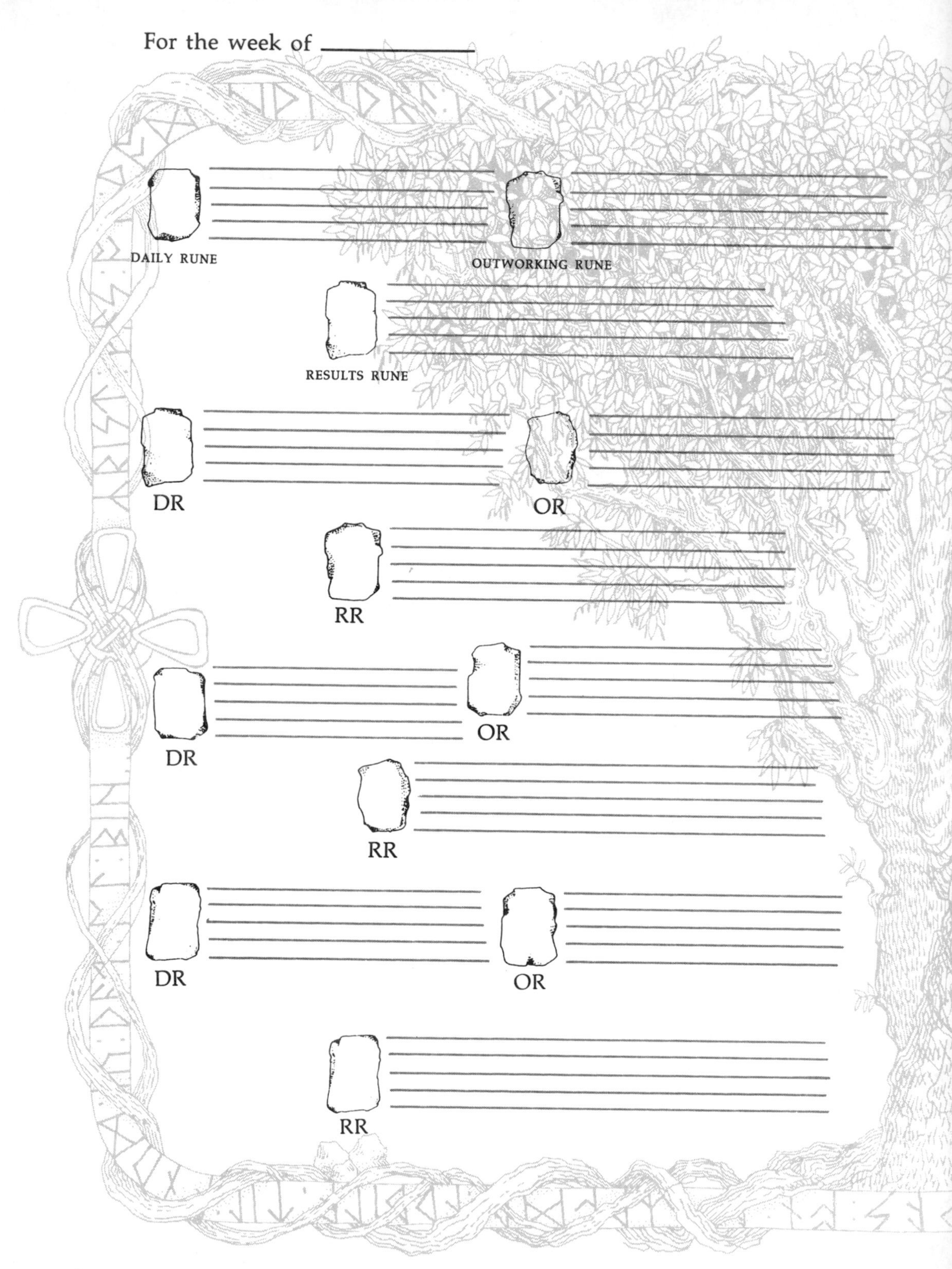

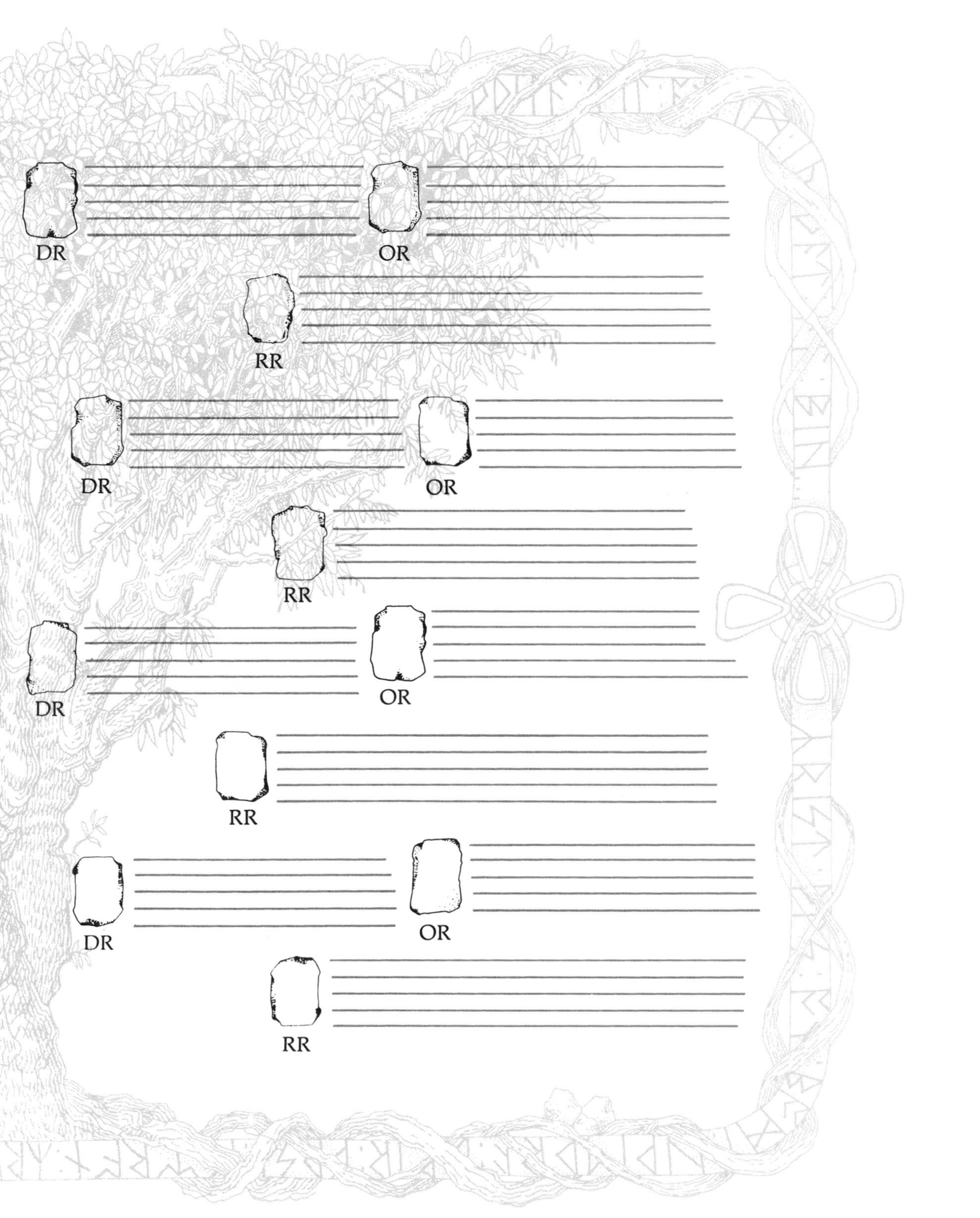
DR
OR
RR
DR
OR
RR
DR
OR
RR
DR
OR
RR

For the week of ____________

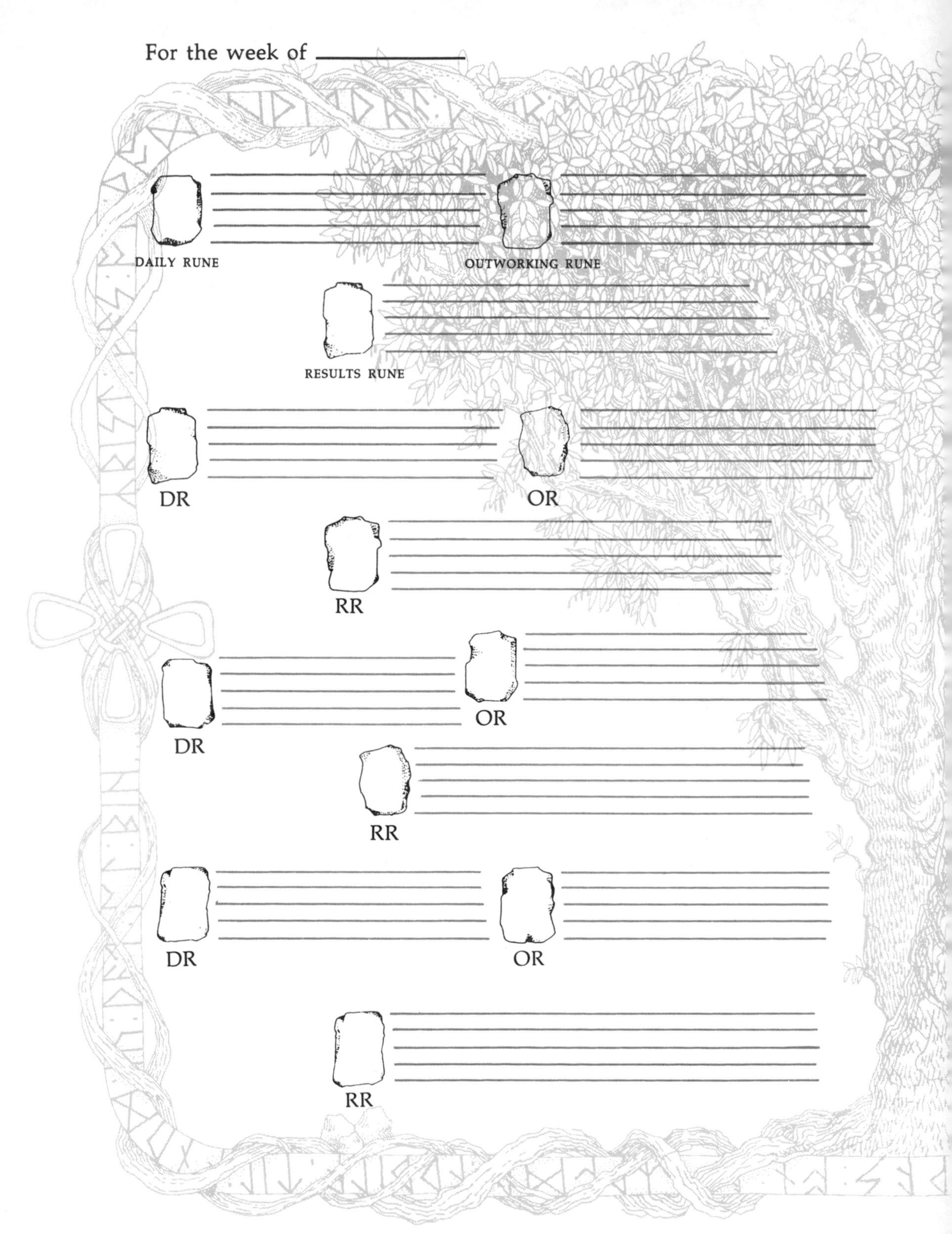

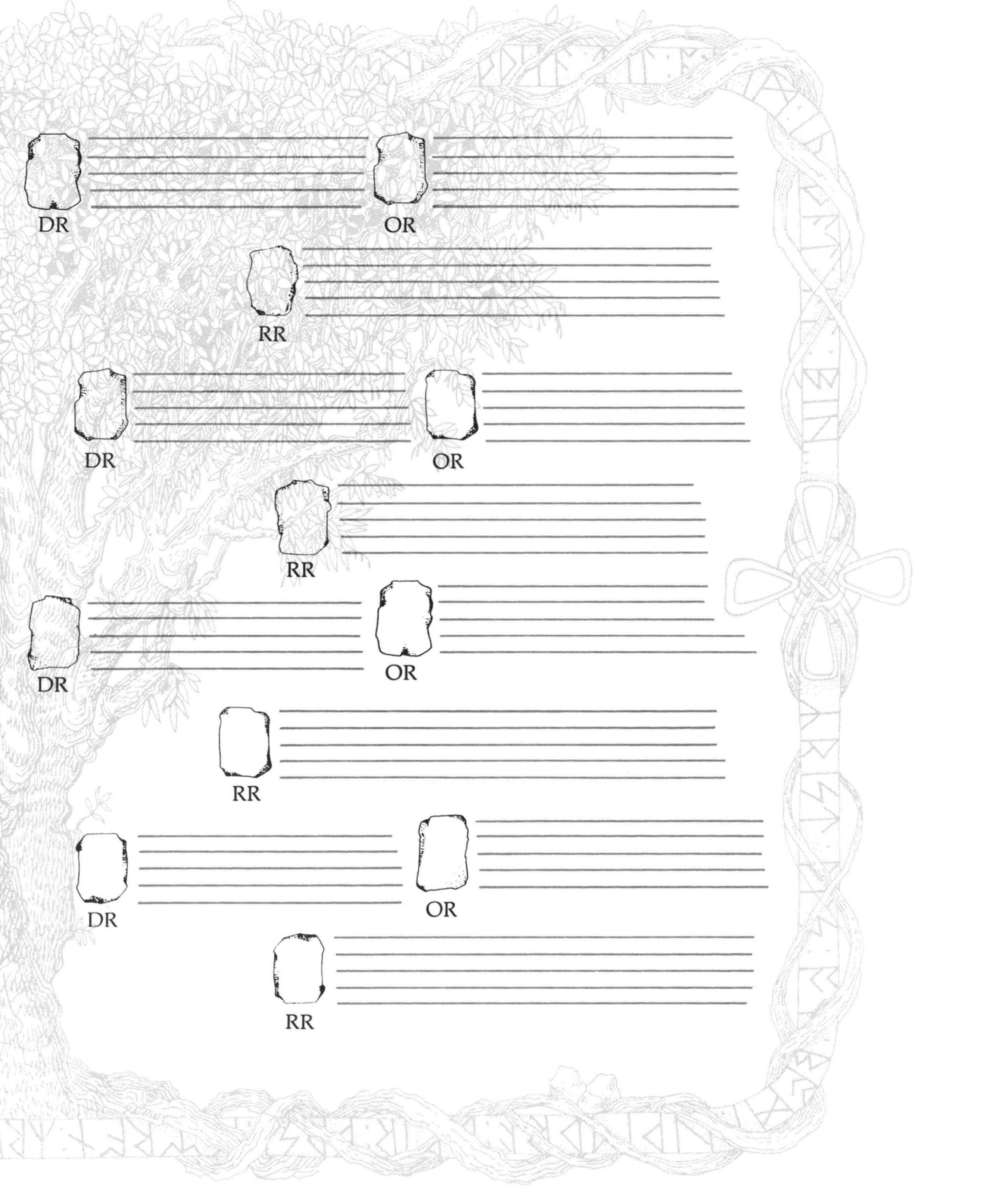
DR
OR
RR
DR
OR
RR
DR
OR
RR
DR
OR
RR

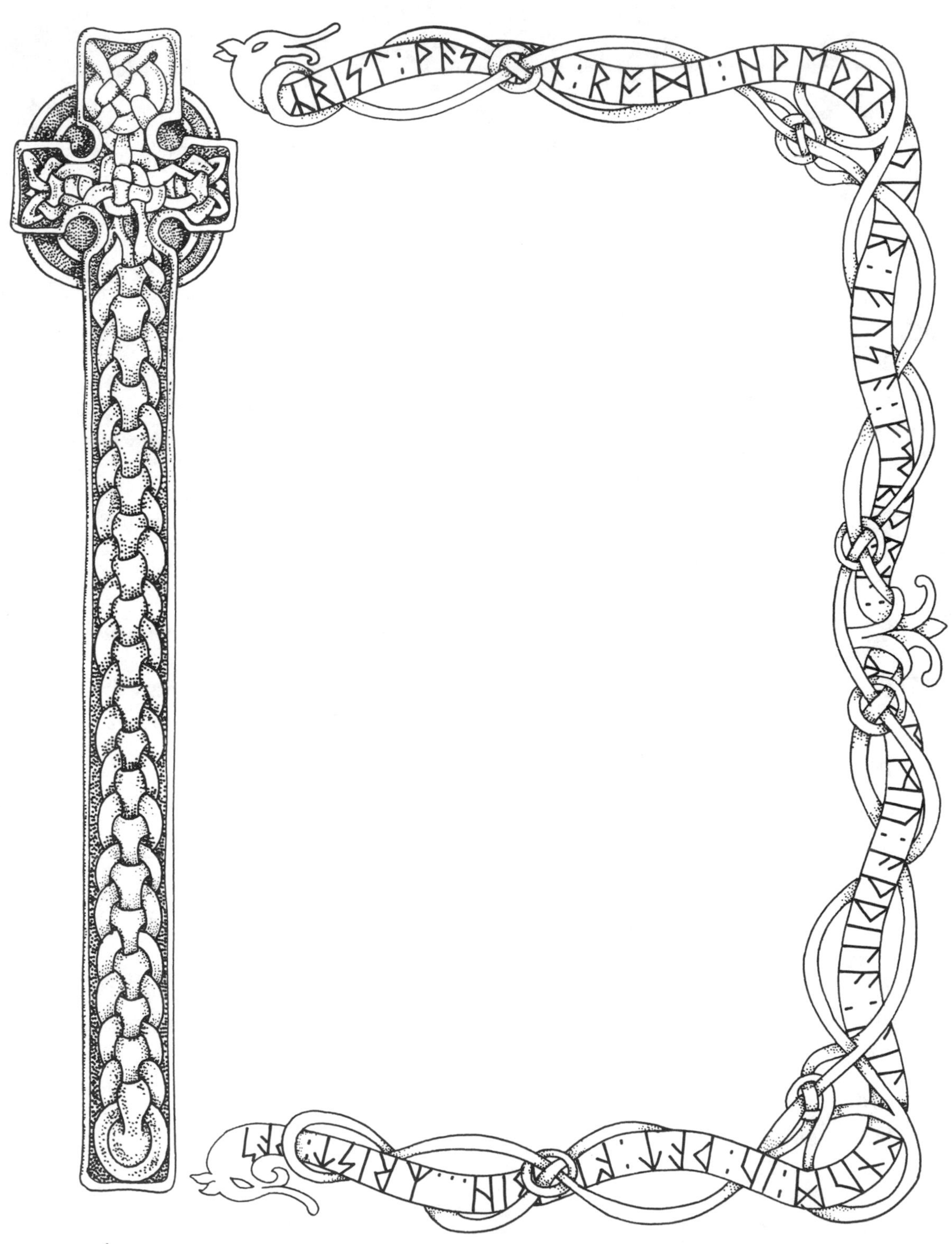

Water Runes Ceremony

This lovely ceremony is linked to the Rune ᛚ, *Laguz,* whose attributes are "water, fluidity, the ebb and flow of tides and emotions, of careers and relationships." There is a ceremonial quality to this Rune casting in that you may perform it, consciously, whenever your body comes in contact with water. It is a ceremony, moreover, that is happily suited to anyone who is alone. It is a cleansing ceremony, a healing ritual. It is simplicity itself.

Whenever you dip your hands into water or take a shower or jump into a pool, a lake, the ocean, think of these words:

I cleanse myself of all selfishness,
Resentments,
Critical emotions toward my fellow beings,
Self-condemnation and
Ignorant misinterpretations of my life's experiences.

As you wash or bathe or swim, you may wish to repeat this little *Prayer of Intention* a number of times. Watch what comes to mind as you repeat the words, aloud or in silence. Observe what you feel. Or, simply repeat the Prayer with love and gentleness, for it is not a hair shirt you are putting on; you are not making yourself wrong. Rather, you are embodying in words a yearning for more clarity, more light in your life, a cleaner passage through this world.

Some of you may find the demand to "cleanse" yourself excessively authoritarian; it may evoke religious practices that remind you of a harsher time. Rather than "giving up" old ways of being that no longer suit the person you are becoming, you may choose to transmute or transform all selfishness, all resentments into their *light opposites,* repeating the Prayer in the following way:

I bathe myself in generosity,
Appreciation,
Emotions of praise toward my fellow beings,
Self-acceptance and
Enlightened understanding of my life's experiences.

The way you relate to the *Water Runes Ceremony* will depend upon your own temperament, your own needs. As you work with it, you may decide to modify it, shape it to your satisfaction. That is correct action, and it is to be encouraged. For at all times, in all ways, working with the Runes is a cooperative venture, an exercise in co-creation.

As there are five elements to the Water Runes Ceremony and its Prayer of Intention, you may wish to construct a special spread to accompany the ceremonial words. Some people select a Rune to take with them into the water, in a pouch or worn as an amulet around their neck. Some people will select a Rune on the matter of Self-condemnation and Self-acceptance on one day. On another day, they might draw a Rune relating to Selfishness and Generosity. Others will draw a Rune about a particular life experience that has hardened in memory as being distasteful, shameful, embarrassing, or sinful, asking for "new Light" by which to grow in understanding of the truth and appropriateness of that life experience. The permutations, as always with the Runes, are endless.

The occasions for performing the Water Runes Ceremony are limitless. There is no activity that is less sacred than any other. Washing the dishes, the dog, or the pickup truck will do nicely, as will bathing the baby, watering the lawn, or standing in the rain.

You may wish to write out the Prayer of Intention and tape it to the shower wall, the splashboard over your sink, on the water cooler. When the words run and dissolve, write them out again and stick them up again. Let the Water Runes Ceremony flow with your life.

For those who like to know the provenance of things, the suggestion for this ceremony came from M. Gompert of Kuranda, North Queensland, Australia. It was, he explained quite simply, part of his way of growing. And now it is available to become part of yours.

WATER RUNES CEREMONY

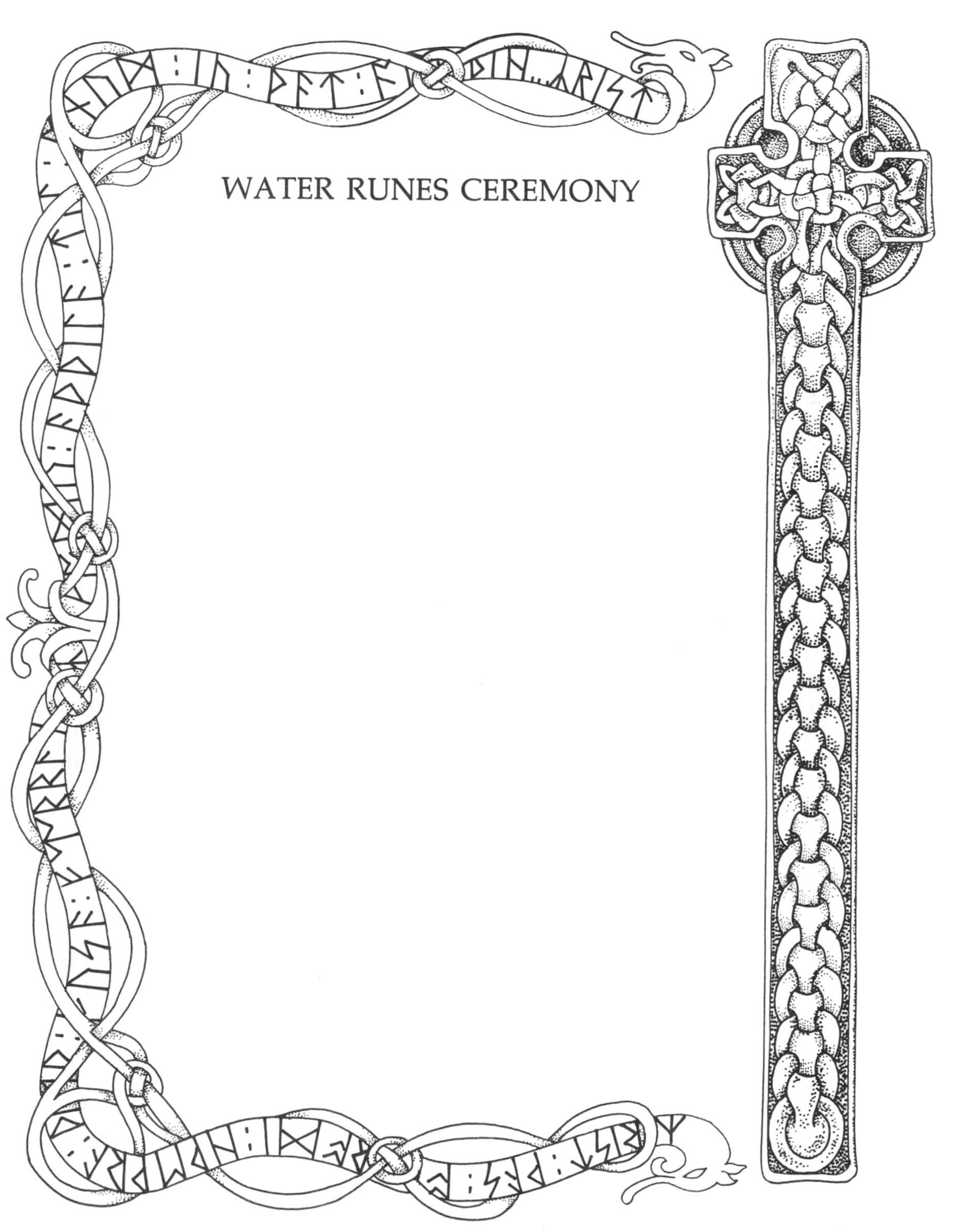

For the week of ____________

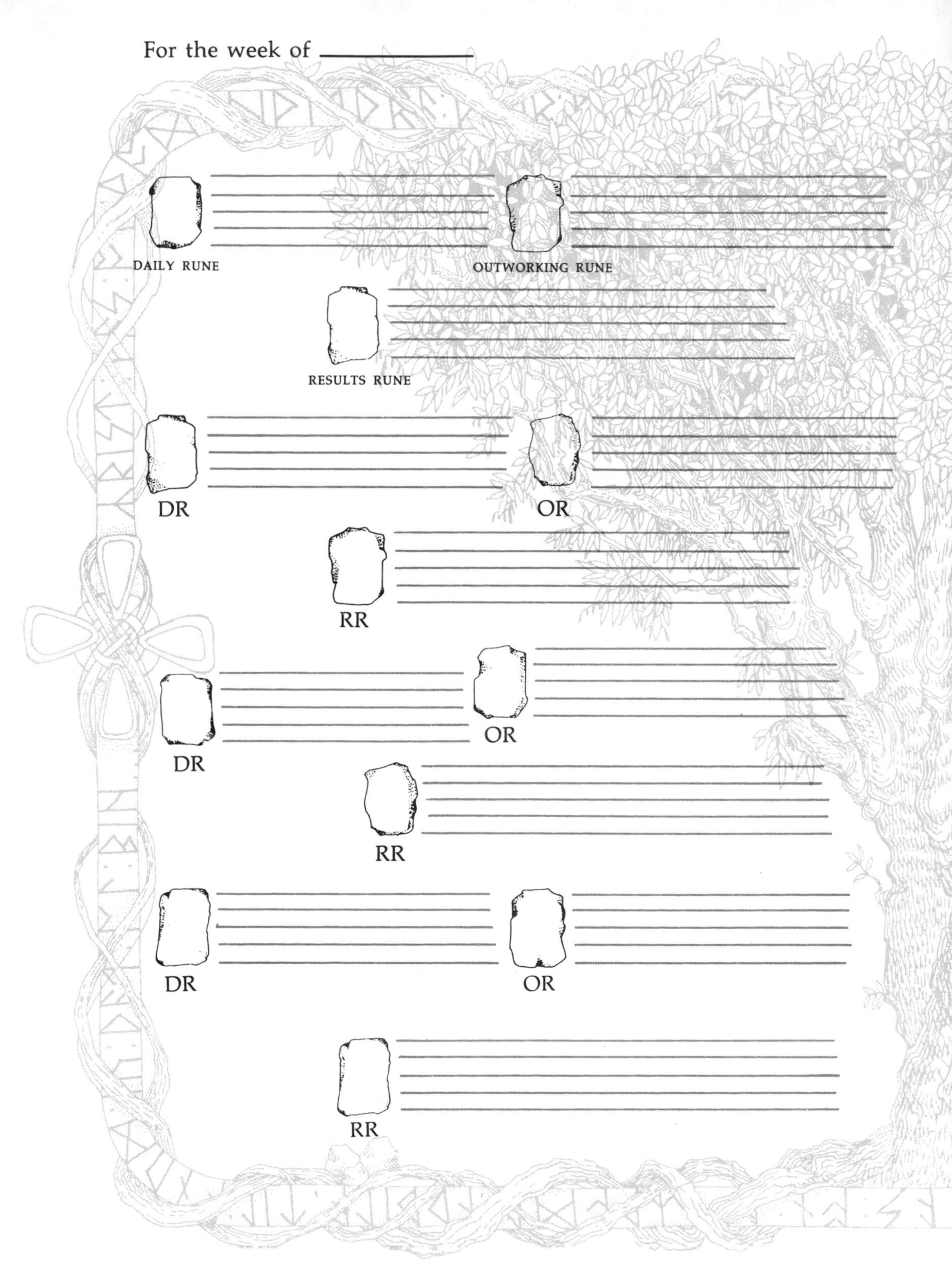

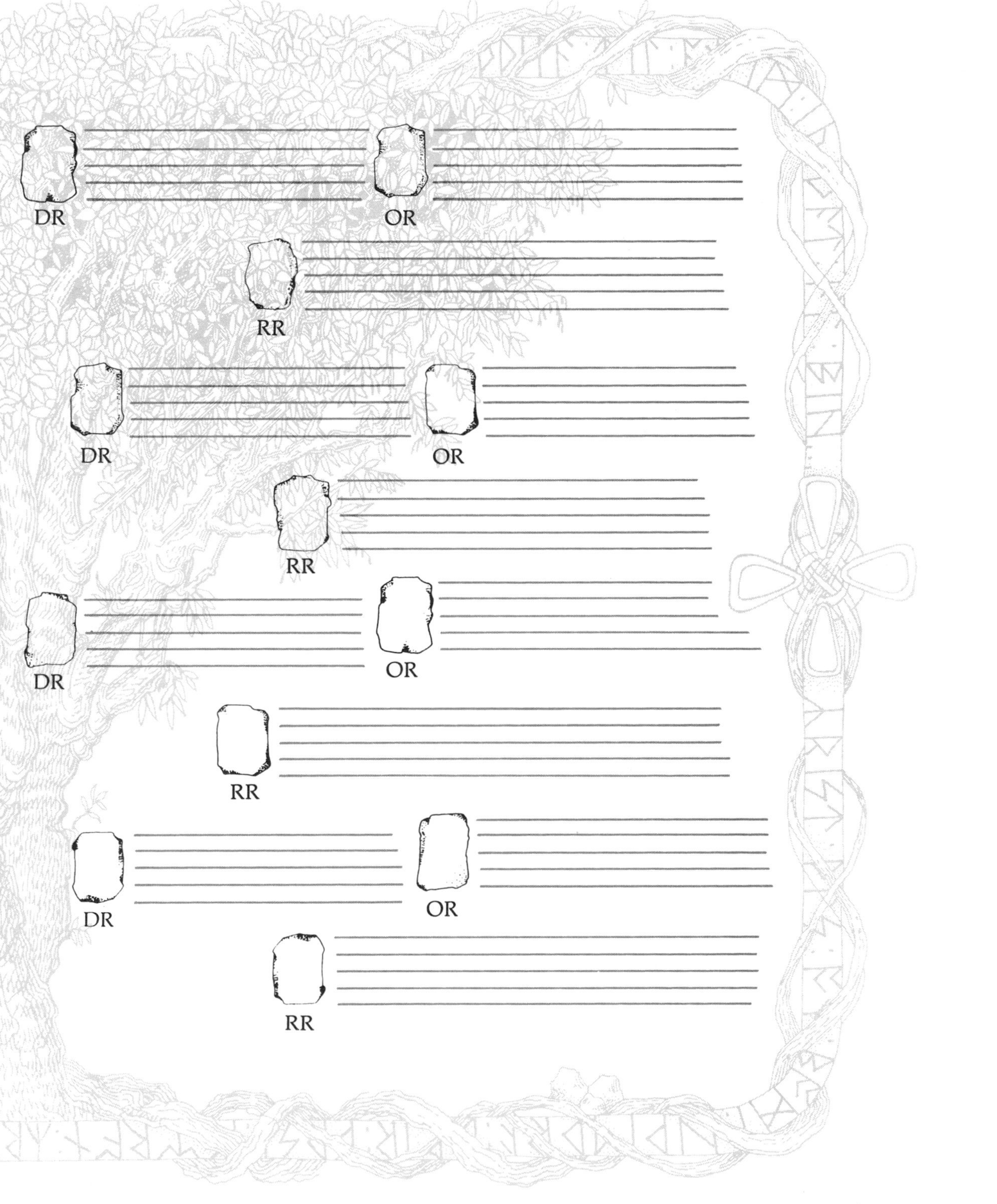
DR
OR
RR
DR
OR
RR
DR
OR
RR
DR
OR
RR

For the week of ______________

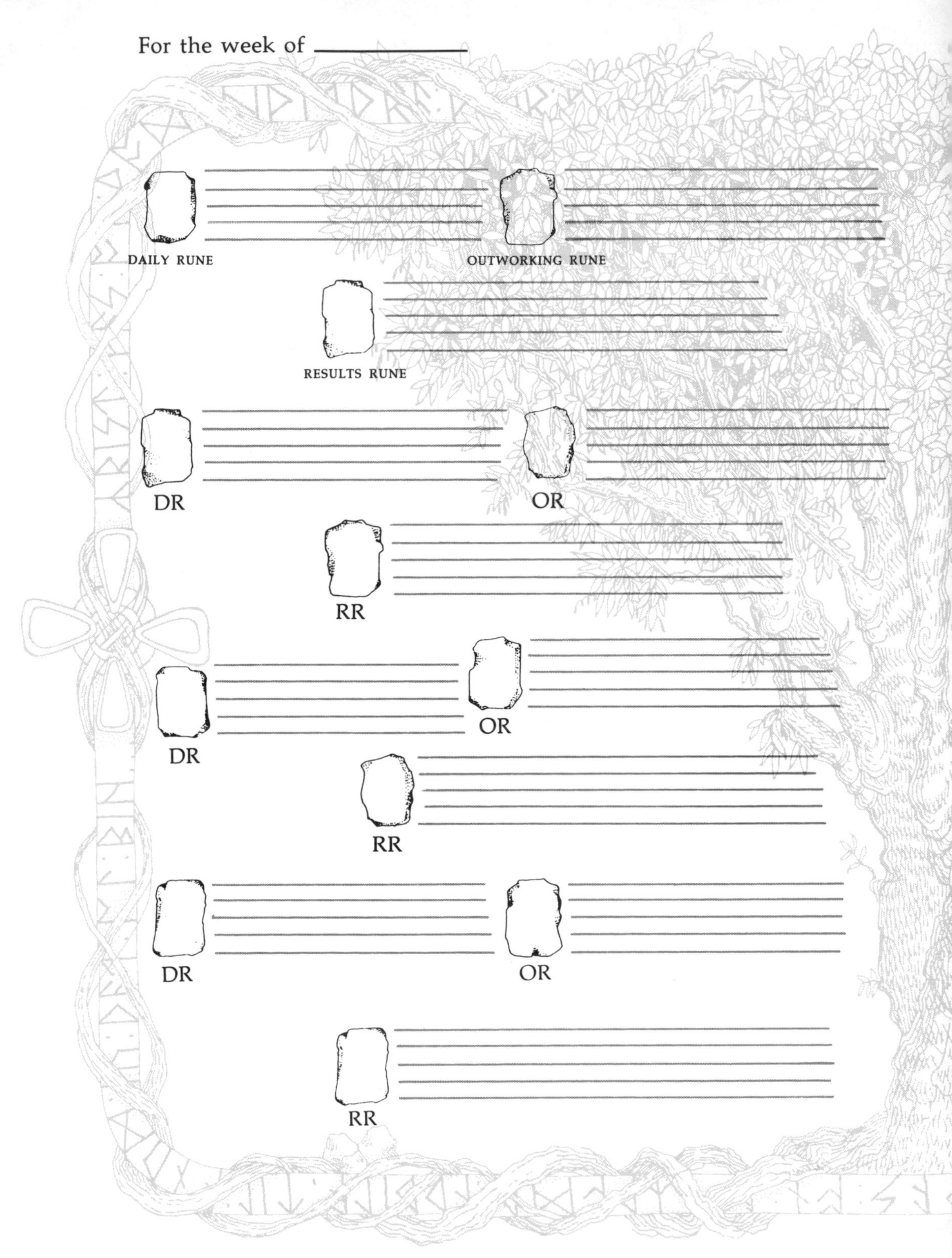

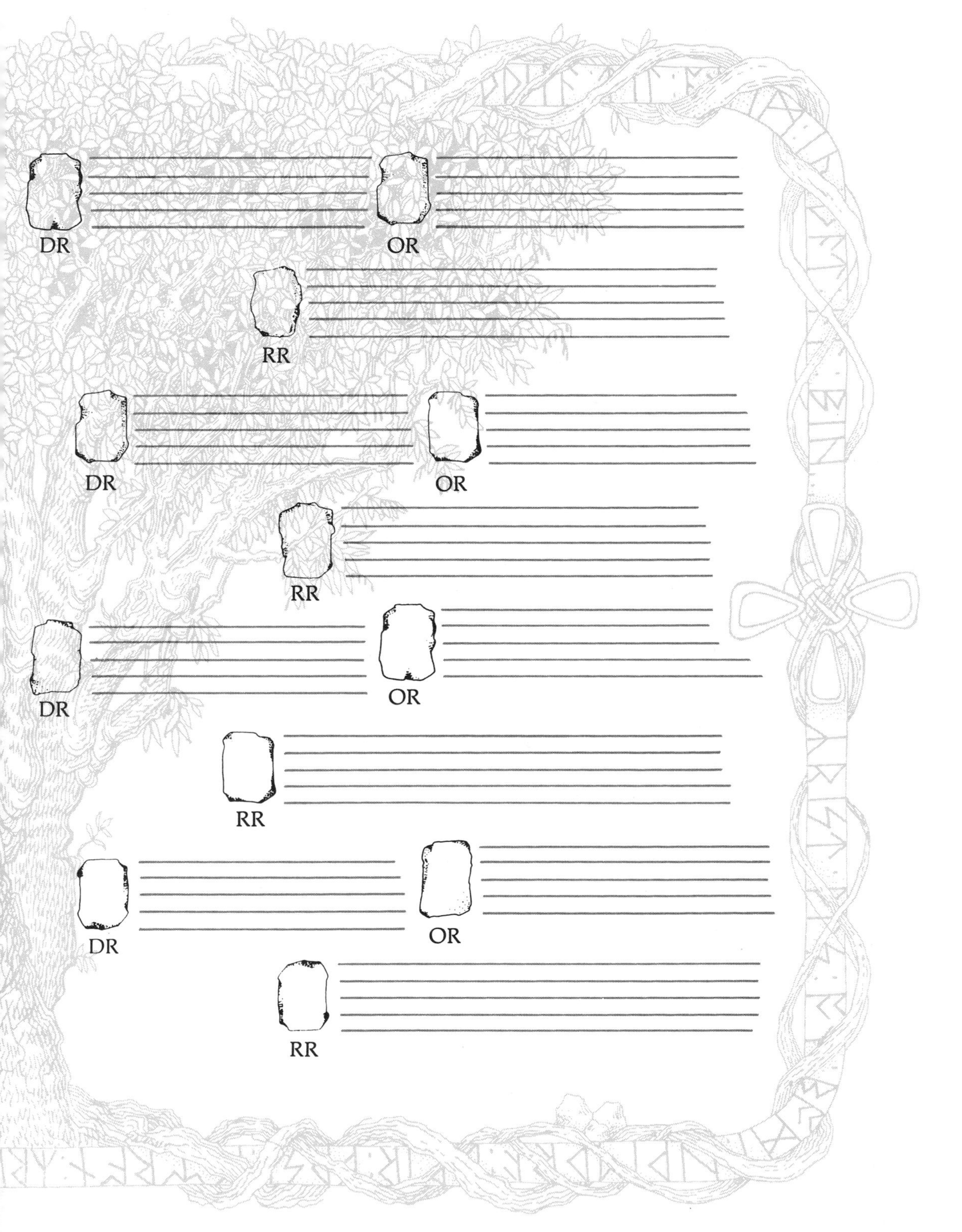
DR
OR
RR
DR
OR
RR
DR
OR
RR
DR
OR
RR

For the week of ____________

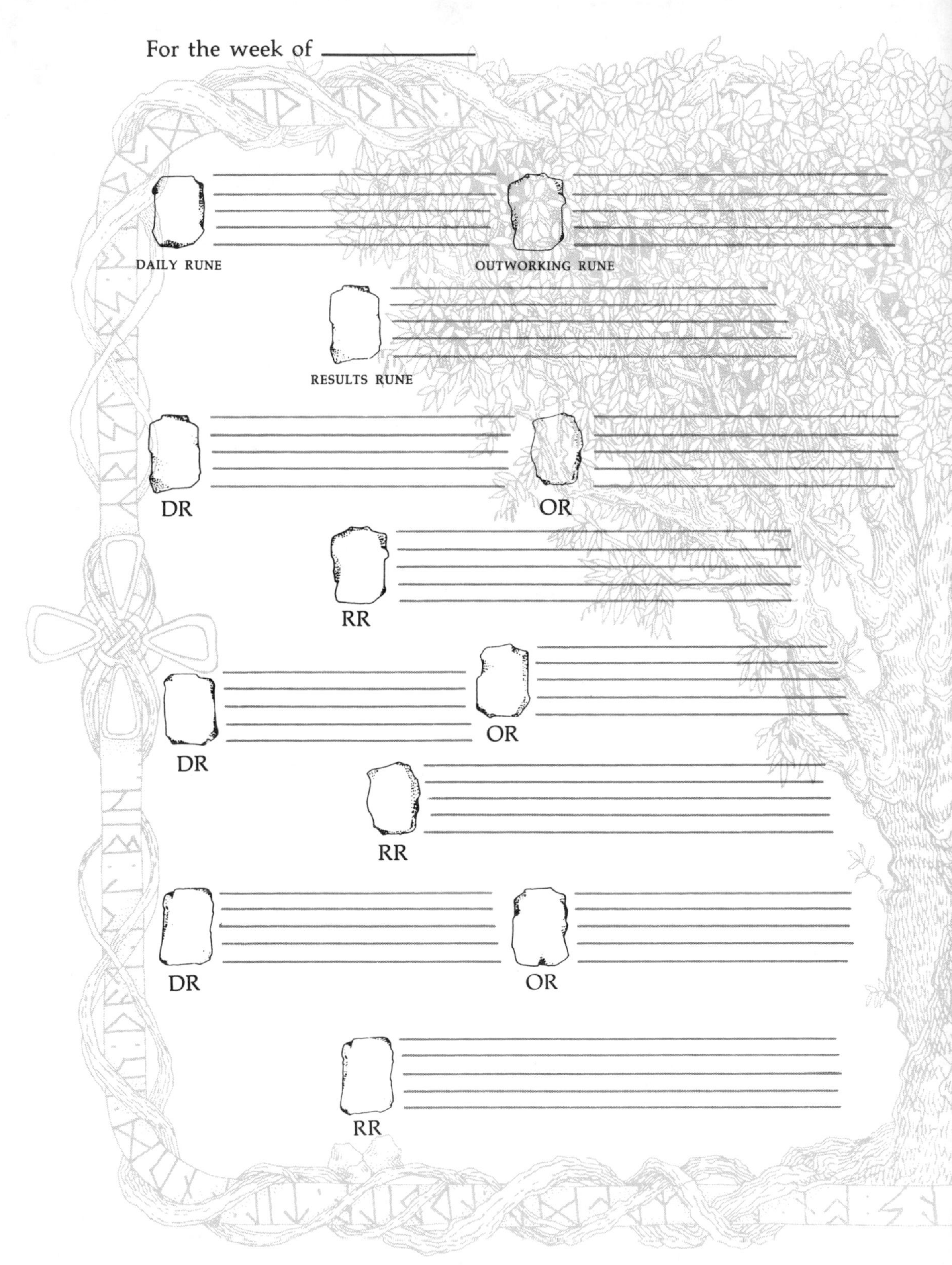

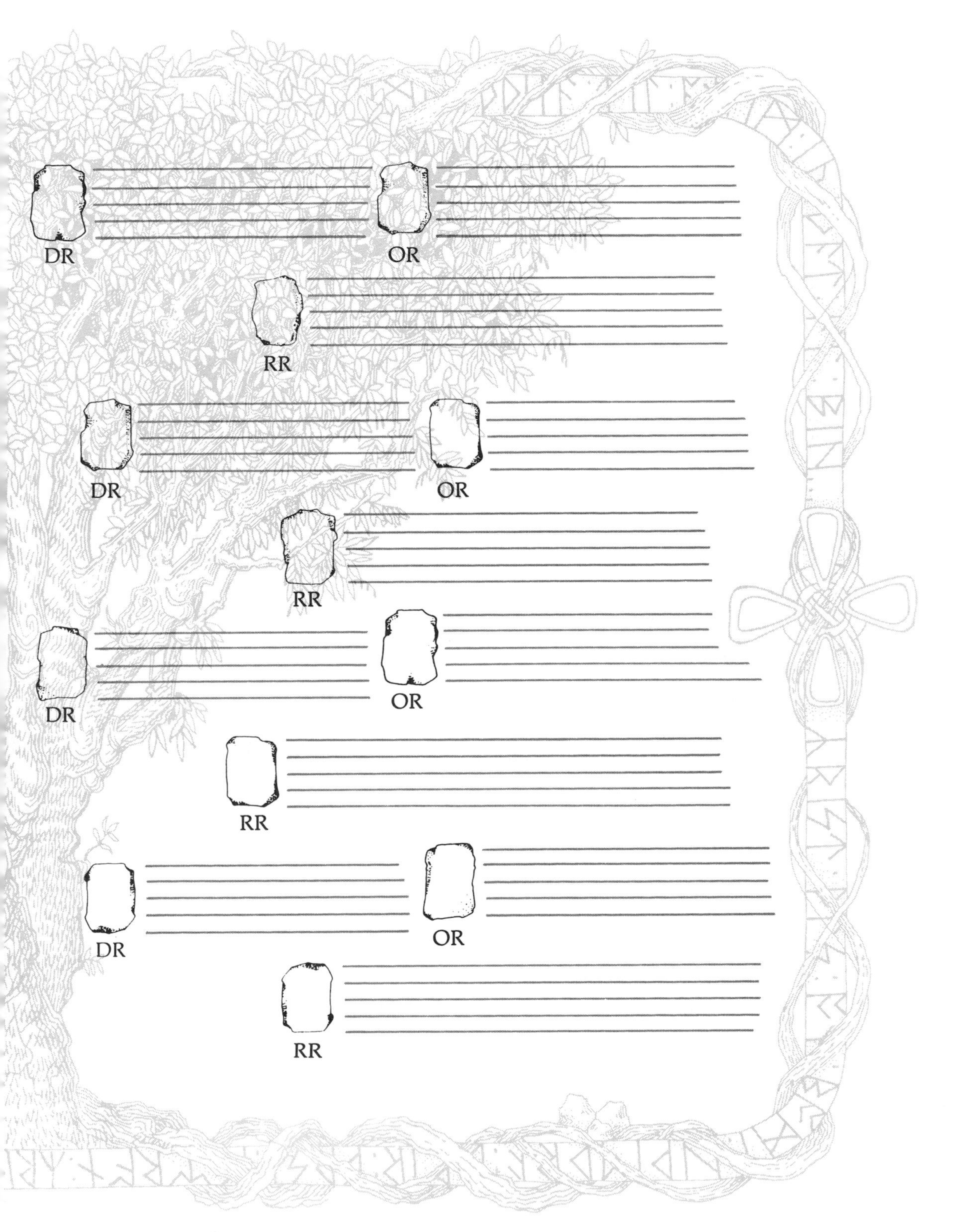

DR
OR
RR
DR
OR
RR
DR
OR
RR
DR
OR
RR

For the week of ______________

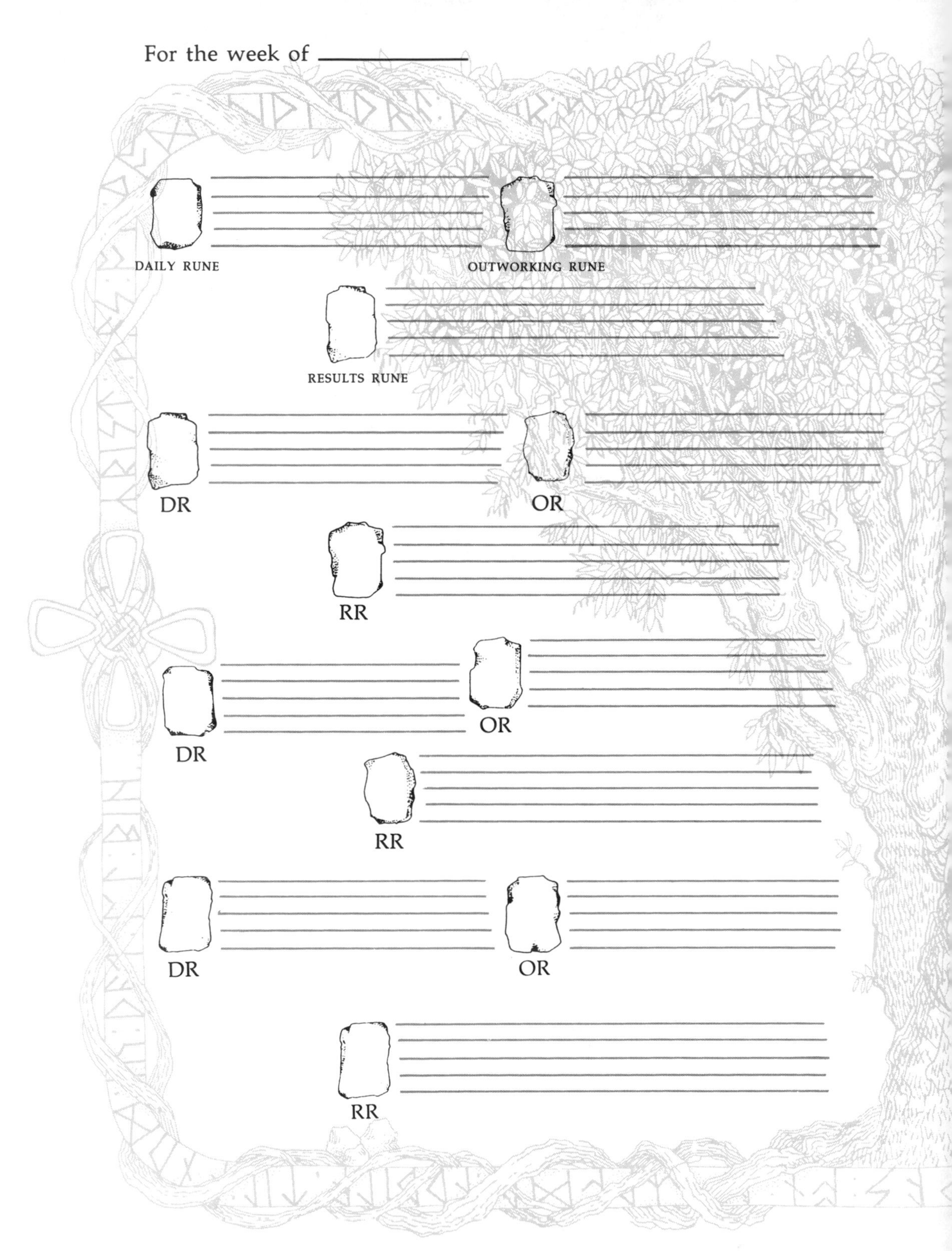

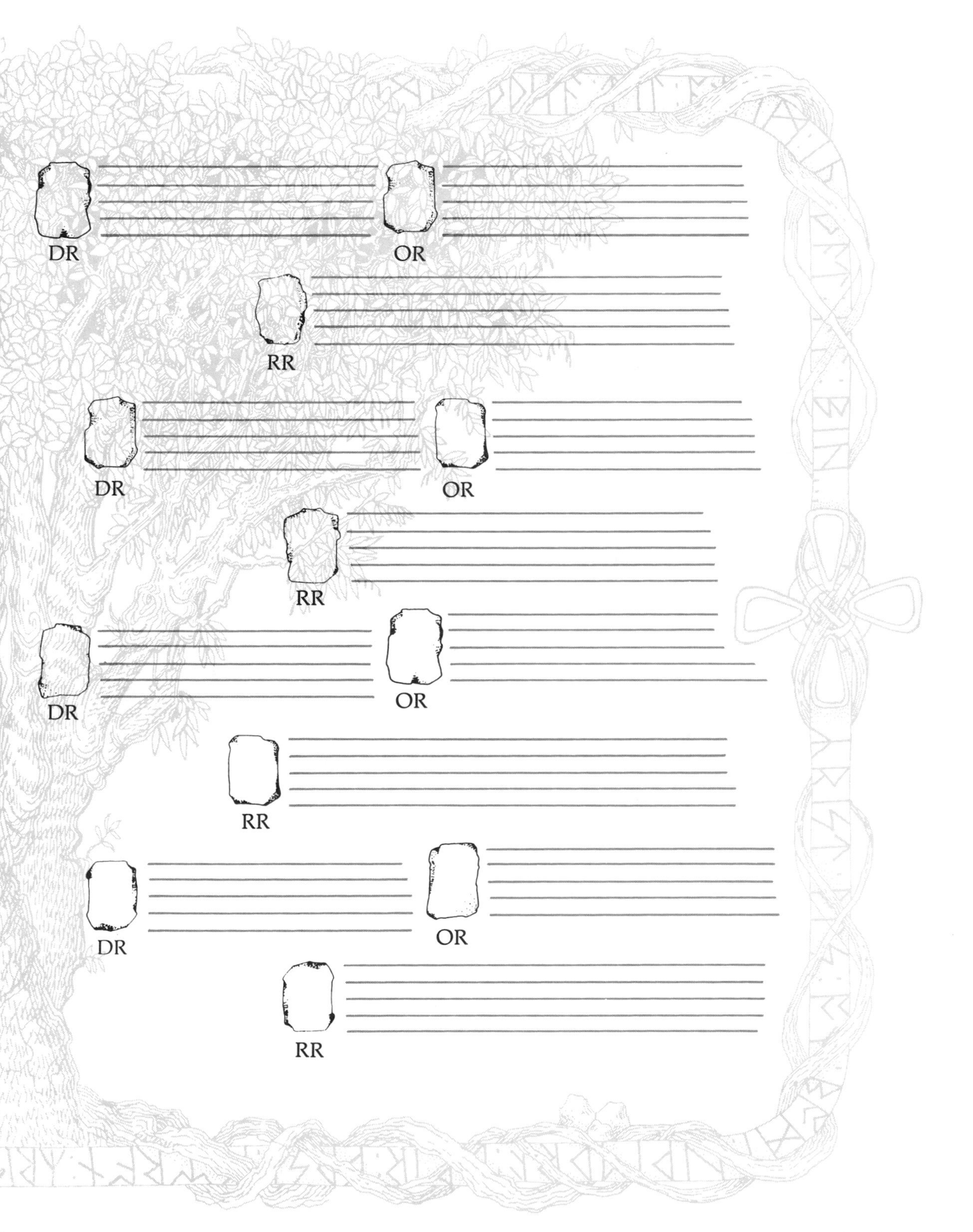
DR
OR
RR
DR
OR
RR
DR
OR
RR
DR
OR
RR

For the week of ____________

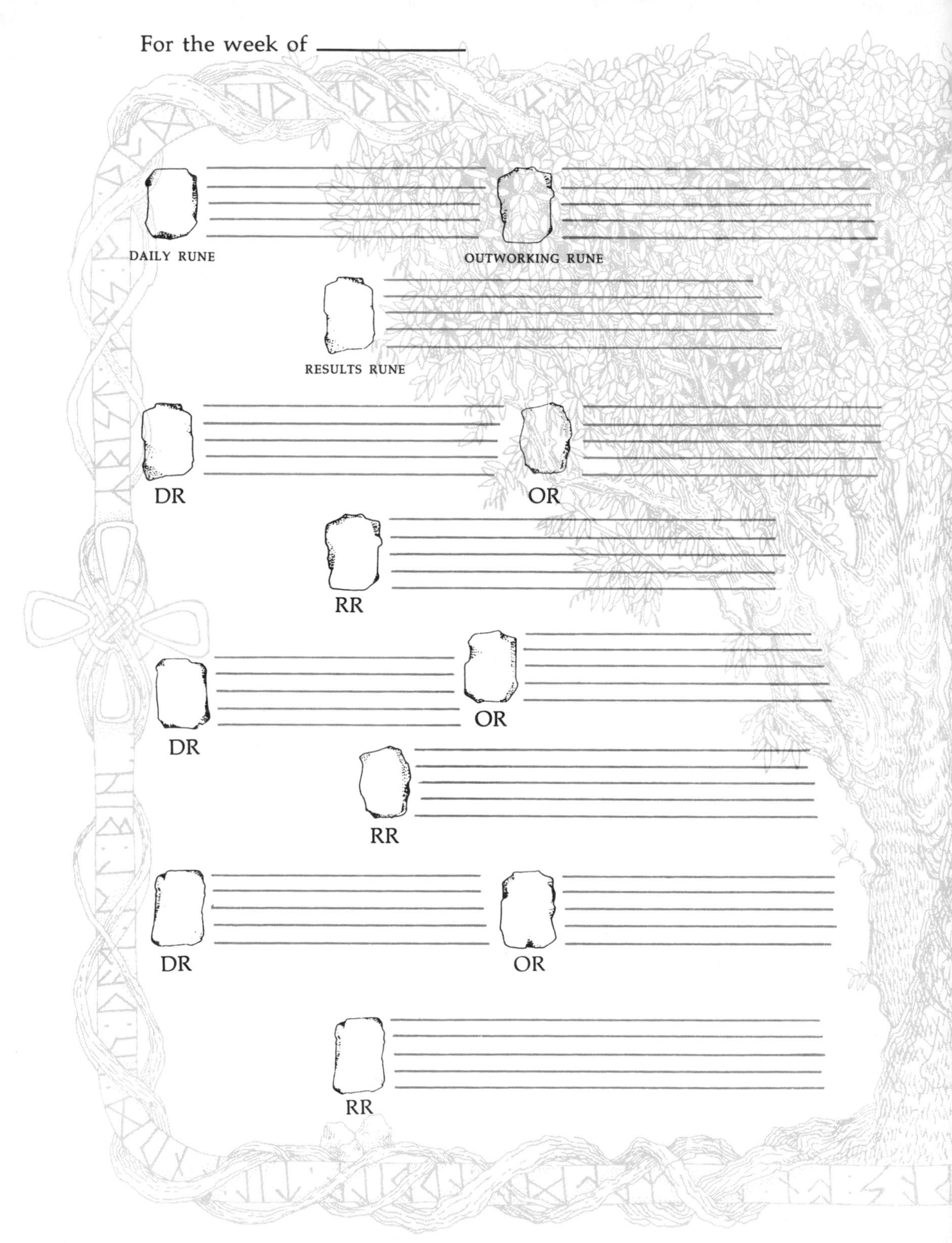

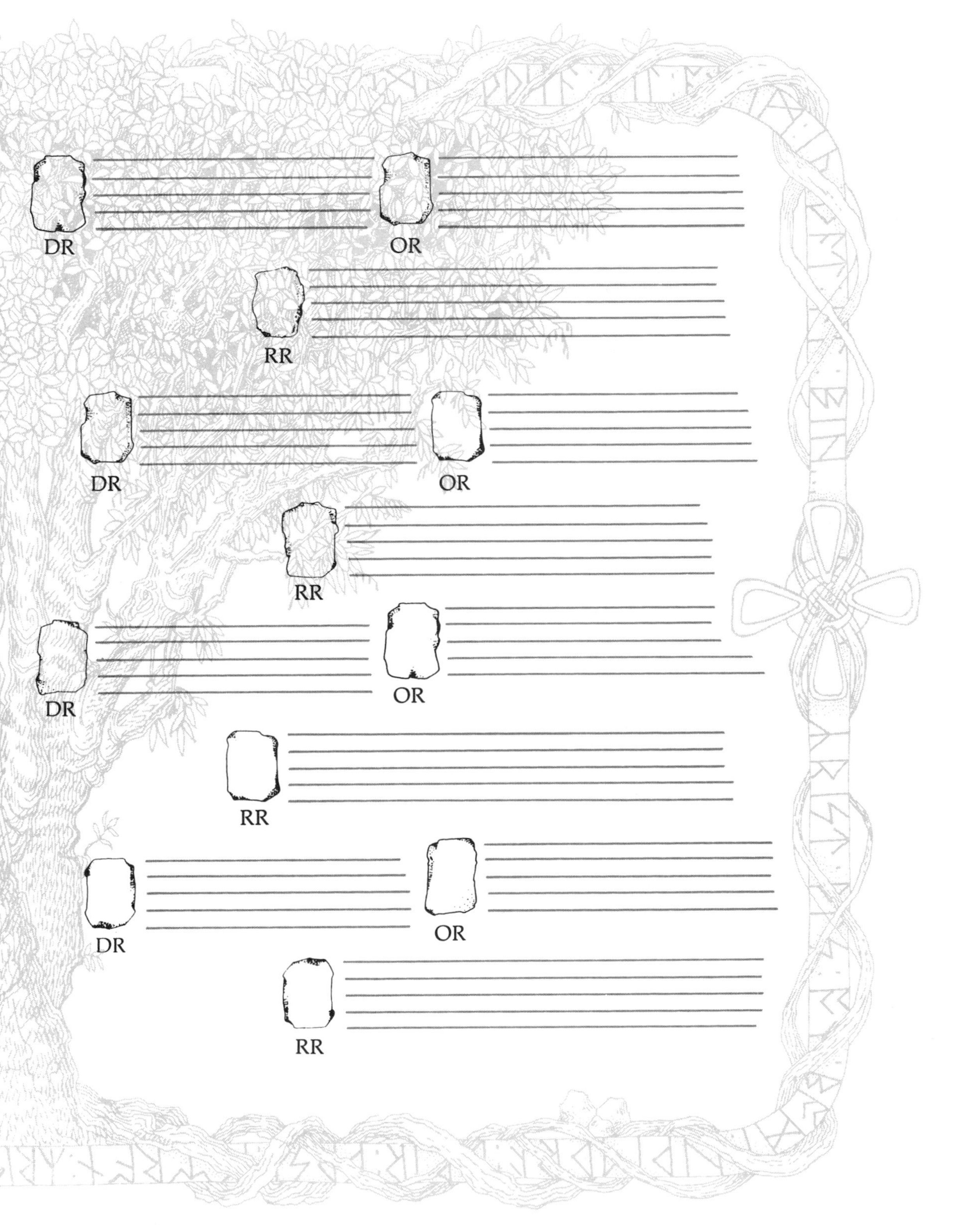
DR
OR
RR
DR
OR
RR
DR
OR
RR
DR
OR
RR

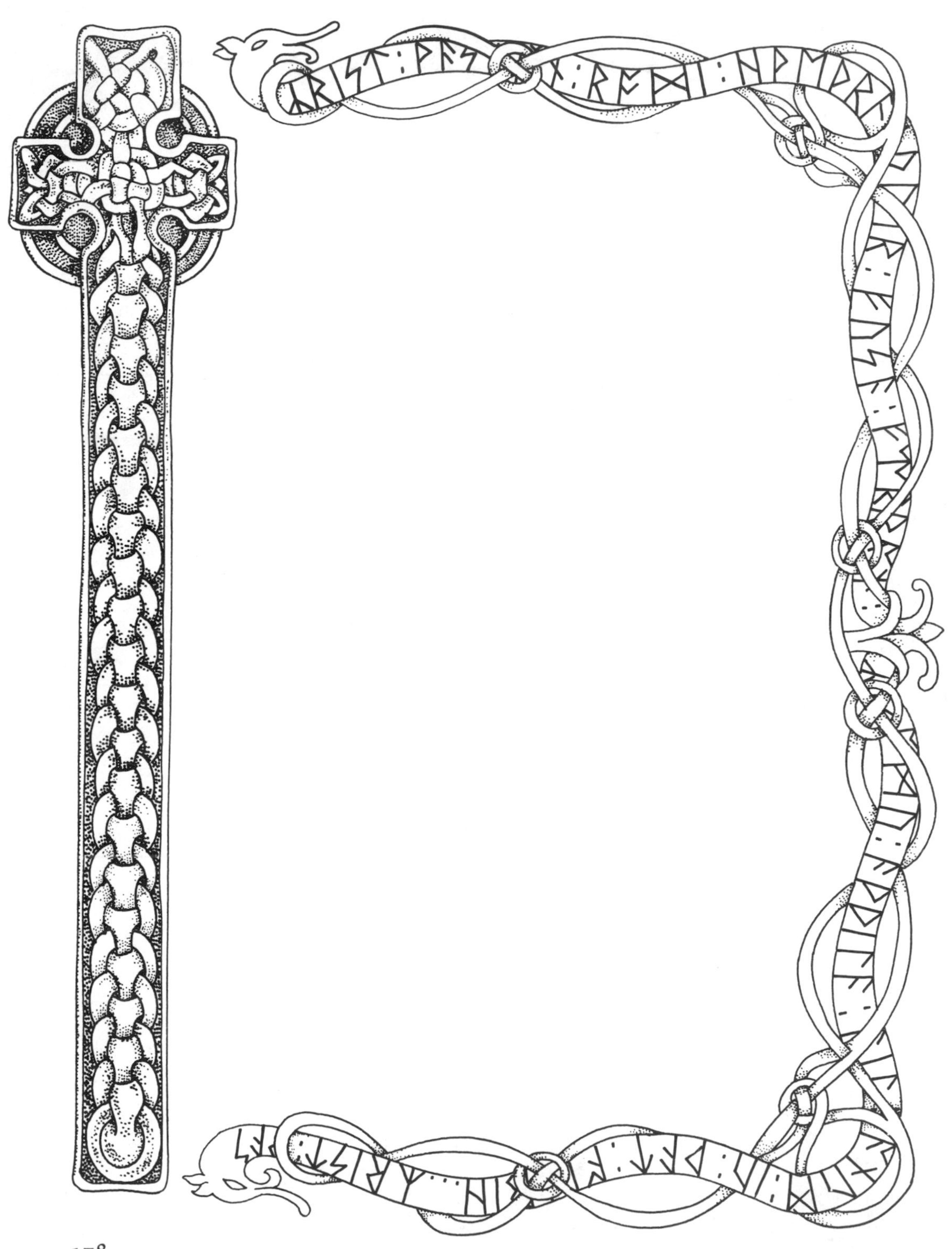

Runes of Comfort for the Bereaved

as it Tolstoy who said, "My life is merely a box in which to keep my death until its time?" How is one to manage the unthinkable? We can begin by thinking about it, facing it, exploring the depths of pain. Up to now, a natural and creative attitude toward death has been largely missing from the fabric of our culture, but that is beginning to change.

Fine work is being done in the field of thanatology. The strength of the hospice movement is growing throughout the world. In the United States there is a dedicated group of experienced people who minister to the dying, notable among whom are Elisabeth Kübler-Ross, Ram Dass's Hanuman Foundation, and Stephen Levine, author of *Who Dies? An Investigation of Conscious Living and Dying,* * a book simply filled with wisdom.

What follows are some suggestions for thinking about death and dying in a new way.

---

*Stephen Levine, *Who Dies? An Investigation of Conscious Living and Dying* (Garden City, N.Y.: Doubleday & Company, Anchor Books, 1982).

RUNES FOR THE DYING

Your friend is dying and you are sitting by his bed. There is not a lot of time left. Ask yourself, "What is still unresolved between us? Have we any unfinished business?" List all the issues, then turn to the Oracle. Draw a Rune for each issue. In this, as in all areas where the ground is wisdom and love, the Runes are unfailing allies.

If the dying person has troubled thoughts about someone who is not present, have them select a Rune for that absent relationship. Record what is said. Perhaps there will come healing words and new understandings which you can later convey to the absent friend. Surely these words will be precious: precious to the dying one who speaks them, knowing that they will be delivered; precious to the one who receives them, knowing the high moment from which they come.

RUNES FOR THE BEREAVED

A young man whose mother had recently died in a car crash wanted to know what his mother would have advised him with her "dying breath." He drew ↑, *Teiwaz,* Warrior Energy. "Be a Spiritual Warrior—that's exactly what she would have told me!"

"When my grief was choking me," said a Florida woman about the death of her twin sister, "I picked a Rune on the issue 'What would Clara be saying to me now?' and got ᛝ, *Inguz,* Fertility and New Beginnings. I began to laugh and laugh for I had just kept my promise to spread her ashes on the roses."

If you have unfinished business with someone who has died, simply take a moment to visualize the person you want to remember. Use a favorite photograph if you have one. Then make a list of the matters you would have liked to discuss, the things you wish you had shared but didn't. Draw a Rune on each issue and meditate on the response. Letters received from people who have worked with the Runes in this way indicate that the results are invariably heartening and clarifying.

This process is not to be confused with séances or night letters "from beyond the veil." Perhaps what the Runes do here is access our deep knowing about that person, knowing which is lodged in our own subconscious. When we hear the voice of Truth, we recognize it.

The little prayer that follows is the result of a meditation on one such Rune casting when ᛞ, *Dagaz,* the Rune of Breakthrough and Transformation, was drawn.

RUNES OF COMFORT FOR THE BEREAVED

I am the Life and the Light and the Way
The earth is my Garden
Each of the Souls I plant as seeds
Germinates and flowers in its season,
And in each I am fulfilled.
There is no cause for grief
When a blossom fades
But only rejoicing for the beauty it held
And praise that my Will is done
And my Plan served.

I am one with all creatures
And none is ever lost
But only restored to me,
Having never left me at all.
For what is Eternal
Cannot be separated from its source.
I am with you all,
And each of you is my Favorite Child.
Feel my Love
Enfold you now and evermore.

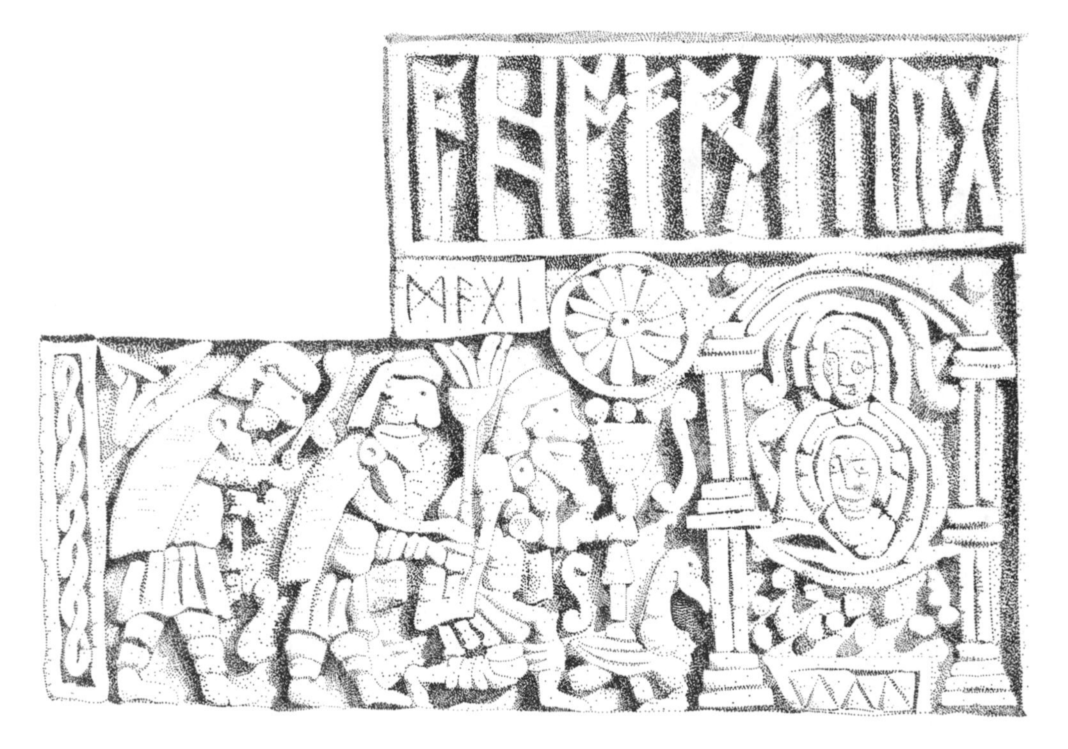

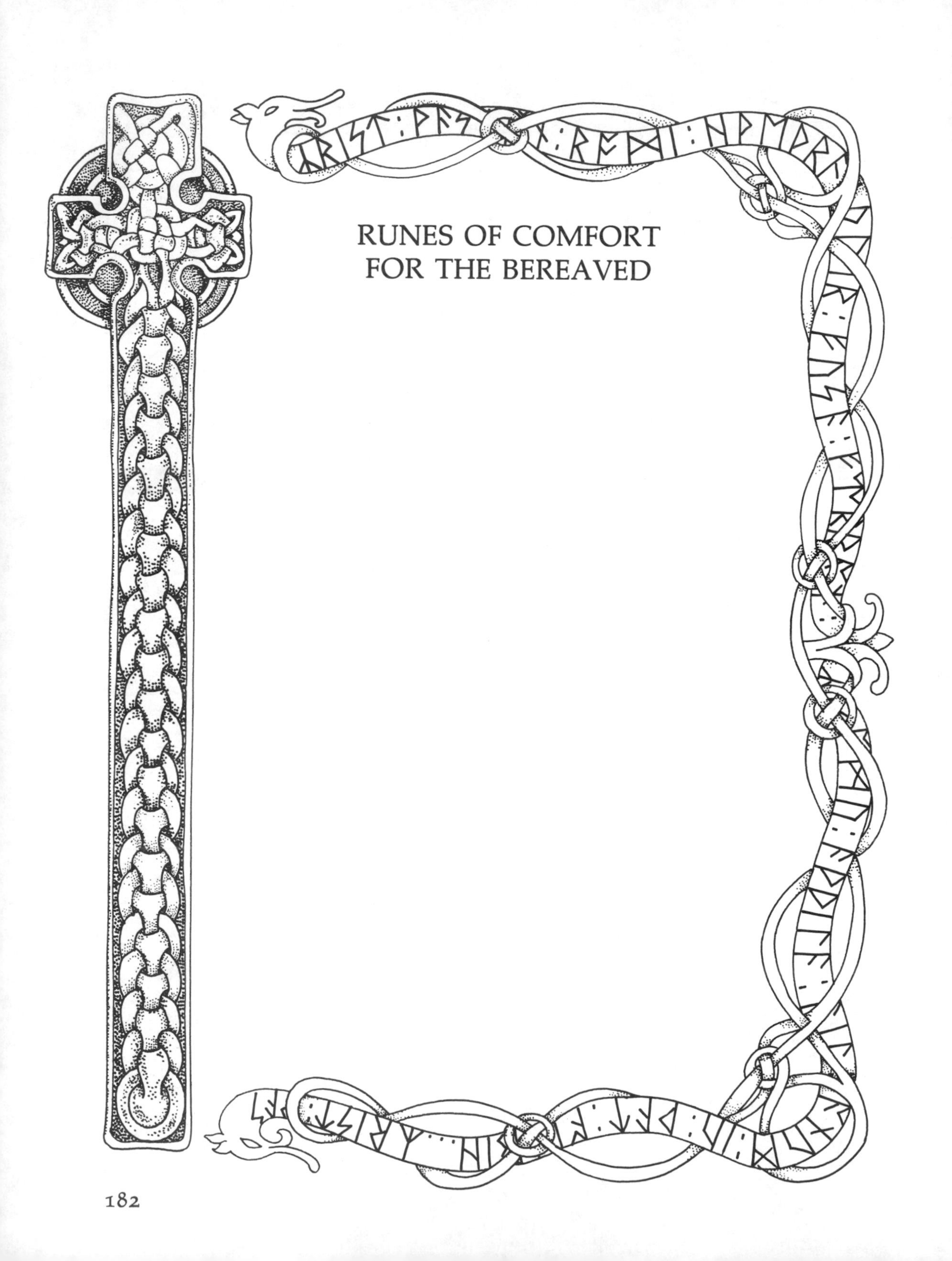

RUNES OF COMFORT FOR THE BEREAVED

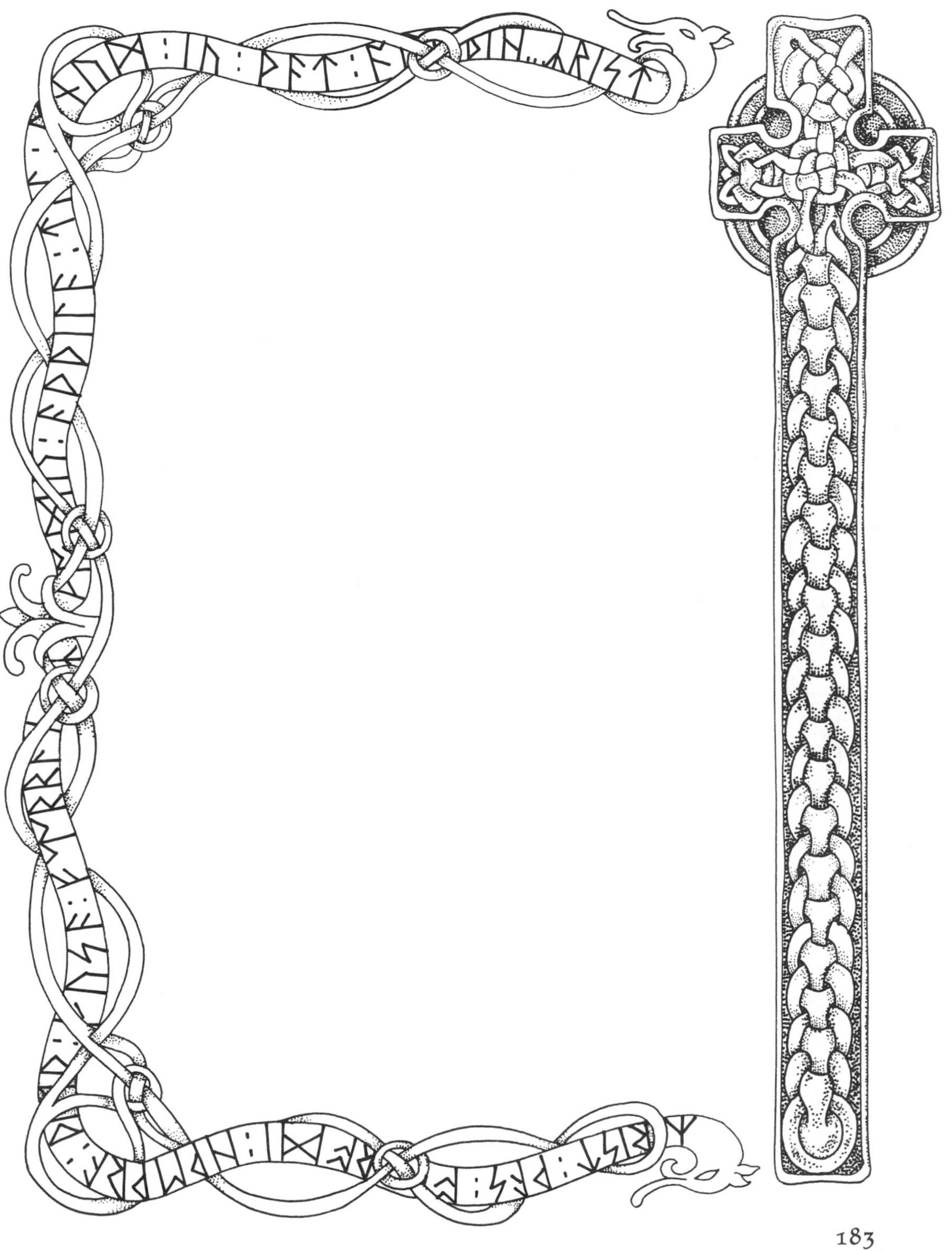

For the week of ______________

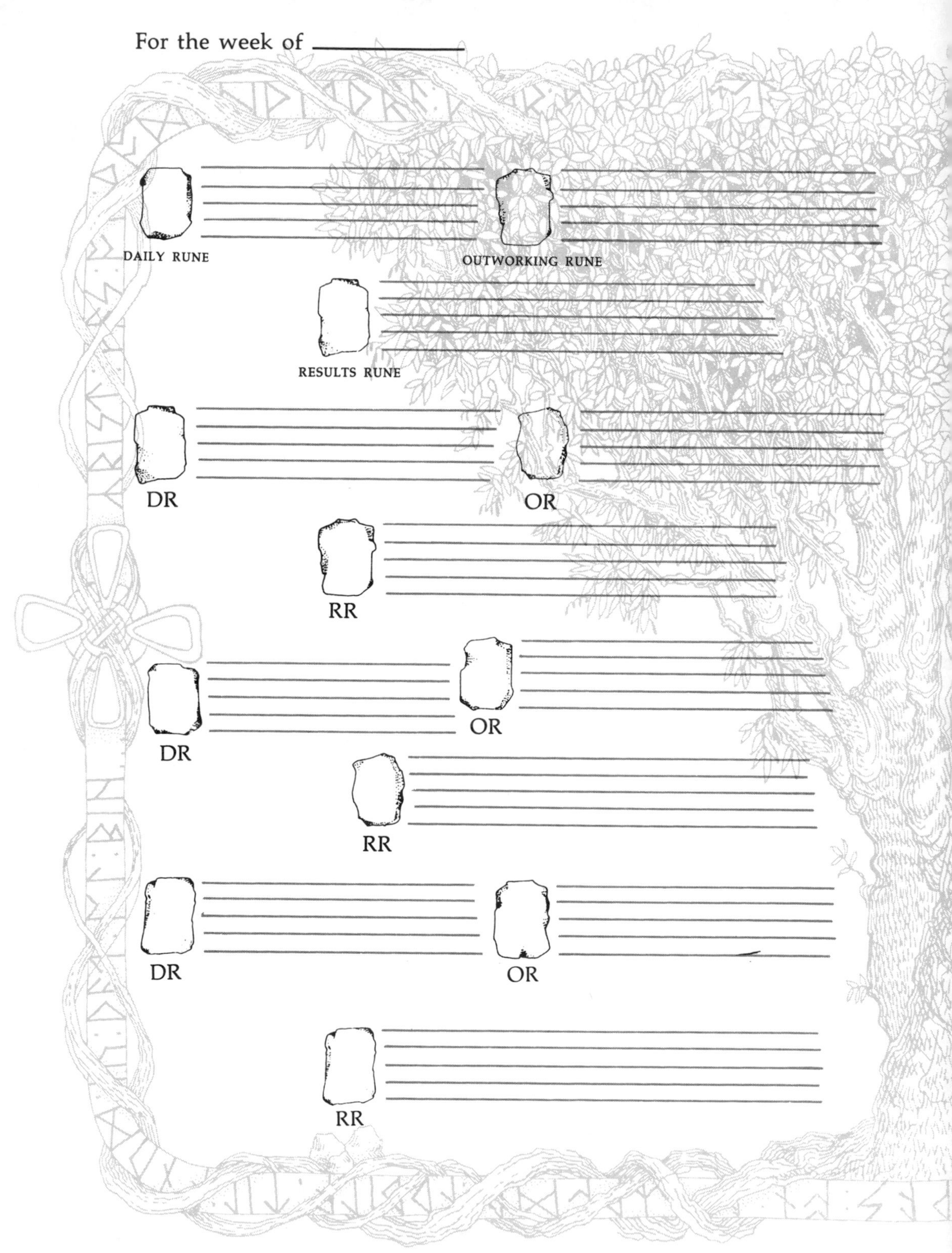

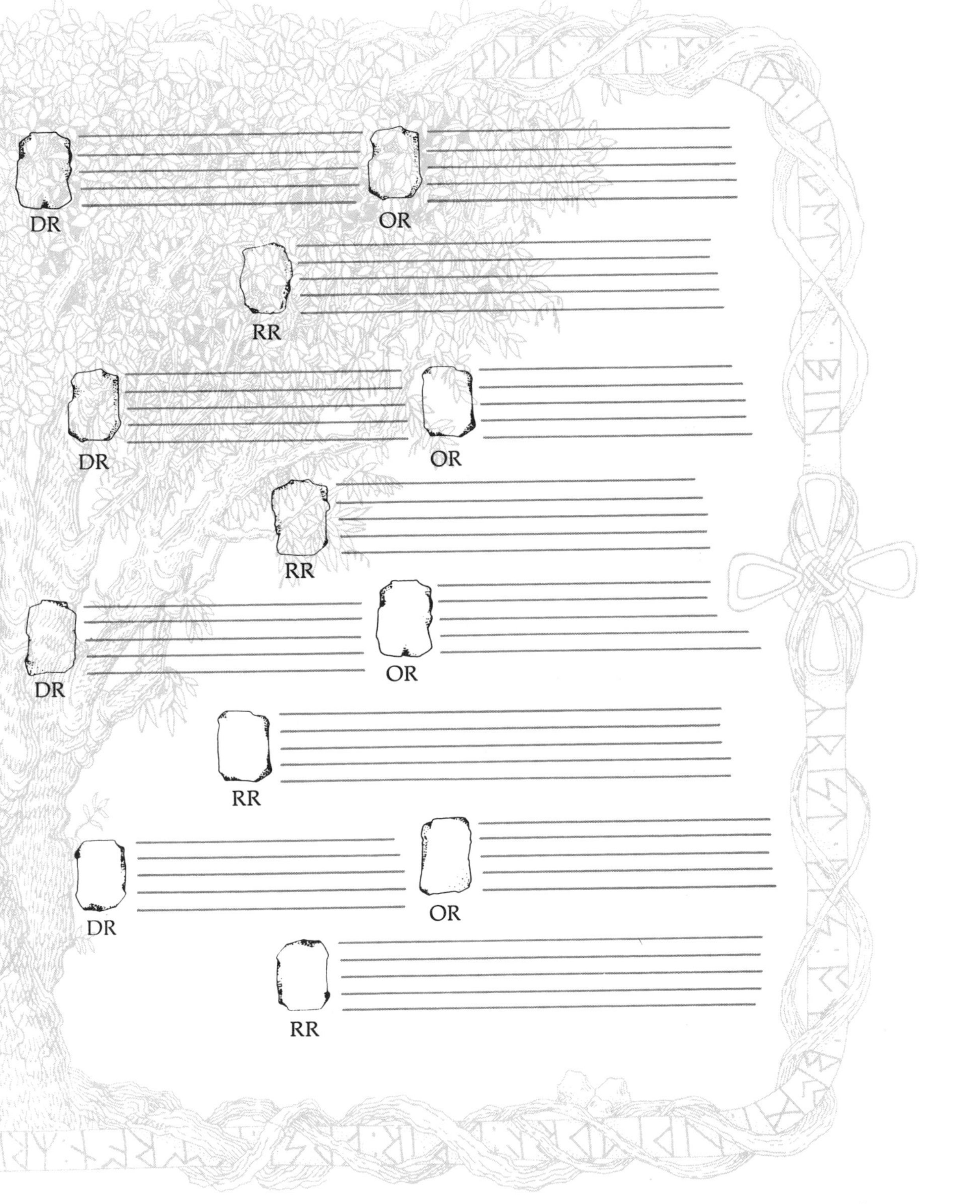
DR
OR
RR
DR
OR
RR
DR
OR
RR
DR
OR
RR

For the week of ___________

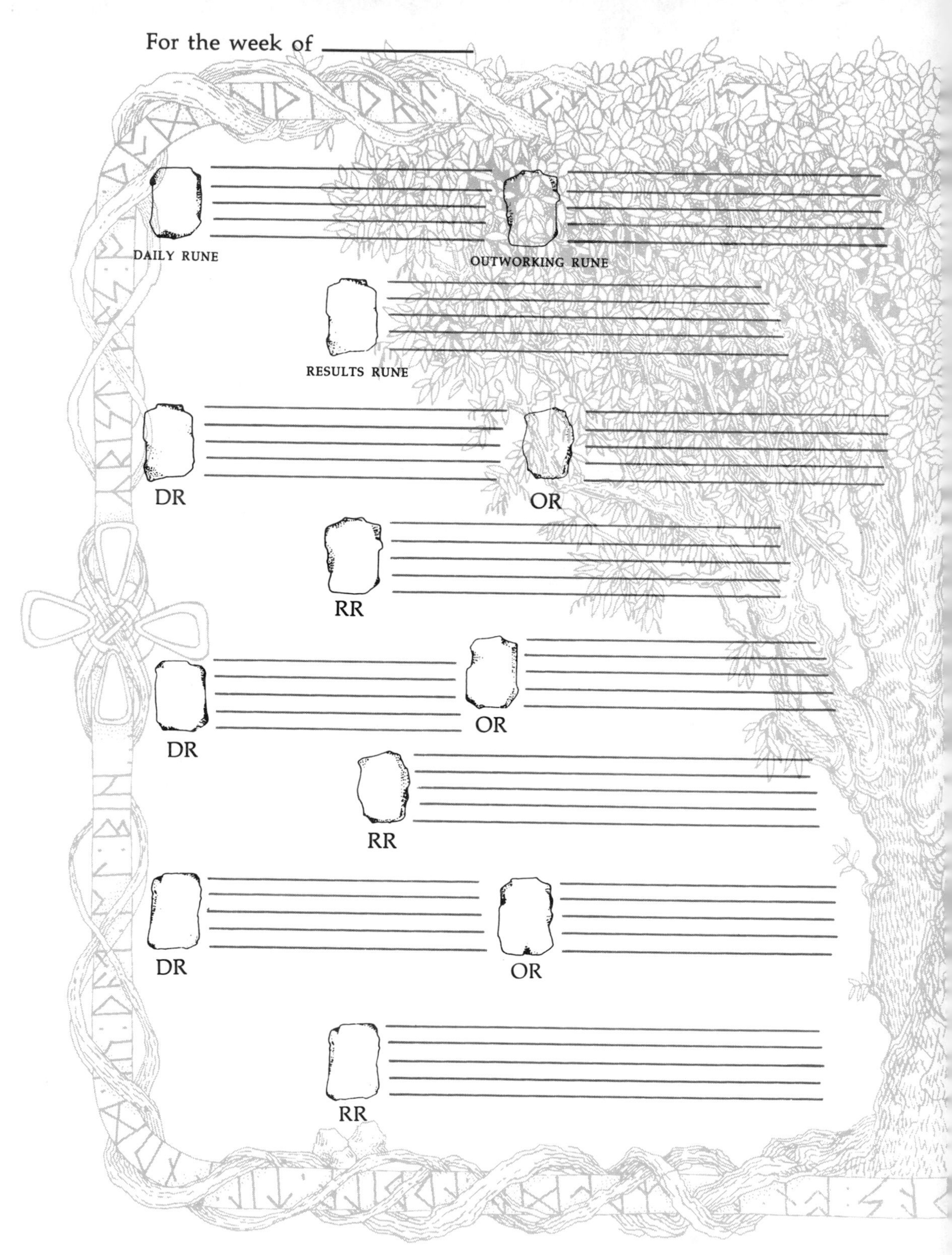

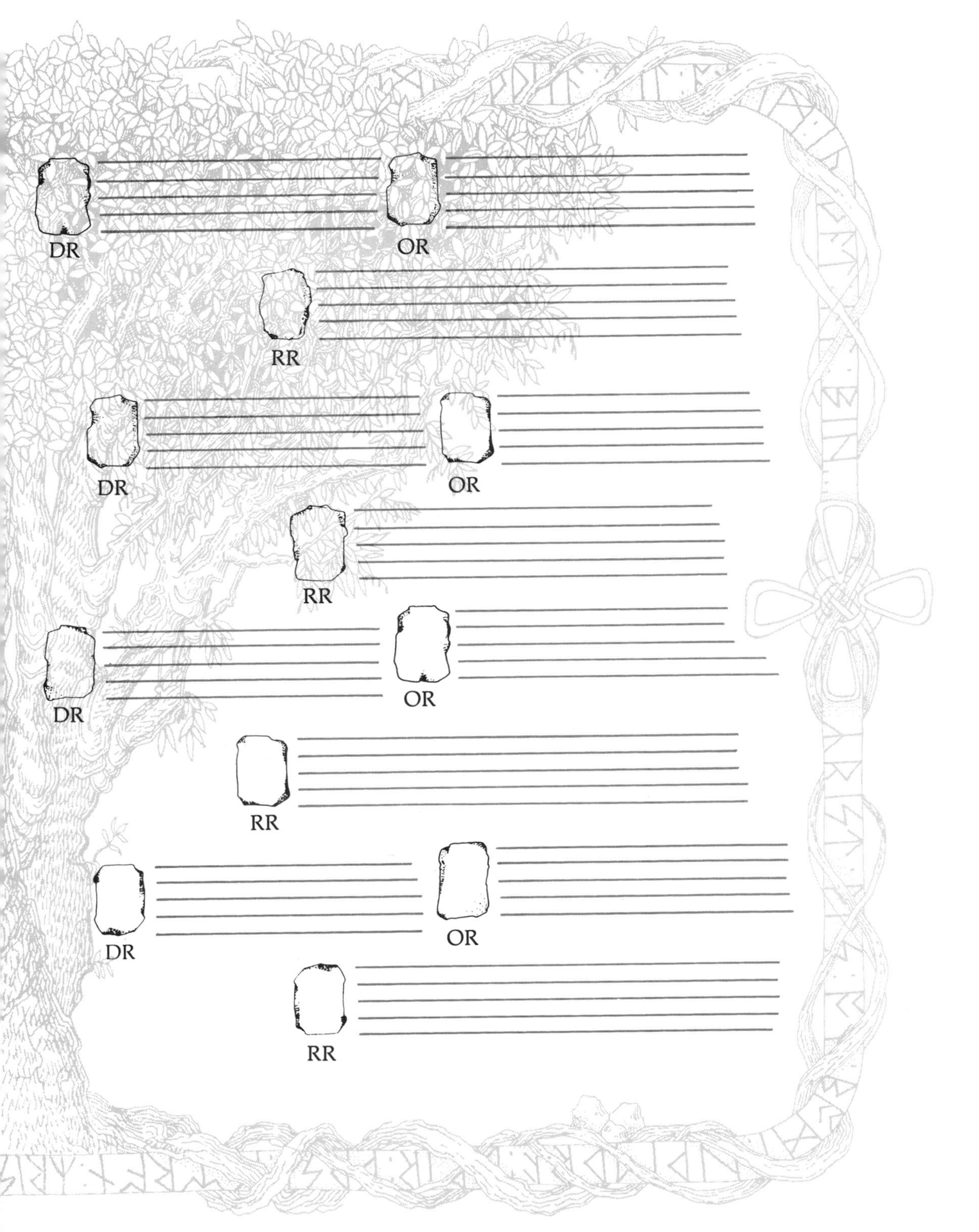
DR
OR
RR
DR
OR
RR
DR
OR
RR
DR
OR
RR

For the week of ____________

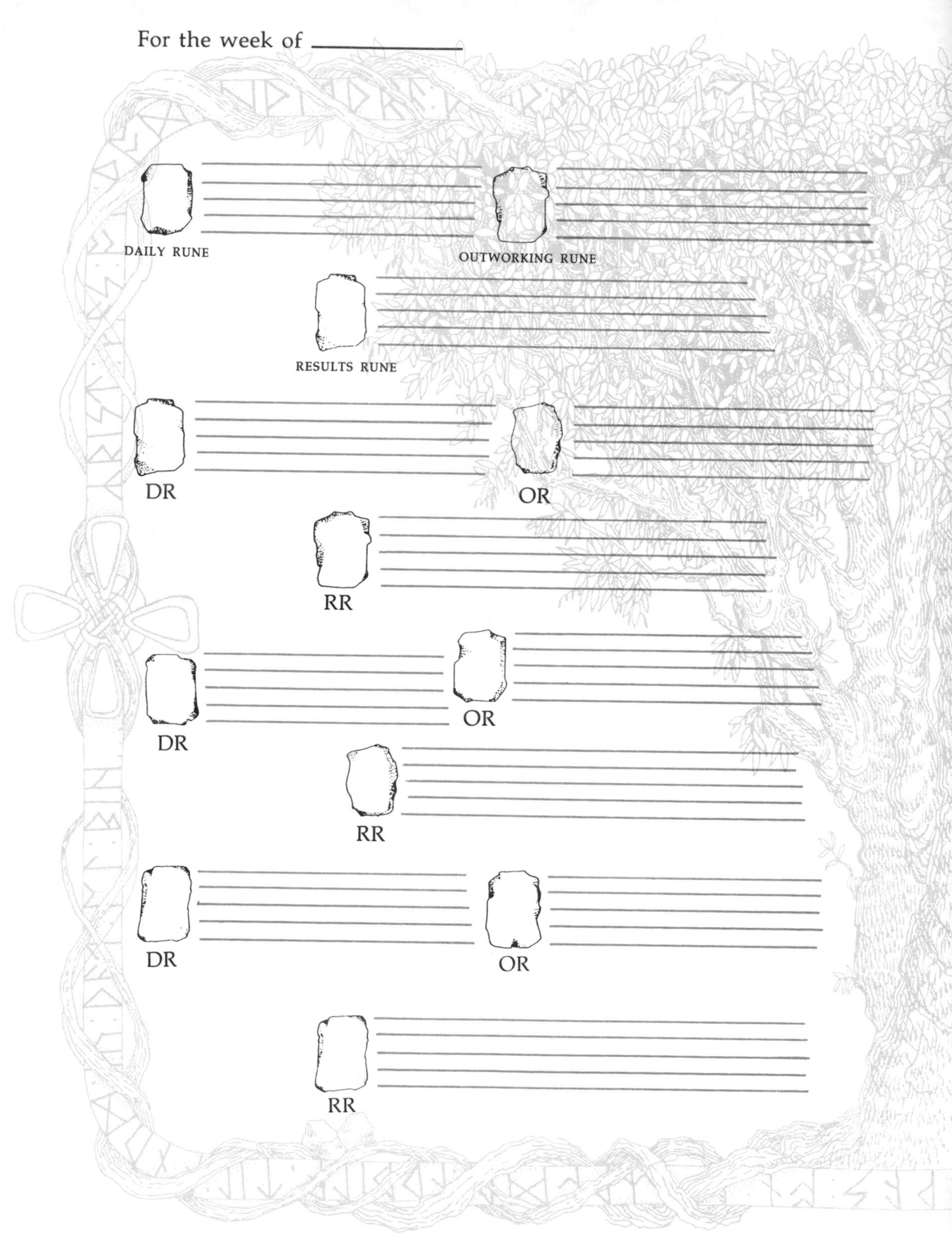

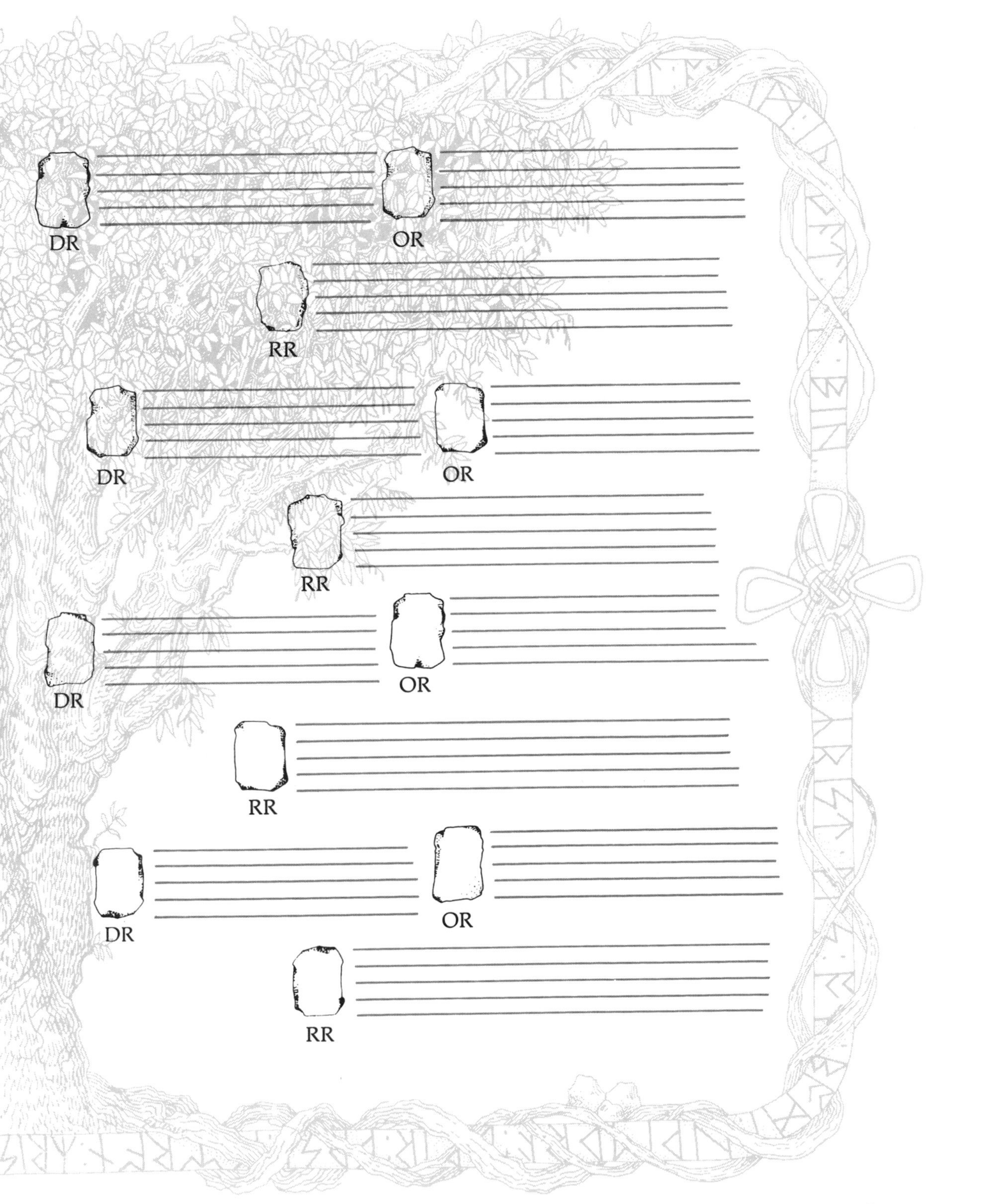
DR
OR
RR
DR
OR
RR
DR
OR
RR
DR
OR
RR

For the week of ____________

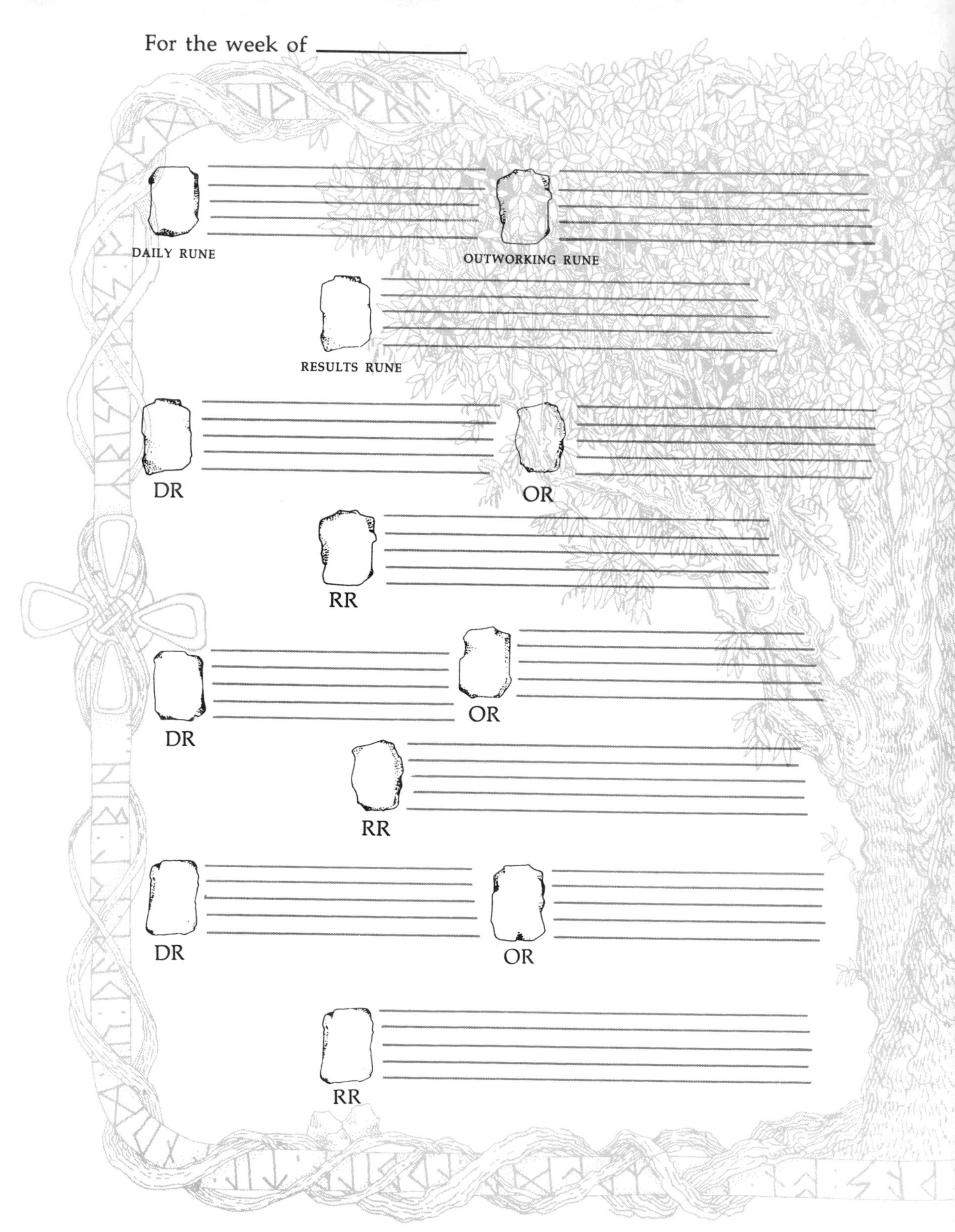

DR
OR
RR
DR
OR
RR
DR
OR
RR
DR
OR
RR

For the week of ____________

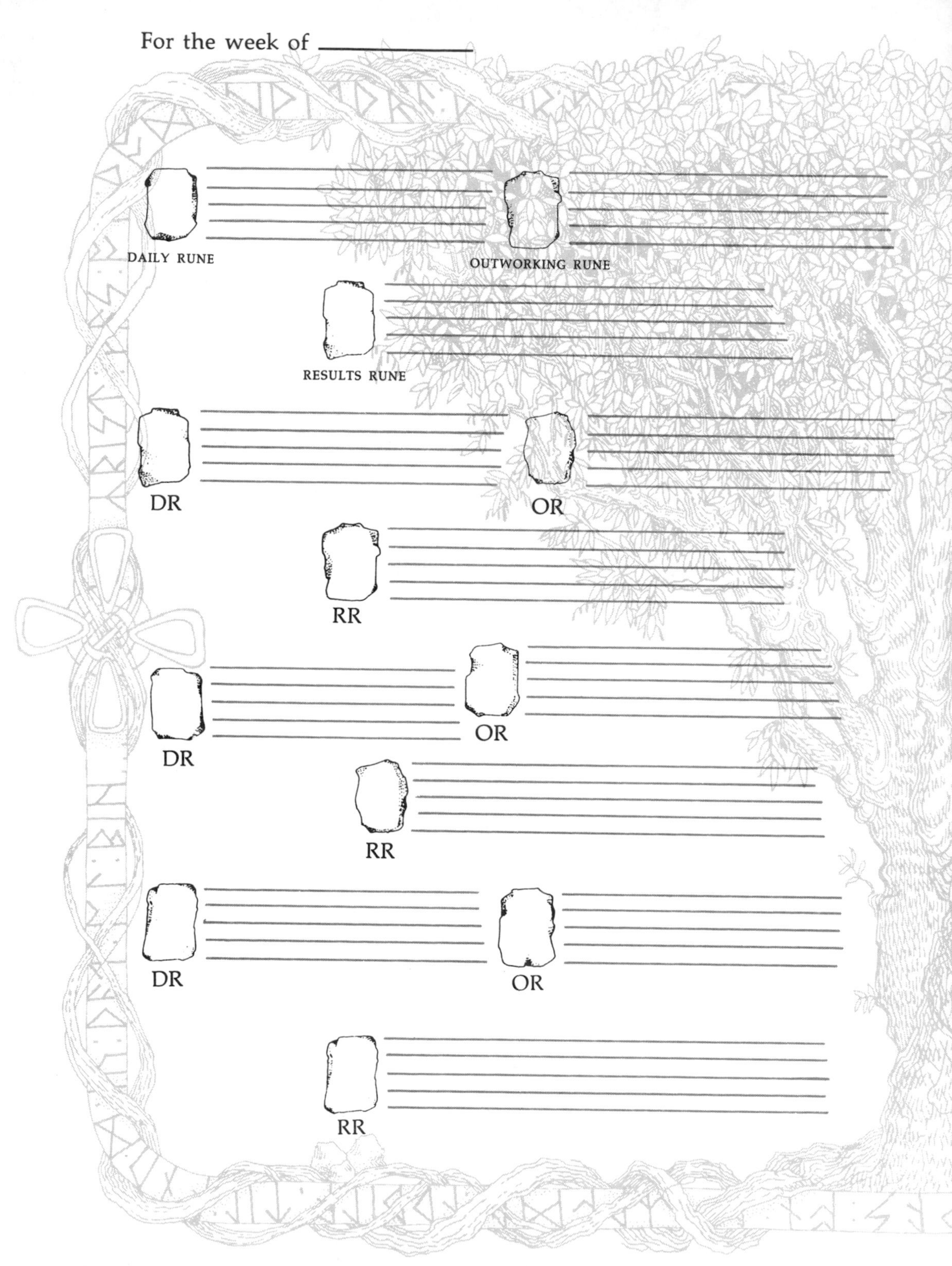

DR
OR
RR
DR
OR
RR
DR
OR
RR
DR
OR
RR

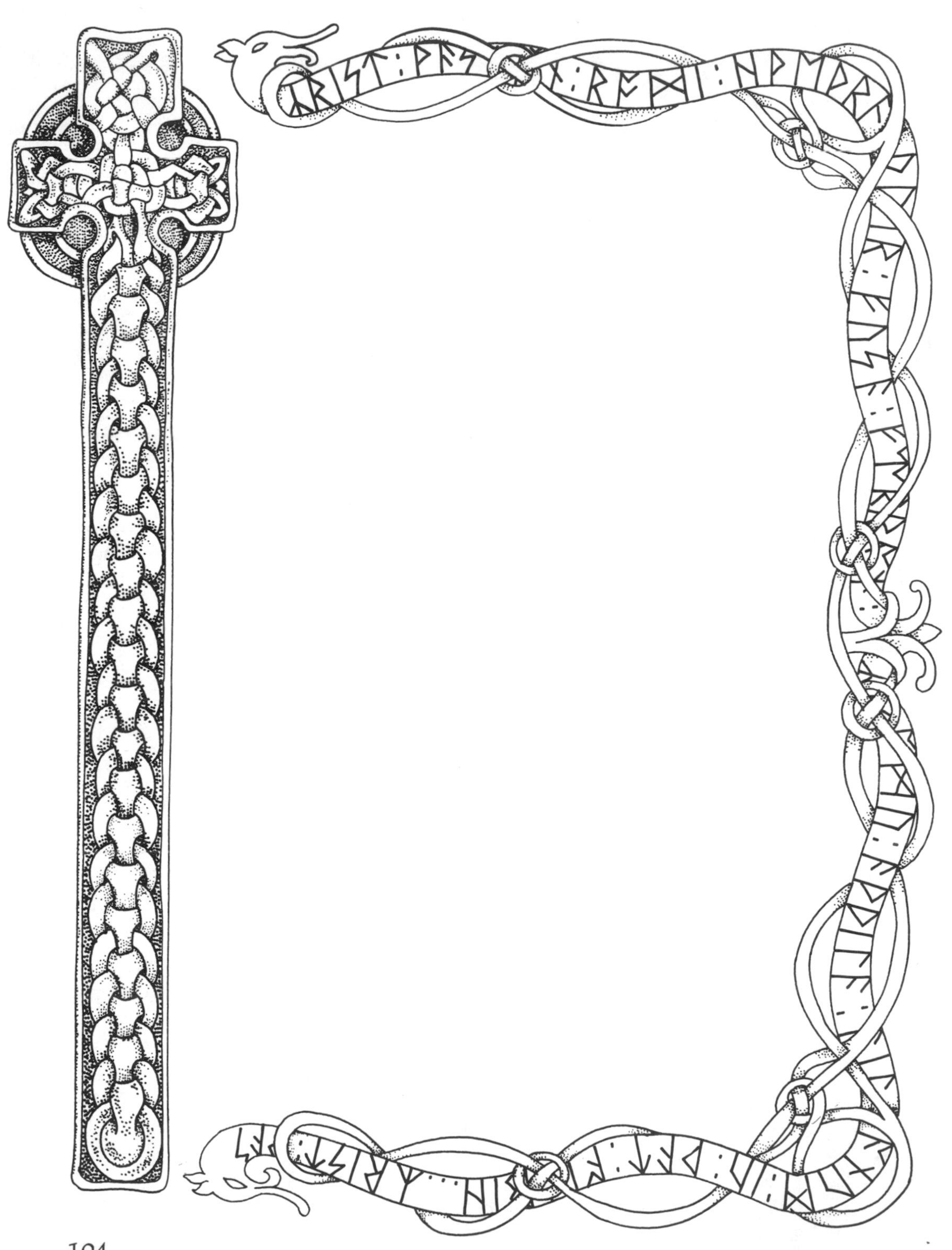

Rune Talk

As you work with the Oracle, questions may arise concerning the practice and philosophy of *runemal,* the art of Rune casting. Here are a few of the popular favorites.

"ARE REVERSED RUNES 'BAD'?"

Some people, drawing a Rune Reversed, go into primary shock and prepare to duck. But the Runes, Upright or Reversed, merely describe *what your nature requires of you at the present moment.* Remember the words of ᚨ, Ansuz: "Even a timely warning may be seen as a gift." Think of the Reversed readings as amplifying and specifying your present condition. Neither good nor bad, at their most intense, Reversed readings are nothing more than the obstacle expression of the energy carried by the same Rune in its Upright position.

"BUT THE RUNE I PICKED DOESN'T APPLY TO MY ISSUE"

A small percentage of those drawing a Rune for the first time will respond with these or similar words. When this happens, you are being provided with a teaching opportunity. Almost invariably the Runes are going into *Runic override:* The unconscious of the querent has been engaged and is addressing a more significant issue. Sometimes this happens when people decide to test the Oracle with a trivial question. Take a few moments to discuss with them ways in which the selected Rune might relate to some other aspect of their life. You will, more often than not, observe a sudden dawning of awareness in their eyes as they begin to connect the Rune reading to their true area of concern.

When your issue is ignored, the Runes are saying, "You wanted to ask a question, and I've got an answer for you, but you will have to think of the question yourself."

"WHAT IF I HAD PICKED A DIFFERENT RUNE?"

The first and most obvious answer to this question is, you didn't. You picked this Rune. Chances are, if you pick again on the same issue, you will draw a different Rune. The Runes are acting in their capacity as a biocomputer. Enter a demand and the computer prints out the most appropriate response; a second demand on the same issue will be interpreted as a request for more information. Try it yourself and you will see that, taken together, the two "printouts" combine to broaden and illuminate your understanding of the issue.

"DO THE RUNES TELL MY FUTURE?"

Often people assume that the art of Rune casting should be of service to them in getting a "fix" on the future. But what is the future? It is the intentions you formulate *now* bearing fruit. It is the actions you take—or do not take—today. It is the words you utter or withhold, moment to moment. The decisions you make, including no decision, leave in their wake results, stepping-stones that bring you one pace at a time to what we call "the future." For what else is the future except another "now" formed from all our intentions, actions, words and decisions.

Confront the issues that challenge you in your life now, letting the Rune stones serve to clarify your intentions, moderate your actions, temper your words and help you commit your decisions to the outworking of the greatest good for all concerned.

"THE USE OF *self* AND *Self* IS CONFUSING."

A footnote in the Introduction to *The Book of Runes* states that "the term *self* is used to represent the little self or ego-self, the *Self* to signify the Higher Self, the All-Knowing or Witness Self, the Watcher Within."

In ᚷ, *Gebo,* the Rune of Partnership, there is a challenging statement: "God always enters into equal partnerships." But the truth is, you have to start by being a good partner to yourself. Otherwise, how can you hope to understand the ways of the Divine? There is a cultural shadow that falls over the matter of this sacred partnership. We are inclined to discount and disparage "ego" as something bad, something to be suppressed and subjugated. The adjective "egotistical" suggests conceit and selfishness. In fact there is even a flavor of the misuse of power when we think about ego.

The Concise Oxford Dictionary defines ego quite simply as "the conscious thinking subject," indicating that ego is the necessary ground for self-change, for human process. Perhaps ego can be regarded as the hallmark of being in this body, in this world. The personal signature of the Higher Self. That aspect of our Divinity that is to be polished and honored.

Ego disorders are plentiful but they can be set to rights. The ego does not require beating into submission, but rather a more conscious understanding of the quality of power represented in its proper relationship to the Divine Self.

> *Theorem:* A harmonious relationship between the Self and the self is a function *not* of "power over" but of being "in partnership with."

It is well to consider again here the opening words of the first Rune ᛗ *Mannaz,* the Rune of the Self:

> The starting point is the self. Its essence is water. Only clarity, willingness to change, is effective now. A correct relationship to your Self is primary, for from it flow all possible correct relationships with others and with the Divine.

Remember: God always enters into equal partnerships.

Glossary of Rune Terms & Concepts

Daily Rune: (DR) a forecast of what will require your attention during the day. Also called "The Rune of Right Action," this Rune, drawn in the morning, amounts to a personal weather forecast for your day.

Results Rune: (RR) how you met the challenges this day has brought. A Rune that evaluates the way you have conducted yourself. Your grade for the day.

Outworking Rune: (OR) As your day unfolds, if you require a "course check," draw a Rune to determine your current position. Likewise, draw an Outworking Rune (OR) for insight into any challenge that arises for you or a friend during the day; see how the Outworking Rune (OR) relates to your Daily Rune (DR).

Comments Space: Extra space has been provided at the week's end. This is for notes, thoughts, observations, useful quotes, additional spreads and readings.

Five Week Month: a contemporary Runic tradition. No one ever feels there is "enough time." The Five Week Month is intended to alleviate the pressure. While some days of the fifth week are consumed by the traditional calendar, the rest allow for the pressure of events that call for extended evaluation or comment. Feel free to expand into the space provided for tomorrow.

Rune Play Page: found every five weeks, in case the extra days still do not give you sufficient writing space. This page permits you to record extended spreads, to enumerate page numbers where similar situations accessed different Runes, different insights. On the Rune Play Page you may wish to record new ways you discover for using the Viking Runes.

Runemal Page: on which to lay out the first spread you undertake for a new Rune casting technique. Some people find it useful to note on the

Runemal Page references (the page or the date) when, in future, they utilize this same spread. *Runemal* means "the art of Rune casting," and this page is intended for the practice of the apprentice in this art, as it serves the greater art, that of self-change.

Extra Rune Blanks: to be added by you as needed. Draw in the blanks by hand wherever you wish to do a spread. See the Sample Week, the space for Friday, 3/15, for an example of converting the Daily Rune readings into a Three Rune Spread (page xx)

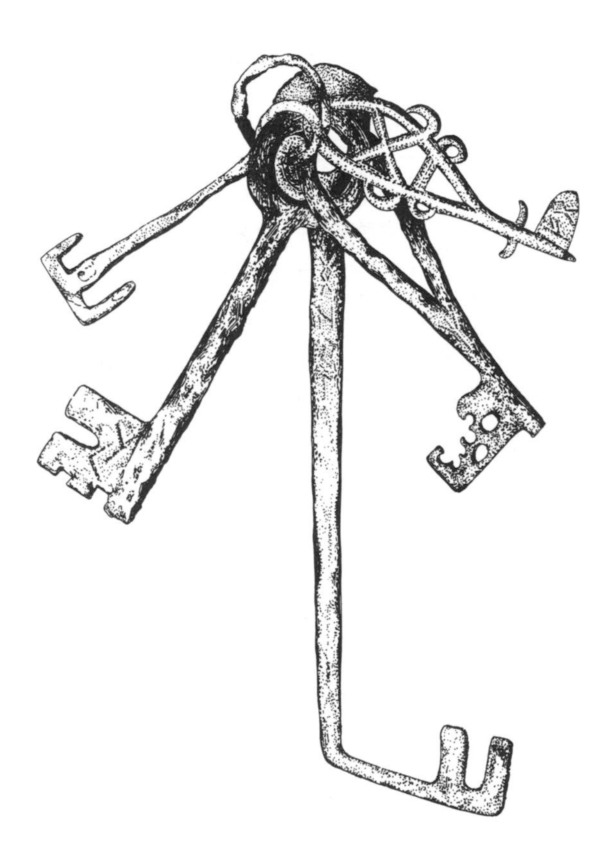

Memo from The RuneWorks

NEW TECHNIQUES

Work with the new techniques, then send us the insights you receive. What astonished you when you played *Night Runes?* What did you notice when *Doing Ing* that we may have overlooked? What is missing, for you, from *A Destiny Profile?* What "wait-till-you-hear-this" effect did you get from doing *Runes of Healing?* TYPEWRITTEN LETTERS ARE A BLESSING. Printing and clean handwriting run a close second.

Since Runecraft is so newly restored to us, this remains *an information and idea-gathering period.* Help us to serve you better by telling us what you need to know. Share with us your creative ideas for new Rune projects, keeping information exchange as your first priority. Especially suggestions for ways to make *Rune Play*—its record pages—more useful, clearer, more fun. For this we thank you in advance.

THE NEW ORACLE NEWS & RUNE DIGEST

The RuneWorks is a clearinghouse for information regarding Runecraft. Four times a year we publish a newsletter, *The New Oracle News & Rune Digest,* which tells where and when Bronwyn Jones and Ralph Blum are doing Rune Workshops; the names of people around the country you can be in touch with to start your own Rune Network; addresses of our correspondents in other countries; new techniques and studies by historians, linguists, and other scholars in this expanding new field of self-work.

Subscription Information: Subscription for one year (four issues), is $12.00. If you live outside the United States, please send money orders in U.S. dollars only, and add $5.00 to cover the cost of first class mailing to:

The RuneWorks
P.O. Box 24084
Los Angeles, CA. 90024

Single back issues are available for $4.00 and one full year of back issues may be purchased for $15.00.

MAIL ORDER

For those of you who may have had some difficulty in finding copies of *The Book of Runes* or *Rune Play* in your local bookstores, ask them to order it or write to us at The RuneWorks and we will provide you with copies. One of our primary functions these days is to act as "bookstore backup," so please write to us if we can be of help.

THE RUNEWORKS CATALOGUE

If you wish to be placed on the mailing list for the RuneWorks Catalogue, please send your name and address to The RuneWorks. The catalogue will evolve and grow with our changing interests and will include information about new products ranging from Runic Christmas cards to Rune pendants, and special sets of Rune stones.

As always, we look forward to hearing from you.

Ralph Blum

About the Author

A writer, lecturer, and publisher, Ralph Blum is also a student of the oracular sciences.